W9-BNS-383

Editorial and Opinion

**Recent Titles in
Democracy and the News**

Editorial and Opinion

The Dwindling Marketplace of Ideas in Today's News

Steven M. Hallock

Foreword by John Downing

Democracy and the News

Jeffrey Scheuer, Series Editor

PRAEGER

Westport, Connecticut
London

Library of Congress Cataloging-in-Publication Data

Hallock, Steven M.
  Editorial and opinion : the dwindling marketplace of ideas in today's news / Steven M. Hallock;
  foreword by John Downing.
     p. cm. — (Democracy and the news, ISSN 1932–6947)
  Includes bibliographical references and index.
  ISBN 0–275–99330–2 (alk. paper)
  1. Editorials—United States. 2. American newspapers—Sections, columns, etc.—Op-ed pages.
  I. Title.
  PN4888.E28H35 2007
  070.4'42—dc22   2006028553

British Library Cataloguing in Publication Data is available.

Library of Congress Catalog Card Number: 2006028553
ISBN: 0–275–99330–2
ISSN: 1932–6947

First published in 2007

Praeger Publishers, 88 Post Road West, Westport, CT 06881
An imprint of Greenwood Publishing Group, Inc.
www.praeger.com

Printed in the United States of America

The paper used in this book complies with the
Permanent Paper Standard issued by the National
Information Standards Organization (Z39.48-1984).

10 9 8 7 6 5 4 3 2 1

Copyright Acknowledgments

Excerpts from "Two Papers in Joint Operating Agreement Publish Meaningful Editorial Diversity,"
by Steve Hallock, Ron Rodgers, Mike Gennaria, and Fei Wei, published in *Newspaper Research
Journal* 25, no. 4 (Fall 2004): 104–109. Reprinted with permission.

Portions of this manuscript were previously published in the *Newspaper Research Journal*. Reprinted
with permission.

Every reasonable effort has been made to trace the owners of copyrighted materials in this book,
but in some instances this has proven impossible. The author and publisher will be glad to receive
information leading to more complete acknowledgments in subsequent printings of the book and in
the meantime extend their apologies for any omissions.

For K

Contents

Tables

Series Foreword

Democratic societies are widely understood to promote human freedom through political equality—equality before the law and in choosing the lawmakers; and the main instruments of such political equality are voting, representation, and constitutional government. These are indeed basic features of the democratic engine, regardless of the specific design. But while necessary for self-government, they are not sufficient.

The fuel that makes a democratic engine run, and without which it is a mere blueprint, is information: the flow of facts, analyses, opinions, discussions, and arguments that empower citizens for their central role in guiding the machine. Hence, the importance of freedom of speech and, its crucial ancillary, the freedom of the press. Journalism, and media in general, intertwines with the principles and strategies of democratic culture in many ways; democracy runs on conversation and communication. The quality of journalism bears directly on the quality of democracy itself.

Like journalism generally, the editorial page is many things to a community. As Steven M. Hallock observes, it is at once the "community watchdog, agenda-setter and conscience." It is where a community (large or small) can converse with itself, expose arguments to criticism and facts to correction. In every way, it is essential to—if not the very soul of—the democratic machine.

Professor Hallock probes beneath this basic democratic premise, exploring the state of opinion journalism in America. Combining the insights of scholarship with considerable journalistic experience, he examines the importance of a diverse and lively culture of opinion: not just a "market of ideas," but also a "market basket," that is, the need for true competition and diversity, ideological and otherwise, in the democratic marketplace. In the process, he offers both rigorous analysis and a panoramic backdrop of the history of editorial opinion in America since the colonial era.

Sifting voluminous evidence, Hallock shows how the concentration of the American journalistic landscape has narrowed the range and depth of debate. The threat to democracy that he identifies is not remote or hypothetical. It is not something that might happen decades hence, if we do nothing. It is an actual and ongoing process of decay, reflected in, among other things, the paucity of local coverage, the loss of local autonomy in public affairs, and the lack of a true "basket" of diverse voices and ideas.

This series is predicated on the idea that the state and quality of our democracy is inseparable from the state and quality of our news media. There are many ways of exploring the connections between the interlocking spheres of power and mediation and of showing the necessity of informed citizenship for the proper functioning of the democratic machine. *Editorial and Opinion* identifies a critical nexus of those parallel and conjoined universes.

Professor Hallock extends the series into the realm of opinion with a cogent argument that the trend toward concentration and monopolization in the American media represents a triumph of market forces over market baskets, and a genuine limitation on the quality of our democracy. His conclusions and recommendations, echoing those of the Hutchins Commission 60 years ago, are both sensible and timely; and like the work of that sorely underestimated Commission, they also contain, in their adherence to enduring democratic values, elements of the timeless.

Jeffrey Scheuer, Series Editor
September 2006

Foreword

The book in front of you is a robust, questioning, and thoroughly researched exploration, which systematically strips away the comforting shibboleths about our news media that commentators who should know better persist in propagating: "American media are the freest in the world," "U.S. journalism is the world's leader," "America's fourth estate," "vigorous watchdogs of our democratic system." In view of the increasing concentration of media ownership, which in a private ownership system does betoken control if the owners want it, these shibboleths come across as cozy but crass, as comfort food for ostriches. War, pharmaceuticals, the environment, public security, healthy—not just safe!—food, racism, women's opportunities, children's education, eldercare, and technology are only some of the daily cruxes of our existence about which we must depend on our news media for illumination and guidance. As well as on their honesty and determination.

But how far can we depend on them? The history of tobacco, of auto safety, of the Vietnam and Iraq wars, of Agent Orange and the syndromes associated with the veterans of the 1990–91 Gulf War, of school failures, of obesity, of overprescription, of the horse-race politics that keeps television firms afloat, of portraying welfare as unearned luxury and the prison system as a nowhere place on the planet—these are just some of the question marks against the news diet we have been served over the years. "Homeland Security" legislation, the Patriot Act, and other legislative and executive initiatives along the same lines since 9/11 are equally part and parcel of the story.

Steve Hallock does not come to this task as a cynic, nor as a cardboard-cutout East or West Coast sociologist full of denunciatory rhetoric, nor yet as someone determined to shred the United States. He comes as a working journalist of thirty years' experience in various parts of the heartland, deeply committed to democratic debate and to the essential contribution of news media to a strong democracy. He comes too with a doctoral degree in journalism from Ohio University, schooled in the intensive review of evidence and in sifting out casual opinion from considered conclusions. Not least, he comes with a quiet conviction in favor of the enduring strengths that since 1776 we Americans have generated in our social tissue.

So we had better focus on what Hallock has to say. His critiques are based upon very solid information, gleaned not only from in-depth study of the contemporary economics and politics of our news media but also from searching interviews with twelve working editorialists and journalists of varying political opinions across the nation. Their degree of unanimity, given their spectrum of political opinion, is deeply worrying regarding the shrinkage of the news media as sources for informed debate. Hallock is very thorough, separating out locations where there is a newspaper competition—increasingly rare ever since the 1920s —from those where editorial functions are separate but business location and operations are jointly operated, and these again from today's metroplex newspapers. He traces the historical evolution of the decline in newspaper competition, comparing past with present. And, no mere Jeremiah, in the final chapter he reviews a series of practical options for reinvigorating our increasingly stifled system of news diffusion and analysis.

It is happier and cuddlier to join the ostriches, to hymn the praises of our republic while fixing our eyes straight ahead, to resonate with the reassurance of the famous "It's morning in America" Republican radio commercial of the 1984 presidential election, and even to hand a blank check to our commander in chief because father knows best in times of trouble.

But an adult republic demands adults. Able to think, to be informed, to stand up to power, and to reconstruct shaky edifices. Media reform is vital to our future, and this study is a strong contribution to current debates toward that goal.

Not only this. Autocrats around the world, who always wish we had fewer freedoms against which their subjects could compare themselves, can stand up and toast, along with their coteries of well-heeled cronies, every time the economic and political bands around our news media draw a little tighter and the oxygen of our debate gets a little thinner. The United States is under their close scrutiny. We have responsibilities beyond our frontiers, not as a policeman but as a working democracy.

So in closing, Hallock and I at the time of this writing have known each other just one year, both newly arrived colleagues in our College of Mass Communication and Media Arts. I am more than pleased to be able to contribute side by side with him to the same dynamic project and here to endeavor to draw readers' attention to the contemporary urgency of his book.

John Downing, Founding Director of the Global Media
Research Center at Southern Illinois University, Carbondale

Preface

The man who gave me my first job as an editorial writer in the late 1970s is dead now. So I will never know why a politically conservative Idaho publisher like Alvin Ricken hired a left-leaning Coloradoan like me to write opinions for his newspaper. When I asked him, it usually was in the heat of editorial debate over such issues as hospital competition in Pocatello, a college town of maybe 40,000–50,000 a couple of hours north of Salt Lake City where a privately owned, Mormon-backed hospital firm was competing with a tax-supported county hospital to be the community's hospital services provider. Or over the benefits (his viewpoint) and dangers (mine) of nuclear energy as proposed by the stockholder-backed and privately operated utilities versus the benefits (my viewpoint) and bureaucratic inefficiency (his) of government-produced hydro-electricity. In those moments of argument, our voices raised so that the features editor's ears, just beyond Ricken's open office door, crooked in our direction, when I stopped in exasperation and asked him why he had hired me in the first place, the best I got was "hell if I know."

I do know why I took the job. And it wasn't the money, though for the time—this was during the latter days of the administration of President Jimmy Carter and the early days of President Ronald Reagan—the money was appealing. When Ricken telephoned me to discuss the job as editorial page editor of the 22,000-circulation *Idaho State Journal*, the first sentence he spoke after I identified myself was a question: "I saw your ad in *Editor & Publisher* magazine seeking work as a newspaper writer, and I'm wondering if you would be comfortable with fifteen-thousand dollars a year." After I immediately replied "yes" (I was an unemployed, unpublished novelist who a year before had left my last newspaper job as a $150-a-week reporter) and we had the salary negotiations out of the way, he told me the job would be as an editorial writer. I told him I had never done that, so he suggested I write two sample editorials and mail them to him. I did, and I was hired within the month.

Rather than the money, it was something else that appealed to me, which I expressed to my wife after I hung up the telephone. "They want to pay me to write opinions." Never before had anyone of authority sought out my opinion on anything having to do with government or social policy. And for the rest of my newspaper career, writing my opinion—participating in agenda-setting and fulfilling the traditional watchdog-role function of journalism, second-guessing mayors, governors, senators, and presidents—remained the lure and the reward of editorial writing. I did it for better than a decade before eventually becoming a features editor and then a newspaper editor.

Even after I left full-time editorial writing, I never stopped writing opinion pieces, be they regular columns for the sections I supervised, editorials and columns for the newspapers I edited, or op-ed pieces for other newspapers. As Roy Campanella once said about being paid to play the game of baseball, I sometimes wondered over the fact that I got paid for offering my opinions to the public.

Over the next four years as editorial page editor of the *Idaho State Journal*—interrupted by a stint of a little over a year as a jazz critic for the *Arizona Republic* in Phoenix—I learned a lot about editorial writing from studying the editorials of others. These included the editorials of my Idaho colleagues and some large-circulation newspapers I regularly read. One thing I discovered in those days as a young editorial writer was how editorials can differ in ways other than simple political ideology. I learned how they can vary in more subtle but just as meaningful ways such as tone, or in framing—in how they spin a particular topic. For example, from Bill Hall at the family-owned *Lewiston Morning Tribune*, I learned the power of sarcasm and humor in opinion writing; from Chris Peck's editorial page in Twin Falls, I learned the strength of straight logic founded on solid reporting; from Jim Boyd's editorials at the *Idaho Statesman*, a Gannett newspaper in Boise, I learned the value of brevity. From my reading of editorial pages that included not only these Idaho pages but those in the *New York Times* and the *Christian Science Monitor*, I learned that a regular reader of a well-done editorial page will not need to go anywhere else in the newspaper to keep up on current events and that editorial pages also are documents of history. And I learned that Americans cherish the opportunity to participate in political and social debate through letters and guest columns, and that editorial pages besides setting political agendas also are places that can harbor fine writing on subjects that range from gardening and music to literature and sports—or that can be home to empty, poorly phrased hack nonsense. But no matter the quality of writing, editorial pages are a place in the newspaper that over a period of time take up all of the major topics of the day and sometimes the minor ones—from wars, taxes, health, and welfare to diet and entertainment.

From my colleagues in the Northwest at convention gatherings of editorial writers, I learned that some of them did not enjoy the sort of autonomy I did. Ricken had promised me he would never order me to write an opinion with which I disagreed, but he reserved the right to kill one he didn't like—and he did this frequently. This differed from the experience of a staff editorial writer at a large West Coast daily who matter-of-factly reported over drinks at a Port Angeles pub that his job was to write the consensus of the editorial board even if he did not agree with it. "I am a professional writer," he said. I discovered that some of these editorial writers had gone into the field in a process similar to horses being put out to pasture; publishers who no longer needed or valued their services on the news pages had forced them into the editorial section. For others, like me, editorial writing was an opportunity to engage in the Democratic forum and process, to trade in the marketplace of ideas.

And during my years as an editorial writer, I learned that while political parties, faces, and players change, most of what concerns us Americans remain the same: taxes, which either are too high (Ricken's viewpoint) or that could use a boost if it means better social services (mine); crime and punishment, one ought to fit the other (his) or we should avoid fixed sentencing and such drastic measures as capital punishment (mine); foreign policy, which, if done properly, would mean using armed might to intervene in the internal affairs of other nations and building up our nuclear arsenal (his) or placing greater reliance on diplomacy and negotiations (mine). So just as death and taxes are certainties of our existence, they, along with such regular editorial fare as racial issues, education, crime rates, budgets, education, and weather, have over the years made frequent and repeated topical visits to the commentary page.

Perusal of the editorial excerpts that open the chapters of this book, taken from Allan Nevins' excellent 1928 collection and analysis of editorials, *American Press Opinion: Washington to Coolidge, A Documentary Record of Editorial Leadership and Criticism, 1785–1927*, attests to the consistency of U.S. political topics and problems. These editorial snippets deal with issues that include race relations, the character of a president and his administration, political corruption, the fraudulent election of a president, a womanizing governor and presidential candidate, a mistaken war policy, and campaign finance abuse. All of these are issues that have revisited the nation's editorial pages in recent years.

Finally, from experience and from my colleagues, I discovered some general verities about editorial pages and editorial writing that, while quantitative studies may not bear them out, stand up to the qualitative experience test. Readers and politicians do pay attention to editorials. Elected and appointed government officials, be they on the left or right or in the middle, are viewed as scalawags or heroes depending on the political leanings and perceptions of the readers. I learned from studying the language of editorials that the nation is replete with policies that are "short-sighted," the United States has a plethora of problems that need to be "addressed," politics is filled with the need for "statesmanship, leadership and compromise," there are some issues that are too complex for immediate opinion and that therefore need "further study," others present obvious solutions that are "much needed," some public policy matters call for "dire" and "immediate" redress, and for every foreign threat that falls, from Nazism and communism, another, such as terrorism, will arise to take its place.

My experience in writing editorials and my passion for opinion writing and the nature of the editorial as an expression of opinion led me to conclude that the newspaper editorial is a logical avenue for the exploration of some of the larger issues and problems of today's newspaper journalism such as competition, particularly as measured in political ideology differences; ownership patterns; and the declining numbers of daily newspapers as the industry marches onward toward monopoly and chain, corporate ownership.

To this end, I began my research by formulating some questions that I would put to a limited number of newspaper executives to help me organize and frame my research. Modifications of these questions will appear near the end of this book in the form of a survey of editorial writers, but at the beginning, I simply wanted to get a feel for the research topics I planned to explore. For this preliminary survey, I selected three people: John Craig, former editor of the *Pittsburgh Post-Gazette*, because I was familiar with that newspaper, it was one that I respected not only for its editorial pages but for its reporting and writing in general; Richard Aregood, former editorial page editor of the *Star-Ledger* in Newark, New Jersey, and the *Daily News* in Philadelphia, Pennsylvania, before that, and a winner of the Pulitzer Prize for editorial writing, because I had frequently read his editorials while he was with the *Daily News* and I respected them for their strength of conclusion and for their clear, terse, and forceful language; and Lynnell Burkett, former editorial page editor of the *San Antonio Express-News* and 2004 president of the National Conference of Editorial Writers, because of her position as an officer in a national editorial writing organization, lending her an opportunity to speak on editorial writing as one familiar with issues and problems of the trade.[1]

These three members of industry, as we in academia call the newspaper business, offered some thoughts and ideas that will arise in this book, ranging from opinions on the importance of editorials and competition to observations about media ownership, and editorial writing and its power. Burkett and Aregood, for example, recalled editorial battles they had waged with the competition. Burkett, who was with the *San Antonio Light* before it was closed, remembered what she termed a "heated" editorial debate over the proposal for a new library in downtown San Antonio.

"As I recall, the publisher of the other newspaper adamantly wanted the old library kept, so we really went at different directions in that one," she said, adding that her newspaper argued on the grounds that the old library was antiquated and that a new library would better serve the community than would a refurbished one. "Our position prevailed, we did get a new library. I think the nature of the opposition was that they were worried about whether it would stay in the downtown area, which it did."

Both papers published several editorials on the subject in the late 1980s, she said. "We took it on as a crusade, our paper did, to get a new library. We really went hard on local issues, crusades, an agenda, that sort of thing; they were more traditional in their approach. The other newspaper was reactive, the *Light* was proactive at the time."

Aregood also recalled an editorial battle over a downtown building—a pro-posed convention center in Philadelphia—by the *Inquirer* and the *Daily News*, both owned by the Knight Ridder group.

"The *Inquirer* really loved the idea of locating a Pennsylvania convention center downtown," he said. "We thought it would be best to locate it elsewhere in the city. It was pretty vigorous; all the powers that be were pushing. We were fortunate that at that time the traditions of John S. Knight were still very much alive, the publisher favored it (downtown location), but he was an old-time Knight Newspapers publisher, and he didn't impose his will on us. I thought that was mighty nice of him. They won, by the way."

The newspapers also frequently differed on political endorsements, Aregood said. "Editorial competition was alive and well. There was a time when there was competition from the world's sleaziest tabloid, the *Philadelphia Journal*, even. It was kind of a European down market tab, plus there was the *Bulletin*. So there were at least four voices going at it at some points."

Aregood and his colleagues agreed on the value of vigorous editorial competition.

"It's sort of like the way I look at film critics," Aregood said, arguing that newspaper positions offer reliable barometers of public opinion and that a marketplace of opinion is important for informed debate. "If you know the critic, you are able to make your own choices. If you know your newspaper and what its typical positions are, you're much more capable of judging those positions. I think that's universally true. I suspect that the dittoheads that get their informa-tion with only one slant are pretty much limiting themselves; they don't get to hear the other voices. I think newspapers nowadays have overcompensated for being the only voice in the community, and many of them don't say anything, which is not a particularly good thing."

Having two editorial voices, Burkett said, provides an opportunity for differen-ces of opinion. Plus, "you have double the clout if you both agree on something. Beyond that, you have more of an opportunity for voices from the community, and voices period." Citing contributions from syndicated columnists, community-based commentators, and letter writers, she argued that a variety of viewpoints is beneficial. "The more voices, the more active, the merrier, as far as I'm concerned."

The community also relished the competition, responding in letters to the edi-tor and in feedback to the newspapers when the Hearst corporation bought the *Express News* from Rupert Murdoch and then closed down the *Light* in 1993, she said. "The community really did react as though they were losing something."

Craig also viewed competition in terms of a marketplace of ideas, in which dif-ferent voices compete in a debate, through a newspaper forum in the democratic process. "The point I'm pushing," he said in response to a question regarding what he viewed as the importance of editorial competition, "is serious differences of opinion, or serious discussions about the issues of the day, and that's not just because it's black and someone else says it's white. You present effective arguments and present an opportunity for people to differ with them."

Serious and vigorous discussion of the issues of the day has suffered, in Craig's view, from newspaper conglomeration and monopolization. "Mainly, what I think has happened is, we are eccentric in the best sense of the word, and that is what's been lost, it's become more homogenous. *USA Today* has become almost the embodiment of what you get when you are afraid to offend anybody, you want to be fair, and so on. It's just a big bore."

Aregood, while concerned about possible homogenization fostered by chain ownership such as that of Gannett, which owns *USA Today*, also worried about the power of a corporation to influence editorial position. "I think the days of big corporations dictating editorial policy are over. But I think a lot of strong positions make a lot of corporations nervous."

The questions surrounding conglomeration and monopolization go beyond mere ownership, in Burkett's view. Sometimes, she argued, newspapers can benefit because of their distance from the corporate ownership. "There's another way to look at it. If it's a local owner, that person could very well be more worried about offending than a corporation located elsewhere, and so it could cut either way."

Fear of offending businesses and corporations was cited by the editors as one of the major drawbacks of ownership trends that include monopolization and group ownership. Aregood, for example, cited a loss of editorial vigor due to fear of losing advertising revenue. Business concerns, he argued, get in the way of editorial integrity. "I think they chicken out, it's a business decision," he said. "The right-wing page of the *Detroit News* has been defanged because of the chains. I've been doing this long enough to know that somebody's been making a business decision, which certainly doesn't do the product any good."

Craig offered a similar concern. "From the point of view of business, making more money, selling more ads, you don't want to offend anybody. If you want to become successful within the profession, it's the same thing."

Two of the editors believed they were reaching the public, or at least important components of the public, on their editorial pages, while one believed that the power of the editorial has diminished over the years.

"Look at (Horace) Greeley," said Aregood when asked about the power of editorials of the past compared to that of the present. "He was wrong a lot, but people certainly read him. The abolition newspapers clearly had their influence. I'm not denigrating the power of editorials, otherwise I've wasted the last 40 years or so. I just don't think they've had the same impact as they did years ago. I can't return to 1893, so I don't know how people reacted then. From this vantage point maybe we're thinking they're a lot more popular than they were."

Burkett said that a readership survey conducted recently by her newspaper found greater readership of editorials than had been expected, including a finding that editorials enjoyed a greater readership than did the sports pages, which long have been regarded as leaders in reader popularity. Craig, though, said he didn't worry so much about the numbers of readers he was reaching as he did about the types of readers—the power elites—who come to the editorials. "The leader group, politicians, corporate CEOs, they pay more attention to editorials than do other people," he said. "There's nobody who looks at it like they do... I often write editorials; there's just about three or four people I want to read them."

Aregood offered a similar sentiment, mentioning that the New Jersey state treasurer was coming to visit the newspaper's editorial board the next day. "He cares what we do." The editorial, Aregood said, "is a way to get a message out to a more thoughtful audience than the people who watch the local Fox News."

The editors agreed that newspaper editorials will remain a part of the American media menu, at least in some form. And, as might be expected from those who make their living writing their opinions, they concurred on the value of the editorial—but for varying reasons. Craig, for example, cited the process of citizenship in a democratic government. "I love opinion, and I think it's the most important thing a newspaper does, without a doubt," he said. The editorial "is tangible evidence about what values and ideas the newspaper both embraces and puts forward. It is tangible expression of the nature of its citizenship."

Burkett saw the value of the editorial in its role of providing community dialogue. "It's the heart of the newspaper, it's the soul of the newspaper, it's the conscience of the community. It's where the community can have a conversation with itself, so if you believe that it's the soul of the newspaper and the conscience of the community, then that's pretty heavy, pretty important."

Aregood argued on behalf of the editorial's appeal to the intellect. "I think it's important because you have some people who are willing to do the work of breaking down issues and presenting them," he said. "Maybe they do present them with a spin. Even the *Wall Street Journal* editorial I find valuable, even though I disagree with them. It keeps thought alive, provides ammunition that somebody might use for their next cocktail party." Much newspaper content is filled with clichés, is redundant, and does not contribute to "anything intelligent," he added. "But we try to do that on the editorial page. We try to be intelligent, we try to be reflective. We're currently studying tax policy; I don't know who would do that if there weren't an editorial page. I guess a newspaper is the closest you get to diving deeply into subject matter for the average person. For 35 cents a day you get whatever profundities we produce."

I agree with all of this, and then some. As one who has made a living writing editorials, as a newspaper editor, and thus a gatekeeper who had decided what news my community would and would not find on my pages, the editorial page was the place that I considered nearly sacred. I have worked for editors who came to accept spelling and typographical errors in the newspaper at large, but not on the editorial page because, as one editor explained to me once, it is the one page that represents the newspaper's most important role—as community watchdog, agenda-setter, and conscience. I came to agree with these editors when I moved into their chairs.

Because of the importance that editors and many publishers lend to editorials and opinion, because editorials do represent bias and political ideology, because editorials try to exert leadership and to apply pressure to public decision-making, because those in the community who decide whom to tax and what roads to build and what classes to offer students pay attention to the editorials of their local newspaper—for all of these reasons, I have chosen the newspaper editorial to explore what this nation has lost and is losing in a diminishing marketplace of ideas.

Acknowledgments

This book is the result of three years of study and research that have given me the opportunity to learn from scholars who are recognized leaders in their respective fields. They include my doctoral dissertation committee members at Ohio University: Dr. Pat Washburn, who chaired my committee and introduced me to the rigors and art of historical research and writing and also oversaw a project that became my first published journal paper; Dr. Joe Bernt, who led me through a content analysis project that became a conference paper and part of this book and that helped immensely in refining my method; Dr. David Mould, who oversaw another historical research project that also became a conference paper, portions of which appear in this book; and Dr. Alonzo Hamby, distinguished professor of history, who provided intellectual stimulation and whose guidance contributed to the historical research of this book. Also, Dr. Dan Riffe introduced me to content analysis and oversaw a research project that became a conference paper and then a published journal article. His patience in instruction of statistical research methods to a mathematics-challenged former journalist was appreciated. I also want to thank my colleague, Dr. Ron Rodgers, who worked on one of these projects with me and helped me develop a coding method to identify and quantify ideological and subject variances in newspaper editorials; his friendship and support are valued. In addition, I want to thank the Scripps Howard Foundation for the teaching fellowship program that enabled me to undertake this research. Finally, I thank my wife, Joanne, who frequently accompanied me on my out-of-town research jaunts and who endured my doubts and shared my intellectual curiosity. All of these individuals contributed to this book; any faults of method or logic are mine exclusively.

Introduction

*In a war with England we shall need numerous armies and ample treasuries for
their support. The war-hounds that are howling for war through the continent
are not to be the men who are to force entrenchments, and scale ramparts against
the bayonet and the cannon's mouth; to perish in sickly camps or in long marches
through sultry heats or wastes of snow....*

*A nation that can debar the conqueror of Europe from the sea, and resist his
armies from Spain, will not surrender its provinces without a struggle. Those
who advocate a British war must be perfectly aware that the whole revenue aris-
ing from all British America for the ensuing century would not repay the expenses
of that war.*

—New York Evening Post, April 21, 1812, on the coming
War of 1812 against England[1]

The sprawl and aesthetic blight of billboards in her community bothered
Barbara Funkhouser. Then editor of the Gannett-owned *El Paso Times*, the largest newspaper in the West Texas city, Funkhouser decided in the early 1980s to
undertake an editorial campaign. It would consist of news stories followed by a
series of editorials on the billboard, or outside advertising, industry. She wanted
to look into its local effects and usage, and into attempts to legislate and regulate
such advertising, which dated to the campaign in the 1960s by former First Lady

Mrs. Lyndon B. (Lady Bird) Johnson to beautify America and its roadways. On the editorial page Funkhouser intended to call for city legislation to more rigidly regulate, but not necessarily eliminate, billboard advertising.

Funkhouser was expecting resistance from business-friendly city officials. What she was not prepared for, though, was censorship from her supervisors at Gannett, a company that has traditionally trumpeted the editorial freedom enjoyed by the chain newspaper organization's editors.[2] One day, before she had the opportunity to publish any editorials on the subject, she received a telephone call from her newspaper's in-house publisher nixing the campaign. So much for local editorial autonomy, she said some years later. "That lasts about ten minutes."[3] Other than the publisher telling her that he had heard from Gannett executives upset about her proposed campaign, she does not remember a lot about her anti-billboard efforts. She does recall, though, that Gannett owned an outdoor advertising company, which it since has sold. And she remembers "the hell I got" over the proposed billboard editorial campaign.[4]

What this episode demonstrates is not so much whether owners of chain newspapers allow their local editors full editorial autonomy. The extent or lack of such autonomy depends upon the chain involved, though there is evidence at least of a homogenizing effect on editorial position and policy by chain newspaper owners.[5] What Funkhouser's experience does speak to, however, are two phenomena regarding this country's media that came under increased scrutiny and research in the waning years of the twentieth century and the early years of the twenty-first.

One is the dwindling number of competing daily newspapers, including those involved in JOA (joint operating agreement) arrangements that enable separately owned newspapers, such as the morning *El Paso Times* and its then-rival, the now-defunct *El Paso Herald-Post,* to combine business and production operations while maintaining separate and competing editorial departments. Though the *Herald-Post* did not take up Funkhouser's billboard campaign, what is important here is that it could have; as a competing voice in El Paso, the Scripps Howard-owned *Herald-Post* offered an alternative outlet of information, opinions, and agendas. Had the issue of billboards become important to other community leaders besides Funkhouser, these leaders could have taken the issue to the competition; and the *Herald-Post* was free to take up such a campaign unrestrained by Gannett, had its editors so desired. Without the existence of the competing newspaper, that option is gone.

The closure of the *Herald-Post* in 1997 added El Paso to the ranks of U.S. cities that had traditionally enjoyed newspaper competition only to find themselves one-newspaper towns as part of a downward trend of such communities. The number of U.S. cities with daily newspaper competition totaled 502 in 1923.[6] This had declined to 288 by 1930. As of 2003, eleven cities had separately owned competing English-language daily newspapers housed in separate headquarters, and thirteen had newspapers involved in JOAs (see Table I.1).[7] These

Table I.1   U.S. Cities with Competing Daily Newspapers

	JOA cities	Separate newspaper cities
	Birmingham, AL (2)*	San Francisco, CA (2)*
	Tucson, AZ (2)*	Washington, DC (2)*
	Denver, CO (2)*	Honolulu, HI (2)*
	Salt Lake City, UT (2)*	Chicago, IL (5)*
	Fort Wayne, IN (2)*	Boston, MA (2)*
	Detroit, MI (2)*	Columbia, MO (2)*
	Las Vegas, NV (2)*	Trenton, NJ (2)*
	Albuquerque, NM (2)*	New York, NY (4)*
	Cincinnati, OH (2)*	Wilkes-Barre, PA (2)*
	York, PA (2)*	Kingsport, TN (2)*
	Seattle, WA (2)*	Green Bay, WI (2)*
	Charleston, WV (2)*	
	Madison, WI (2)*	
Total	13 (26)	11 (27)

*Number of newspapers in that city.
Source: Melvin Mencher, *News Reporting and Writing,* 9th ed. (New York: McGraw Hill, 2003), and
   Editor & Publisher International Yearbook 2003 (New York: Editor & Publisher, 2003).

twenty-four cities offering newspaper editorial competition took in a total of fifty-three newspapers based within these communities.

As for the hundreds of cities that had daily newspaper competition in 1923 but that no longer enjoyed daily newspaper competition as of 2003 and the thousands of other cities and towns that never had such competition, they are served by monopoly newspapers (many of which are group-owned and supervised by absentee owners or boards), by dailies that experience some competition from weekly or semiweekly newspapers, by weekly or semiweekly newspapers only, or they have no newspapers at all.

Accompanying the decline of competing daily newspapers in the United States has been a decrease in newspaper readership as measured by daily circulation. The country at the beginning of 1930 had a total daily newspaper circulation (excluding Sundays) of 39,589,172 serving a population of 122,698,192.[8] By 2003, the nation's population had more than doubled that of 1930, to 292,654,345, an increase of 138.5 percent, while daily newspaper circulation stood at 55,186,157, an increase of just 39.4 percent.[9] So the ratio of population to circulation in that time period declined significantly.

In 1970, the year that Congress passed the Newspaper Preservation Act codifying JOAs, the total daily newspaper circulation in the country was 62,107,527, serving a population of 203,302,031. So, the newspaper industry between 1970 and 2003 experienced a net loss in circulation of 6,921,370, a decrease of about 11.1 percent, while the population grew by 89,352,314, an increase of nearly 44 percent.[10]

CONGLOMERATION, CROSS-OWNERSHIP, AND CONVERGENCE

The other phenomenon at work in the story of the stymied El Paso billboard newspaper campaign is the conglomeration and concentration of media, including newspaper, broadcasting, entertainment, and other information companies, and how such concentration affects media coverage. Besides the business arrangement of the *El Paso Times* with its JOA sister paper, the other important consideration of the situation that Funkhouser faced was the cross-ownership factor. Gannett's interests in the billboard industry at that time conflicted with the newspaper editor's interests in taking on the billboard industry. This sort of media ownership pattern has prompted some media analysts to argue that recent trends toward greater concentration and monopoly in information industries pose a threat to a functioning democracy because of the resulting decline in media competition and in the marketplace of ideas. Journalism educator and former newspaperman Ben Bagdikian articulated the problem in his book *The Media Monopoly*. As discussed by Bagdikian, the trend toward conglomerate media ownership in the last half of the twentieth century included cross-ownership, so that newspapers, television stations, radio outlets, magazines, books, and film companies increasingly had common owners or were overseen by common boards. This means, as Gannett did to protect its billboard business in El Paso, that corporations have greater ability to prevent news that might damage their financial interests from being broadcast or published. This is despite the existence today of large numbers of daily newspapers, broadcast stations, magazines, cable systems, book and magazine publishers, and movie studios that some media analysts cite as evidence of great competition and diversity.

But as Bagdikian wrote in 2000, "If the number of outlets is growing and the number of owners declining, then each owner controls ever more formidable communications power. Furthermore, the growing numbers [of media outlets], ironically, accompany a growing uniformity of content."[11] This ownership trend also touches on economic factors, such as budgets, staff sizes, and resources, that can affect editorial content.

As this book is written, more newspaper conglomeration is taking place. In spring of 2006, the McClatchy newspaper group purchased all of the newspapers owned by the Knight Ridder chain. McClatchy was reportedly in the process of seeking in turn to sell some of those newspaper properties to other interested parties in an industry shake-up that some analysts see as a realignment trend of American newspapers toward regionalized markets.[12] This sale affects some of the newspaper markets analyzed in this book.

Discussion of declining newspaper competition and readership takes in at least one other recent media trend: convergence. Beyond such cultural factors as less free time available to spend reading newspapers, researchers and industry analysts have attributed declining newspaper sales and readership to influences that include the rise of radio and then television and, most recently, the Internet and cable television. Studies have shown that television has replaced newspapers as Americans' dominant source of news, at least at the national level, a trend that has remained steady in recent years. A 1997 study by the Radio and Television News Directors Foundation found that television was the primary source of information for 56 percent of the general public, followed by newspapers at 24 percent, radio at 14 percent, magazines at 1 percent, and online (Internet) at 1 percent.[13] A 1991 study found that cable television has shared increasingly in this trend, bringing more channels and options to consumers of media information.[14] Similarly, a 1992 study found cable eating into the traditional superiority of both broadcast television and radio from 1980 through 1989. Cable outlets offer an increased volume and frequency of information dealing with national and international topics if not local and regional subjects, which find relatively more air time on local broadcast affiliates.

A 2000 study of media usage found a gain for Internet over the previous four years accompanied by a decline in local and network television news and newspaper usage. The researchers offered no explanation for this decline but concluded that the Internet was not necessarily the cause of it. They measured the decline as follows: from 70.8 percent in 1995 to 59.4 percent in 1999 in regular usage of local television news, from 67.3 to 60.4 percent for network television news, from 59.3 to 54.2 percent in regular usage of the daily newspaper. During the same period, Internet usage increased from 5.3 to 34.5 percent.[15] The authors did report, however, a complementary rather than a competitive relationship among consumers of Internet news, newspapers, and radio news, and they found that people who use the Internet are more likely to read newspapers than people who do not use the Internet. The same does not hold for television.

A study conducted the following year found a "moderately high degree of overlap or similarity between the niches of the Internet and the traditional media on the gratification-opportunities dimension," though Internet news demonstrated superiority over other news media except cable in categories that included content variety and availability of news at differing times of the day.[16] These findings are relevant to the discussion in this book because they are evidence of a diversification of usage within new media (i.e., Internet and cable television) and of convergence in media usage.

The 1997 Radio and Television News Directors Foundation study cited above supports this finding of complementary usage: "Among those respondents who regularly read a daily newspaper, 64 percent go online and 66 percent are AOL (America Online) subscribers." A "State of the News Media 2004" *Quill* magazine assessment found that despite the rise of online and alternative journalism outlets, "media consumers still enjoy reading, even though a 'one-size-fits-all' newspaper format may not work in the future."[17]

Complementary use of online, broadcast, and print media was touted by journalism professor Janet Kolodzy in a 2003 *Columbia Journalism Review* column.

Convergence, she wrote, "can also harness the benefits of online, broadcast and print to provide news to people when and where they want it. Few people get their news from one source anymore. Just look at all the ways people got news about the war in Iraq. They used TV for immediacy, online for diversity, and print for context."[18]

Also, the 1997 Radio and Television News Directors Foundation study found that other factors, such as gender and education levels, played roles in media usage, and "people's level of political knowledge is powerfully related to how interested they are in news and public affairs, and is less strongly related to which dominant media source they use."[19]

This study noted one other variable that is important to consider in looking at media usage and the significance of medium selection. Two-thirds of the study's survey participants cited information about their towns and communities as news in which they were "very interested." This was followed by news about their state or the region of the state in which they lived. Consumers who "report a high level of interest in local news show little interest in information about the larger world," the study reported. "These people tend to rely on newspapers and television, gender and generational differences are less severe, and college graduates and online users express little interest."[20]

Finally, the Radio and Television News Directors Foundation study found some reliance on professional gatekeepers of information: A "significant portion, 29 percent, 'say that a news editor is in a better position to select what might be of interest to them.'"[21]

That consumers of information place a high priority on localism is important for the purposes of this book, for which the research suggests meaningful findings regarding localism in editorial diversity. This, along with the observation that consumers often look to editors to help them wade through information, indicates that newspapers or newspaper companies continue to play a key role in providing information, analysis, and opinion, particularly on matters of local and regional interests. A 1991 study attested to this, finding that while people rely most on television for three types of national news, "clearly it is newspapers they turn to for local news."[22] And a 1983 study found that newspapers prevailed over television as a source of state government news.[23]

The decline of competing local daily newspaper voices diminishes not only the availability of local and regional news to consumers but also the availability of competing opinions and ideas, not just at local levels but at all levels. Social thinkers, historians, and political analysts have identified such diversity of thought—a marketplace of ideas—as essential to a functioning democracy.

THE MARKETPLACE OF IDEAS METAPHOR

John Milton argued in his *Areopagitica* in 1644 that truth will emerge from a multitude of ideas in an atmosphere of free thought and individual rights. He wrote that in a head-to-head confrontation with falsehood, truth will win out. "So Truth be in the field, we do injuriously by licensing and prohibiting the misdoubt of her strength. Let her and Falsehood grapple; who ever knew Truth put to the worse in a free and open encounter?"[24] John Stuart Mill expanded the marketplace concept beyond individual rights and truth-finding to one that would facilitate a democratic government through a citizen-based process of decision-making. As Fordham University communications professor Philip M. Napoli suggested in 2001, "Mill was among the first to conceptualize free speech as serving an extended social good beyond the rights of the individual."[25]

The marketplace of ideas metaphor took on legalistic and political/democratic ramifications and interpretations in twentieth-century U.S. Supreme Court decisions and governmental policies on behalf of democratic ideals. At the same time, it has been invoked by political and media analysts who cite a free and diverse marketplace of beliefs, in which citizens choose from an abundance of ideas, as vital to fostering robust debate in maintaining and promoting a democratic form of government. As J. A. Smith argued in his 1981 study of the relationship of the marketplace of ideas to freedom of expression, while the marketplace metaphor has come under some criticism when applied to the press, the concept nonetheless has become established as basic to the notion of free expression.[26]

Robert A. Rutland, in his 1987 study of the newspaper editorial debate sparked by the 1787–88 ratification of the U.S. Constitution, spoke to the vitality and significance of the editorial discussion in which the nation's intellectual and political elite realized that "something fundamental had happened to the political process in the new Republic." He agreed with Jefferson that the best preservation of the nation's liberty is through public debate.[27] In the context of the media's role in informing the public, Steven H. Chaffee and Donna G. Wilson argued in 1977 that communities of diverse opinion "would seem to be functioning more in the manner of the Jeffersonian ideal than those communities where few problems are perceived as important, and where there is little diversity of opinion or change in perspective over time."[28] David Pearce Demers, an ardent defender of corporate ownership of newspapers, has conceded the importance of the marketplace and a pluralistic social system, arguing in 1996 that one of the strengths of corporate media ownership is that it will ensure and even increase a diversity of ideas and thinking, thus keeping intact a political dialogue that is vital to a democracy.[29]

These media analysts were building on a journalism-based marketplace foundation articulated in 1947 by a distinguished panel of scholars and intellectuals that formed the Commission on Freedom of the Press, better known as the Hutchins Commission. The panel, whose members included Columbia University economics professor John M. Clark, Yale law professor Harold D. Lasswell, former U.S. Assistant Secretary of State Archibald MacLeish, noted philosopher Reinhold Niebuhr, Harvard history professor Arthur M. Schlesinger, Harvard law professor Zechariah Chafee Jr., and University of Chicago Chancellor

Robert M. Hutchins, cited Milton's "victory of truth over falsehood" notion in observing that

> public discussion is a necessary condition of a free society and...freedom of expression is a necessary condition of adequate public discussion. Public discussion elicits mental power and breadth; it is essential to the building of a mentally robust public; and, without something of the kind, a self-governing society could not operate.[30]

The commission again invoked the marketplace metaphor when it argued that U.S. society needs accurate and truthful information. "We need a market place for the exchange of comment and criticism regarding public affairs. We need to reproduce on a gigantic scale the open argument which characterized the village gatherings two centuries ago."[31]

The American media, observed the commission, framing its comments in a context that included a discussion of the "Big Business," profit-driven emphasis of the press and newspapers, were not meeting these needs.

> The news is twisted by the emphasis on firstness, on the novel and sensational; by the personal interests of owners; and by pressure groups. Too much of the regular output of the press consists of a miscellaneous succession of stories and images which have no relation to the typical lives of real people anywhere. Too often the result is meaningless among widely scattered groups whose only contact is through these media....When we look at the press as a whole, however, we must conclude that it is not meeting the needs of our society. The Commission believes that this failure of the press is the greatest danger to its freedom.[32]

Because the marketplace of ideas concept takes in the notion of ideas competing in a struggle to arrive at a perceived truth, any consideration of the marketplace of ideas concept in a newspaper market should include an analysis of competition. As with the debate over effects of ownership, researchers and analysts are divided on the importance and contribution of competition to a diverse marketplace of ideas. Some observers—including Michael W. Drager who, in a study of the editorial page content of 105 newspapers, found little diversity among the papers[33]—have questioned whether competition actually brings about editorial diversity. But others have argued it is vital to maintaining a marketplace of ideas. These range from Theodore L. Glasser, who wrote in 1984 that the First Amendment fosters "divergent points of view" that promote "an informed citizenry,"[34] to the U.S. district judge who in 1972 upheld the 1970 Newspaper Preservation Act on the grounds that it preserved editorial independence.[35] Discussions of the benefits of media competition cite not only Jeffersonian ideals but also *laissez-faire* economic theory, which argues that a free and competitive media market is one operating in classic capitalistic fashion and fostering a range of ideas whose merits are decided by the consumers.

Bagdikian, writing on behalf of media competition in the newspaper industry, discussed the reading habits developed before the rise of mass advertising, when "papers succeeded solely because they pleased their readers." In that pre-mass-advertising era of the nineteenth century, Bagdikian argued,

Readers were clustered in terms of their serious political and social ideas—some were conservative, some liberal, some radical—and they had religious or regional loyalties. Each paper tended to focus a great deal of its information on the preferences of its readers. Because papers were physically smaller, lacking mass advertising, they were cheaper to print.... The result was a wider spectrum of political and social ideas than the public gets from contemporary newspapers. The frequent excess among adversarial papers of the past is the normal social cost of rigorous debate in a democracy.[36]

Regardless of the debate over the benefits of competition, it has played a key role in U.S. media operations, particularly in newspaper markets. Thus, it will be an integral component of analysis and research here, and a review of the literature on the subject of competition will be cited.

The purpose of this book and its research is not to focus on the phenomena of conglomeration and convergence. While these are vital components of the media economic structure and operation, they are dealt with in depth in other venues. Rather, the intention here is to study one effect of these changing dynamics of ownership: diminished competitive newspaper markets. The aim of this book is to help determine how these changing market dynamics are affecting competition and editorial diversity in a forum, newspapers, that traditionally has supplied the American democracy with its marketplace of ideas. The purpose is to analyze what is offered in markets that currently enjoy daily newspaper competition and thus to discern what might be lost if they become one-newspaper markets. It also is to discover what has been lost in those markets that experienced such competition in the past, and thus to look at what is missing in those communities that never have experienced such competition.

EDITORIAL ANALYSIS

The editorial page is the section of the newspaper that serves as a community's conscience, that sets its priorities, that serves as a community sounding board. Journalism educator Gayle A. Waldrop's 1967 description of the editorial page's role in society remains apt. Waldrop argued that the editorial page lends meaning to the complexity of the day's events, takes on the battles of the citizenry, helps free the reader from myths and demagoguery, offers a daily forum for community dialogue, cultivates public opinion, and in the process nurtures democracy. "For the newspaper, the editorial page is (1) a source of personality, of 'conscience, courage, and convictions'; (2) a means of demonstrating that 'A newspaper is a citizen of its community,' a statement which appears in the editorial masthead of the Eugene [Oregon] *Register-Guard*; (3) 'a leaven and a guide to the whole newspaper operation.'"[37] Also, as F. Dennis Hale argued in 1988, the editorial page "serves as a showcase of how that newspaper satisfies its watchdog obligation to oversee and interpret the actions of government."[38] This book will examine that "personality," "conscience," and "showcase."

Editorials reflect content of the entire newspaper. At some point during the year every topic covered in a newspaper, from politics to sports and the arts, draws editorial discussion. Because upper-echelon newspaper executives, including the editor and frequently the publisher, sit on editorial boards, editorials represent content considered by these executives to be important. The process by which editorial boards arrive at their opinions has changed over the years. In the first newspapers of the colonial and Revolutionary War period, single owners reported, wrote, and printed everything in their newspapers, including editorials, which then were hard to distinguish from regular reporting. As the newspaper industry grew and changed, so did this process so that in the modern era, larger and midsize newspapers employ editorial specialists who gather daily with the editor and sometimes the publisher (who reports to an absentee owner in the case of chain newspapers) to discuss editorial topics. The editorial writers bring their own ideas, and agendas, to these daily editorial board meetings, at which these ideas are debated until a consensus is reached. At that point, the group, under the direction and approval of the editor (and sometimes the publisher), agrees on the newspaper's stance. In all editorial debates, the publisher has the final say, followed by the editor and the editorial page editor. The opinion typically thus has come to represent more of a committee and institutional agenda and less that of an individual writer.

IDEOLOGY AND FRAMING

Editorials, the object of analysis for this book's study of competition and the marketplace of ideas, are avenues of opinion and agenda-setting. Thus, they are a venue through which diversity of thought is highly likely to appear in a newspaper and in competing newspapers. Such diversity is defined in two different ways for this book. One is differences in political ideology, such as Republican versus Democratic stances, or conservative versus liberal. Such differences are typically found, for example, in presidential endorsement editorials, in which newspapers not only can differ in their choice of candidates of different parties, most often Democratic or Republican, but also might discuss other political philosophy differences, such as tax and spending proposals and policies. Ideological diversity also might be found in editorials addressing such controversial topics as abortion or capital punishment.

The other editorial difference most analyzed here is framing. This sort of difference is found not so much in disagreements over political ideology but rather in emphasis or focus of editorials, or in what political analysts have labeled as "spin." For example, the editorials of two competing newspapers regarding a president's State of the Union speech might agree with the president's initiatives or proposals and thus offer no evidence of political ideological disparity; but this agreement may be expressed in different areas of public policy. One editorial might focus primarily on the foreign policy aspects of the president's address while the other places its emphasis on the president's domestic agenda. So, while both may support the president, they have selected different programs or policies as being of primary importance. Certainly, in some instances framing is an extension of ideology because it sometimes is done within an ideological context and thus is not necessarily ideologically neutral.

In other instances, though, framing differences clearly are distinctions of focus, and this sort of variance can be just as important as political ideology divergence because it represents a disagreement in agenda-setting, with one editorial board placing more emphasis on foreign policy and its relationship to national security and well-being than its rival, for example.

Journalist and media critic Richard Harwood explained this kind of variance in another way at a forum of the Committee of Concerned Journalists.

> The journalists at the *New York Times* told us the other day that the New York Giants lost a football game by a score of 20-8. Now that was a small piece of truth. But the story of why the Giants lost can be told in a hundred different ways—each story being written through a different lens that is fogged over by stereotypes and personal predilections.[39]

Editorials, like game stories, have different takes and interpretations, and how the editorial writers interpret and use facts and opinions to persuade, to set an agenda, or to scold can bring about an important different meaning for the reading public.

Along with these major differences come other, more subtle variances in editorial framing, such as tone (i.e., a sarcastic, dismissive voice as opposed to a sober and serious treatment) and even editorial placement (i.e., lead editorial versus the third editorial of the day, or even of a day or two later) and length (i.e., a long, ten-paragraph commentary versus a more succinct and less thorough or well-argued five-paragraph treatment).

Finally, gatekeeping—the process by which newspaper owners, editors, and writers determine what subjects receive play and editorial treatment and which ones might be cast aside—is a theoretical element that comes into play in the editorial process. It is an element that, considered here, plays a role in agenda-setting as practiced in selection of topics deemed important for community consideration on the editorial pages of the newspaper.

RESEARCH METHOD

The research and discussion in this book analyzed the content of historical and modern-day editorials to seek answers to the following questions. Have these competing newspaper editorials demonstrated a diversity of opinion and ideas? And if so, what sort of diversity has been found: Political ideology, framing, or something else? Have they offered differences in topic, or in focus on geographical region? What does the decline of such diversity mean to American democracy? Why is newspaper editorial diversity important in an era of increased media informational outlets, such as cable television and the Internet?

Editorials are defined here as unsigned columns that represent the official opinions of the newspaper's editorial board and that appear on the editorial page. Other materials on the same page, such as letters to the editor, reprints of other newspapers' editorials, columns written by syndicated columnists, writers from the community who were not employed by the newspaper, writers who were not one of the newspaper's stable of editorial writers for the opinion page, initialed opinions that appeared in the same location as the editorials, were not counted as editorials. Also not counted were columns carrying such labels as "Hits & Misses" or "Cheers & Jeers," collections of brief observations of just a few sentences. These quick-hit editorial roundups do not stand as fully developed and reasoned editorials; counting them as such would skew the findings and purposes of this study, which are intended to analyze fully developed editorials to discover and study variance of opinion in competing newspapers.

The research method is primarily content analysis of historical and modern-day editorials through secondary and primary sources—books and studies, archival and Internet research. Also, editors of editorial pages involved in the studies of this book were surveyed to determine their attitudes and perceptions of the roles and effects of their editorials.

The modern-day editorial analyses considered daily newspapers in three types of competitive markets. One is direct competition markets, in which the newspapers were in the same community but were owned separately, had separate production and business operations, and were housed in separate headquarters. An example of a direct competition market is Chicago, where the *Tribune* and *Sun-Times* competed. The second is JOA markets, in which the newspapers were owned separately, had competing editorial departments, but were housed in the same building and shared production and business operations. An example of a JOA market is Cincinnati, where the *Enquirer* and *Post* were owned by different groups and competed editorially but shared production and business operations. Findings and a literature review indicate that JOA newspapers operate similarly to separate competitive market newspapers. The third is metroplex markets, in which newspapers of separate but neighboring communities were owned and produced independently but competed for circulation and advertising in a larger metropolitan market. An example of a metroplex market is Dallas/Fort Worth, where the *Dallas Morning News* and the *Fort Worth Star-Telegram* were separately owned and headquartered in communities a half-hour's drive apart but competed for readers and advertisers in a converging greater metropolitan area market.

The scarcity of competing newspapers, either direct competition or JOA, resulted in a limited sample. As of the latest date that this research was conducted, 2004, most such newspapers were in the northern United States (only four of the competitive markets were in the south, in Alabama, Tennessee, Washington, D.C., and West Virginia) and were spread across the continent.

Newspapers for study were not selected randomly but were chosen with the following criteria in mind: They represented competitive newspaper markets across the country (from the East, the Midwest, the West, and the South); they included newspapers of a variety of circulation sizes; and they took in varying types of ownership and operation (group, private, and JOA). The research purposely included newspapers that once belonged to JOA operations that no longer exist, such as those in the Pittsburgh and Tulsa markets, or that were endangered as this book was written, such as Cincinnati and Seattle.

The research of historic and modern-day direct competition and JOA markets included two from the West (Denver and Seattle), three from the Midwest (Chicago, Cincinnati, and Fort Wayne), five from the East (Boston, Wilkes-Barre, Cleveland, Pittsburgh, and Washington, D.C.), and one from the Southwest (Tulsa). Of the twenty-four competitive U.S. markets as of the end of 2003, this research included seven of them, or better than a fourth (29.2 percent) of all of the competitive markets. The two metroplex competition markets analyzed were included in this research primarily to help determine if metroplex competition substitutes for JOA or direct-market competition. The author visited each of the cities involved in the research to conduct on-site archival analysis, except where otherwise noted.

The analyses included a survey of literature on editorials of various historical eras along with the study of historical editorial archives in Washington, D.C., Pittsburgh, Cleveland, and Tulsa. The first city was chosen for study because as the nation's capital it offered a sampling of editorial competition in the center of the country's national political activity. Also, it and Cleveland were cities with direct competition newspapers of which one eventually ceased operations. The other two cities were communities in which newspapers that once competed directly entered into JOAs that eventually failed, leaving each city with only one major daily newspaper.

Historical analyses were not intended as a catchall survey of editorials on every major topic of U.S. history, nor was the selection of eras or issues random. Rather, selection of editorials was deliberate, based on important issues and dates throughout U.S. history, from the post–Revolutionary War era through that of the Penny Press and the early twentieth century. Source material that served as guidance in editorial subject selection included the author's course lecture notes and readings from graduate-level studies in American history, and events and dates selected from the *Encyclopedia of American History Bicentennial Edition*.[40] The 1970 cutoff date of historical research was selected because that is when the Newspaper Preservation Act became law.

Editorials of newspapers in cities that had daily editorial competition as of 2003 also were analyzed. This included archival research in the direct competition markets of Chicago, and Wilkes-Barre, Pennsylvania, selected because they represent, respectively, big-city, historically robust direct competition and small-community direct competition that has become even more rare than such competition in larger urban markets. Also included were newspapers in the JOA markets of Cincinnati, Ohio, and Fort Wayne, Indiana (research has found that JOA newspapers "more closely resemble competitive newspapers in news and editorial content than they do monopoly newspapers").[41] Again, these cities vary in the relative size of their populations and newspaper circulation. A metroplex market archival analysis considered editorials in Pittsburgh/Greensburg and Dallas/Fort Worth. These markets were selected because each is a community that previously had head-to-head competition before one of the competing newspapers (the *Pittsburgh Press* and the Dallas *Times Herald*) went out of business—in both cases, the newspapers that were closed had been purchased by their competitors before they were closed.

Modern-era editorials were not selected at random; the sampling was deliberate. The purpose was to find editorials on similar subjects and during similar periods of time, enabling analysis of editorial disagreement and variety. The sampling was of editorials published during the first month of 2001 and the first month of 2003. The first month of each year was selected because that is a time period during which presidents, governors, and mayors traditionally give their State of the Union, State of the State, and State of the City addresses, assessing the events and issues of the previous year and offering their proposals and visions for the coming year. It also is when legislative leaders begin to lay out their agendas for the coming year. And it is a time when newspapers traditionally discuss on their editorial pages the achievements and failures of the past year and their agendas for the coming year. Thus, this time frame offered subject matter on which competing newspapers would be likely to offer diverse editorial opinions. The year 2001 marked the beginning of a new century and a Republican presidency that led a shift in the nation away from the previous eight years' Democratic Party policies and practices. It was the end of a four-year presidential and election cycle, and it was a time period when political issues and events might be juxtaposed against those of the president's Democratic predecessor. The year 2003 was selected because it offered a lapse of two years for comparison, and it represented an off-year election campaign period.

Editorials were categorized according to geographical focus (i.e., subjects of local, state/regional, national, or international interest; also an "other" was used for topics that might not fit any geographic boundary or that take in more than one geographic area). Frequency of editorials was determined by a count of the editorials for the months studied. Editorials also were counted to determine their frequency on common subjects and according to whether they agreed or disagreed in their conclusions on these shared topics. If disagreement was found on shared-topic editorials, another tally was conducted to determine frequency and percentage of editorials that disagreed for ideological reasons versus those that disagreed in framing.

However, ideological differences in this coding not only were defined as Republican or conservative versus Democratic or liberal arguments and conclusions but also were defined on the basis of disagreement in editorial conclusion not necessarily tied to political philosophy. There is no Democratic or

Republican method of filling potholes, for example, or for routing traffic from the state capital to a community; but newspapers might disagree over whether a pothole-filling project should take precedence over installation of new traffic lights, or over whether an existing route should be paralleled in building a new highway to the capital. These differences are considered here to be ideological differences, defined simply as disagreement in their conclusions. The definition of framing difference relies primarily on focus of the editorial subject, as explained above. For example, two newspapers might agree that the city needs to fill the potholes but they might disagree over the amount of money to be spent on the project or on the mayor's rationale for undertaking the project. Examples of the different sorts of diversity will be offered in subsequent chapters.

Categories devised by Paul Deutschmann were used to count editorial frequency according to subject. These subjects were politics and government, war and defense, economic activity, crime, public health and welfare, education and classic arts, accident and disaster, science and invention, popular amusements, general human interest, and public moral problems.[42] While it could be argued that most of these topic categories ultimately become political issues, selection was based on the primary emphasis of the editorial. One researcher did all of the coding, replicating a method used in a previous study by this author and others, published in the fall 2004 issue of the *Newspaper Research Journal,* which produced an inter-coder reliability of 96.5 percent.[43]

To help further measure political ideological differences, editorials also were analyzed according to whether they agreed with policies and initiatives of the administration of President George W. Bush. This analysis was not limited to single or specific policies; rather, it took in all Bush administration policies and initiatives regardless of topic to ascertain whether the newspapers exhibited a general political trend.

These content analyses sought to answer the following questions: Did the competing newspapers differ in the number of editorials offered? Did the competing newspapers differ in the frequency and percentage of editorials published on local and other geographical topic focus? Did the competing newspapers differ ideologically or in other ways in their editorials and, if so, how frequently and in what percentage of their total editorial frequency? How did the competing newspapers differ in the subject emphasis of their editorials?

Also, a case study was done of editorials in six markets during the U.S. presidential campaign of 2004 to discover if they offered ideological or framing diversity. The analysis was of two direct competition cities (Boston and Chicago), two JOA competition cities (Seattle and Denver), and two metroplex competition cities (Dallas/Fort Worth and Pittsburgh/Greensburg). The research analyzed how these newspapers commented editorially on various issues and events of the 2004 presidential campaign, including endorsement editorials. The study was done through the newspapers' online web pages, enabling archival searches using key words and rendering travel to the six cities involved unnecessary because the Internet offered same-day access to these editorials. Coding for this analysis, done by a single coder, identified four categories of editorials: those that differed for reasons of political ideology; those that differed in framing; those that generally agreed in their analysis or conclusions; and those that did not appear (subjects for which no editorial could be found by one of the two competing newspapers). This research also drew on a tally of editorial endorsements conducted by *Editor & Publisher* magazine, a newspaper industry organ, and published daily during the campaign on its web site, focusing on the markets identified here as being either JOA or direct competition daily newspaper markets (see Table I.1). The six markets and twelve newspapers used for the analysis of the twelve election campaign issues were selected during the summer of 2004.

Finally, an Internet/telephone survey of the editorial page editors of the eighteen newspapers involved in these content analyses was conducted to study the editors' attitudes about the roles of their editorials and their perceptions regarding effects of ownership and new media on the editorial process. The results of these findings, while not statistically valid, are important in their findings regarding editors' approach to and opinions about their work.

EDITORIAL COMPETITION SCANT, BUT RELEVANT

Little in-depth research of editorial page competition has been conducted. Demers included some analysis of editorials in his 1996 book, and newspaper market scholar Stephen Lacy included some study of the effects of competition on editorials in his 1986 doctoral dissertation and elsewhere. Also, researchers have produced a number of studies on editorial effects, which will be considered further in this book. Other than broad discussions dealing with the importance of newspaper competition and of the marketplace of ideas to the democratic process, little research has been found of editorial focus on diversity and competition in the context of the marketplace of ideas. Such research is important because of the historical, political, and cultural significance assigned to diverse opinion and thought by the nation's founders and by legal and historical scholars, jurists, and observers. Analysis of editorials in this context is logical and meaningful because editorial pages are the place in a newspaper where ideas and opinions pertaining to political and social subjects are likely to be consistently presented, where such journalistic principles as objectivity and fairness are set aside in favor of partisanship and argument, and where the readers are most likely to seek out and find ideas and opinions with which they agree or disagree. The newspaper editorial page is where a vigorous political, cultural, and social discussion and debate is most likely to take place and thus is a likely focus of an analysis of newspaper content as evidence of a thriving—or dying—marketplace of ideas. It should be noted, however, that newspaper editorials can, and do, sometimes differ in their opinions and findings with content elsewhere in the newspaper, including signed opinion columns and even in some news coverage. Editorials do offer, though, a reliable measure of official news-paper opinion and ideas that can be compared and quantified.

CHAPTER SUMMARIES

This book's chapters are divided according to market and method. Chapter 1 offers a brief historical overview looking at how editorials helped shape the nation's political and cultural history, defining it and separating it from its European roots.

Chapter 2 offers an analysis of newspapers involved in head-to-head, or direct competition, beginning with an historical treatment and followed by analyses of modern-day competitive newspapers.

Chapter 3 analyzes modern-day editorials in JOA markets, and Chapter 4 offers the same sort of analysis for metroplex markets, using the same method.

Chapter 5 analyzes the editorials of all three kinds of markets during the 2004 presidential campaign, and Chapter 6 presents the results of the survey of editorial page editors.

Chapter 7 draws conclusions from the findings of the three research methods employed and offers ideas on how newspaper competition can be maintained in a national marketplace of increasing conglomeration and monopolization.

CHAPTER 1

Of Slavery and Sunsets

Some time during the last week one of those outrageous transactions—and we really think, disgraceful to the character of civilized man—took place near the northeast boundary line of Perry, adjoining Bibb and Autauga Counties, Georgia. The circumstances, we are informed by a gentleman from that county are, that a Mr. McNeily having lost some clothing or some other property of no great value, the slave of a neighboring planter was charged with the theft. McNeily in company with his brother found the negro driving his master's wagon; they seized him and either did or were about to chastise him, when the negro stabbed McNeily so that he died in an hour afterwards. The negro was taken before a justice of the peace, who after serious deliberation waived his authority—perhaps through fear, as the crowd of persons from the above counties had collected to the number of seventy or eighty near Mr. Peoples' (the justice) house. He acted as president of the mob and put the vote, when it was decided he should be immediately executed by being burnt to death. The sable culprit was led to a tree and tied to it, and a large quantity of pine knots collected and placed around him, and the fatal torch was applied to the pile even against the remonstrances of several gentlemen who were present: and the miserable being was in a short time burnt to ashes. An inquest was held over the remains, and the sheriff of Perry County, with a company of about twenty men, repaired to the neighborhood where this barbarous act took place, to secure those concerned, with what success we have not heard: but we hope he will succeed in bringing the perpetrators of so high-handed a measure to account...

—Washington *National Intelligencer*, July 23, 1827[1]

On the morning of May 30, 1921, a young black man who worked as a bootblack in downtown Tulsa, Oklahoma, went to the top floor of the Drexel building, near the shoe shine parlor, to use the restroom. The operator of the elevator that 19-year-old Dick Rowland rode that day was a white girl, Sarah Page, who was estimated to be 17. A few minutes after boarding the elevator, Rowland reportedly ran out of the elevator after witnesses heard Page scream. The next day, two Tulsa police officers arrested Rowland on suspicion of attempted rape.

The facts regarding the alleged assault are murky, according to Scott Ellsworth's 1983 account of the incident, *Death in a Promised Land/The Tulsa Race Riot of 1921*. No evidence surfaced that Rowland attempted to assault the girl, but one account said he accidentally stepped on the elevator operator's foot and that she screamed when he grabbed her arm attempting to break her fall.[2] Nonetheless, a mob of 300–400 angry Tulsans converged on the county courthouse on the night of his arrest. By 10:30 p.m. the size of the crowd had grown to between 1,500 and 2,000, and a group of armed blacks also had gathered at the courthouse. A shot was fired, and, according to Sheriff Willard McCullough, "the race war was on and I was powerless to stop it."[3]

According to another published account of the riot, up to 300 people died as thousands of white rioters attacked the city's black Greenwood neighborhood, looting stores and setting fire to houses, stores, schools, churches, a hospital, library, hotel, and two newspapers.[4] While the articles and books detailing this riot and events leading up to it agree on the general facts regarding the riot and its aftermath, information concerning the pre-riot period varies. Part of the reason is that the original, bound volumes of the *Tulsa Tribune* for May 31, 1921, have been destroyed. Microfilmed copies reveal that someone tore out a front-page article and removed a portion of the editorial page. But according to James S. Hirsch's 2002 account of the riot, *Riot and Remembrance: The Tulsa Race War and Its Legacy*, the *Tulsa Tribune* published an editorial headlined "To Lynch a Negro Tonight," which prompted seventy-five armed blacks to march on the courthouse. Ellsworth, unable to authoritatively cite an editorial as a cause for the riot, did make reference to an "inflammatory" front-page news article, "Nab Negro for Attacking Girl in Elevator," adding:

> There can be little doubt, however, that this issue of the *Tribune*, then edited by Richard Lloyd Jones, had more to say about the incident. Dr. P.S. Thompson, president of the Tulsa Medical, Dental, and Pharmaceutical Association, stated that the "immediate cause" of the riot "was a report in the *Tulsa Tribune* that threats were made to lynch a Negro for attempted criminal assault upon a White girl, which was wholly without foundation or cause." One informant, W.D. Williams, has a vivid memory that the *Tribune* carried an article headlined, "To Lynch [a] Negro Tonight."[5]

The power, or lack thereof, and readership popularity of editorials are subjects requiring more research. The published studies on the subject of the persuasive power of editorials tend to concentrate on editorials in connection to voter behavior, and they indicate that editorials have at least strong ties to, if not influence on, voter behavior.[6] The Tulsa race riot, however, is evidence of a link of a newspaper editorial to an event—the relationship of the editorial to the riot may be nothing more than that of messenger providing information that in conjunction with other events and decisions led to a riot; or the relationship could be cause-and-effect. What can be surmised, however, is that the *Tulsa Tribune* on that day published information, likely accompanied by an opinion, that at least stoked the flames of riot.

There have been other instances, and stronger anecdotal evidence, of the power of editorials to sway public opinion and to bring about social or political change. An editorial published six years after the Tulsa race riot—dealing with racially inspired violence but in a tack opposite the bigoted stance of the *Tulsa Tribune*—led to action against the Ku Klux Klan in Alabama. Prompted by the flogging of a black man at a country church, *Montgomery Advertiser* editor Grover C. Hall undertook a four-month editorial campaign to publicize Klan brutishness and to bring about legislation to curb Klan activities. He took aim at Alabama's U.S. senator, Tom Heflin. "A bully by nature, a mountebank by instance, a Senator by choice. . . . Thus this preposterous blob excites our pity if not our respect, and we leave him to his conscience in order that he may be entirely alone and meditate over the life of a charlatan whose personal interest and personal vanity are always of paramount concern to him." Hall's editorial campaign encouraged victims of flogging to speak out, leading to the criminal convictions of several Klansmen and a decrease in the number of floggings in the state.[7] Similarly, *Norfolk Virginian-Pilot* editor Louis Isaac Jaffe wrote a series of antilynching editorials during the 1920s that persuaded Governor Harry Flood Byrd to push for legislation that finally was adopted in 1928. The governor said the editorials "had more to do than any other single outside urging in convincing me that I should make one of my major recommendations the passage of a drastic anti-lynching law providing that lynching be a specific state offense."[8] An editorial penned by Jaffe that same year "sparked national interest" in a national antilynching law, wrote historian William David Sloan and co-author Laird B. Anderson in *Pulitzer Prize Editorials/America's Best Writing 1917–2003*, though "Congress would delay in enacting anti-lynching legislation."[9]

The post–World War II Cold War sparked numerous persuasive editorials on military preparedness, international diplomacy and, in one case, a unique call for divine intervention. In 1949, Carl M. Saunders responded to rising international tensions by editorializing on behalf of a day of prayer for world peace. "Why don't we—all of us in America—pray for peace?" Saunders asked in the *Jackson* (Mich.) *Citizen Patriot*. "We've tried rattling our tanks and planes; we've tried calling names; we've tried the United Nations. Let's put first things first—let's have a day of prayer for peace." Two Michigan congressmen picked up on his idea, introducing a joint resolution that gained unanimous approval and led to a proclamation by President Harry Truman that called the country to prayer and to a subsequent designation of Memorial Day as a day of prayer.[10]

The *Boston Herald*'s Don Murray in 1953 wrote a series of more than 100 editorials on national defense that were based on extensive reporting, including interviews with congressional and military experts and a study of documents. They were cited in congressional debate.[11] Lauren K. Soth of the *Des Moines Register* two years later penned an editorial that led directly to a thawing of relations between the Soviet Union and the United States. The editorialist suggested food diplomacy:

> We have no diplomatic authority of any kind, but we hereby extend an invitation to any delegation [Soviet Premier Nikita] Khrushchev wants to select to come to Iowa to get the lowdown on raising high quality cattle, hogs, sheep, and chickens. We promise to hide none of our "secrets." We will take the visiting delegation to Iowa's great agricultural experiment station at Ames, to some of the leading farmers of Iowa, to our livestock breeders, soil conservation experts, and seed companies. Let the Russians see how we do it.[12]

One of the more striking examples of editorial power was *New York Tribune* editor Horace Greeley's urging during the Civil War that President Abraham Lincoln declare an end to slavery. In his 1862 open letter to Lincoln lamenting the president's slow pace in proclaiming the freedom of the slaves, Greeley scolded the president for what some perceived as his tardiness in emancipation, and he urged Lincoln to uphold the Confiscation Act, which granted freedom to slaves who entered free territory. "Most emphatically do we demand that such laws as have been recently enacted, which therefore may fairly be presumed to embody the *present* will and to be dictated by the *present* needs of the Republic, and which, after due consideration have received your personal sanction, shall by you be carried into full effect," wrote Greeley. He called on Lincoln to "publicly and decisively instruct your subordinates that such laws exist, that they are binding on all functionaries and citizens, and that they are to be obeyed to the letter."[13] The editorial prompted a personal reply from the president in an attempt to explain and defend his policy. William David Sloan, Cheryl S. Wray, and C. Joanne Sloan in their 1997 *Great Editorials; Masterpieces of Opinion Writing* credited Greeley's editorial with pushing Lincoln to issue his Emancipation Proclamation.[14]

Editorial writers before and during the Civil War began taking on a more proactive role in commentaries that attempted to guide national policy. They increasingly came to see their responsibility as an agenda-setting one, as evidenced by Greeley's editorial. It was a plea that, in swaying the president, demonstrated the power, through persuasion and agenda-setting, of an editorial to bring action.[15]

EDITORIAL READERSHIP

Relatively little attention has been given to the popularity of editorials by newspaper researchers. Readership surveys, most of them in-house, non-scientific polls by newspapers or by the industry, have included editorials among analysis of other newspaper content, such as local news, features, and sports, in efforts to learn what portions of the newspapers attract the greatest numbers of readers.

In a 1992 speech to the National Conference of Editorial Writers, Belden Associates Vice President John Harper told his audience that research by his company found that 60 percent of regular newspaper readers read for the editorials and opinion columns. "The editorial section is well-read," Harper told the assembled opinion writers in Lexington, Kentucky. "Nearly half of weekday readers read the editorial pages, about the same proportion as those reading comics, food, and sports." He added that editorial page readers "tend to be even older, more affluent, and better educated than the average reader."[16] This suggests that editorial writers are reaching that portion of the population likely to be involved in policy and management of business and public affairs.

A 1994 study of editorial page readership done for the National Conference of Editorial Writers belied the general notion subscribed to by newspaper editors and reporters and of industry observers in its finding that 79 percent of adult daily newspaper readers read or look at the editorial page. Drawing on research by Belden Associates, on a recent Newspaper Association of America Report detailing newspaper readership based on a national survey, on a 1993 study of media and their markets by Simmons Market Research Bureau, and on a review of academic research into readership patterns, the report also concluded that editorial page readership is second only to general news for adult readers at every educational level and ranks ahead of newspaper categories that include sports, business, entertainment, food, and home. "In every income category, editorial readership is higher than that of any other page or section except the category of 'general news'," said the report. "The percentages by income of those who generally read the editorial page range from 81 percent (readers whose household income is $50,000 or more) to 78 percent (income under $20,000)."[17]

While no relationship between editorial page readership and editorial effects can be drawn based on this data, these readership findings nonetheless indicate a greater popularity for the editorial page than has been generally surmised even among newspaper industry participants, observers, and scholars. For those interested in agenda-setting, it suggests that editorials reach an elite readership—folks who hold sway in public affairs. Editorial writers have drawn on the appeal of their pages toward purposes that include a voice in establishing societal agendas and robust political debate in a lively democratic marketplace of ideas.

CULTURAL EFFECTS, AGENDA-SETTING

The effects of newspaper editorials in the formative days of the nation were twofold: to help mold the culture of the United States, particularly in an effort to distinguish U.S. society and culture from other nations', especially European, in the years following the Revolution; and to foster a forum of competing ideas that helped shape and define the politics and society of the United States from the days following the Revolution through the nineteenth century.

While editorials in American newspapers first appeared before 1720, Sloan and his co-authors credit the first widely published American editorial with playing a role in bringing about the union of the colonies and with providing the motto—"Join or Die"—of the American Revolution more than twenty years later.[18] Untitled, that editorial, written by Benjamin Franklin and published on May 9, 1754, in his *Pennsylvania Gazette*, cited attempts by the French to expand their American territory. It complained of the difficulties the colonists faced in defending themselves because of the distance of their motherland. Enemies, he wrote,

> presume that they may with Impunity violate the most solemn Treaties subsisting between the two Crowns, kill, seize and imprison our Traders, and confiscate their Effects at Pleasure (as they have done for several Years past), murder and scalp our Farmers, with their Wives and children, and take an easy possession of such Parts of the British Territory as they find most convenient for them.[19]

What the authors identify as the first editorial, "in the modern sense," was published by editors George Goodwin and Barzalai Hudson in the Connecticut *Courant*, on October 28, 1783. Authored by Noah Webster and appearing under the heading "Hartford," the editorial departed from the newspaper's previous practice of publishing only the titles of laws by providing commentary about an ongoing political debate of the day. Goodwin and Hudson, wrote the editorial historians, "published for the first time a synopsis and *comment* on action taken by the state assembly." The editorial chastised the lower house of Connecticut's General Assembly over the issue of giving full pay for five years of service to officers of the former Continental Army, as proposed by the U.S. Congress. After the legislative body came out in opposition to the congressional pay proposal, the editorial argued that the state assembly's stance would have no "remedial effect."

> But when a people, so much enlightened as the inhabitants of this State, suffer themselves to be duped out of their senses by the foes of our independence and British emissaries, who are scattering the seeds of discord in the regions of tranquility, it seems the design of heaven to punish their blindness by some fatal catastrophe, and harden them, like Pharaoh of old, till they plunge themselves into an ocean of difficulties.[20]

The young American nation, fresh from its victory over the British, began a struggle at the end of the eighteenth century to create a political and cultural identity intended to set it apart from England and from Europe. This effort, beginning with the writing and ratification of a constitution, took aim at molding an exceptional nation of politics, of economic and social institutions, and of artistic expression. This nurturing process, in which the American press would play a key role, would last well into the next century.

Beginning with the politically partisan sheets of the late 1700s and early 1800s and continuing with the wide-circulation, advertising-supported penny presses of the nineteenth and early twentieth centuries, American newspapers reflected and helped shape what their owners and editors viewed as the young nation's unique polity and society through their editorials. These editorialists—mass philosophers, if you will—generally did not offer the cerebral depth of the essayists and philosophers published in the higher-brow journals, treatises, and books of the times. For the most part, they represented, and spoke to, a common and eager readership, and they established a bridge between the working-class populace and the nation's intellectual elite. They took on a leadership role by offering sundry opinions on topics ranging from foreign affairs, finance, and government to politics, slavery, and war. And though these editorialists frequently differed ideologically in their opinions, they shared a method of couching their opinions in nationalistic language intended to portray to their readers—and to the world—positive traits of the developing American politics and culture.

These newspapers wielded considerable power, argued doctoral candidate Charles A. Pilant, because they were the most dominant and accessible source for "general instruction and dissemination of news and views." In his 1989 doctoral dissertation, Pilant extensively cited editorial excerpts from newspapers from 1776 to 1826 to argue that newspaper editors of the post-Revolutionary era and into the early 1800s used their sheets to promote everything American. These newspapers lent the nation nearly divine status, blessed by the almighty and destined to be a distinct and providential haven of freedom through a system of self-government never experienced in the world, he wrote, adding that the editors cursed European ideas and culture, particularly anything British in the years immediately after the Revolution and during the War of 1812. They praised American cultural traits, and they condemned perceived threats to union solidarity. "The editors may or may not have consciously attempted to inculcate nationalistic viewpoints within their readers, but they most definitely expressed such sentiments," he wrote. "The development of an American sense of identity, character, usable past, and common historical ties was essential for any early growth of nationalism. By their constant airings, these editors offered nationalis- tic dispositions to a heterogeneous population."[21]

Though the editorialists of those early postwar days would hardly qualify as purely editorial writers by today's standards—the distinction between editor and pamphleteer was "very blurred," according to editorial historian Allan Nevins—they set out on a course of opinion writing that would set the topical standard for all editorials to follow. "The men who were interested in American public opinion between the Treaty of Paris and the Missouri Compromise were with few exceptions interested in it for political purposes," wrote Nevins. "The close connection between the political pamphlet and the newspaper editorial is amply illustrated by such journalists as Alexander Hamilton, William Cobbett, John Fenno, and J.T. Callender."[22] As for their political influence, these editorialists enjoyed "tremendous" sway, according to Nevins, by the simple fact of a relatively small electorate and a literate population. The republic's population of 17 million in 1840 included 500,000 literate adults.[23]

But concerns besides love of nation and politics drove these editors to promote American culture. These included the improved likelihood of financial success for their newspapers in an environment of stable government, the appeal of the opportunity to be a shaper of history and to assess events and personalities of the era, the sense of power gained by taking on an educational leadership role, and the chance to contribute to "God's grand scheme."[24] Pilant argued that the editors seized this opportunity and in the process became major participants in defining the nation. "Through the pages of their newspapers, citizens garnered information about politics and society. Some had their opinions molded; others saw their ideas mirrored. Society's leaders often observed their views reflected by the press."[25]

Most of the editorials of the immediate post-Revolutionary era—many of them published under pseudonyms—were not placed on separate "commentary" or "opinion" pages like those of later newspapers. They appeared throughout the pages of the newspapers, and they often included opinions on topics vital to the shaping of the nation's governmental and political institutions and beliefs. Not the least of these was newspaper publication of "The Federalist" essays, which Sloan, Wray, and Sloan argued comprise "the greatest work on political science ever produced in the United States."[26] These essays promoted the arguments on behalf of a strong, centralized government as opposed to the Jeffersonian view that a decentralized, locally driven democracy would best serve the republic. Perhaps the most noted of these essays, known as No. 10 and published in the *New York Independent Journal* in 1787, appeared under the pseudonym "Publius." In it, James Madison, the author, defined the two primary differences between the Federalist and the opposing version of democracy. These were as follows: (1) the Federalist, centrist form of government delegates government to a small number of representatives elected to make policy for the rest of the citizens; and (2) this form of government would allow for the extension of government over a greater number of citizens and a larger "sphere" of the country. Thus, Madison argued that the citizens would best be served by "the medium of a chosen body of citizens, whose wisdom may best discern the true interests of their country and whose patriotism and love of justice will be least likely to sacrifice it to temporary or partial considerations....In the extent and proper structure of the Union, therefore, we behold a republican remedy for the disease most incident to republican government."[27]

Despite some opposition from Republican-oriented newspaper editors in an editorial debate among newspapers throughout the states, the Federalists succeeded, and the constitution won state ratification in 1787–88. With the constitution adopted and the nation at peace, editors turned their attention to other matters, including economic issues and extolling the new nation's superiority over other countries. Editors often compared the United States favorably to foreign nations, citing American exceptionalism and divine blessing. An editorial published in the October 29, 1796, *Boston Daily Advertiser* expressed this sentiment: "AMERICA This astonishing country for above 60 centuries, unknown to the rest of mankind [*sic*], and consequently exempt from vices... appears to have been peculiarly formed and concealed by the supreme being for the regeneration of the human race."[28] Editors cited American manufacturing and commerce as segments of American culture that put it on an equal footing with foreign nations. For example, the *Examiner* in 1802 boasted of "[t]he sum of nearly three millions of dollars in the amount of exports of the United States for one year ending in September last! No country in the world, Great Britain and the United Netherlands excepted, ever exported produce, goods, ware and merchandizes to that amount."[29]

Political controversy, though, interrupted the editorialists' praise of American enterprise. One of these issues that earned early and frequent editorial attention was slavery, which was being condemned by some newspapers as early as the late eighteenth century. The *New York Time-Piece* in 1797 called slavery the "Curse of America."

> There are not a few in these States who, notwithstanding all that has been said to the contrary, are still of the opinion that the patriotic Washington, who headed the Americans at a crisis that tried the hearts of men, in the sublime cause of liberty and virtue, will come forward before the ingress of the approaching century (big with the most tremendous events) and shew an example to the world, that the people of republican America will not be the last to advance this grand object, the emancipation of slaves, by such means as the legislative wisdom of the Union shall deem it advisable to adopt.[30]

The ongoing Federalist–Republican political battles raised yet another political threat to national unity. An attempted power grab by the Federalists caused the opinion writers to frame the election of 1800 in terminology that defined it as key in the development of the nation's political identity. In January, Federalist Senator James Ross conspired to give the election to President John Adams through the creation of a committee of seven senators and seven representatives, along with the Supreme Court's chief justice, who would count the electoral votes and announce the winner. Because Federalists comprised the majority of both houses of Congress, the counting process, to be done in secret, favored that party. Republican editor William Duane of the Philadelphia *Aurora* obtained a copy of the bill creating the committee, published it, and attacked it editorially as a danger to national unity. His editorial, published on February 16, 1800, demonstrated the power of the editorialist; it angered Republicans nationwide and roused a public protest that brought a halt to the scheme. The proposed Federalist bill, he wrote, "is an offspring of this spirit of faction secretly working; and it will be found to be in perfect accord with the outrageous proceedings of the same party in our state legislature, who are bent on depriving this state of its share in an election that may involve the fate of the country and posterity."[31]

Federalist–Republican differences, raised in editorial accusations of unpatriotic behavior, again dominated the editorial pages during the war with Britain beginning in 1812. But the editorials regarding this war evoked a different kind of language than the editorials before and during the Revolutionary War. With the U.S. Constitution now established, and with America having declared and won its independence from England, patriotism and nationalism became tied more to the notion of the United States as a country and a government as a separate and sovereign entity than to a general, more abstract idea, such as freedom or liberty or to a particular state. "As the war which now exists...is a WAR waged in defence of the violated RIGHTS OF HUMANITY, and of NATIONAL HONOR," opined the *Western Spy* of Cincinnati on May 7, 1814, "the EDITOR of this paper will support and cherish it...until it shall terminate in a result....Glorious to the INFANT NATION."[32]

After the War of 1812, the editorialists moved on to other issues; but the newspaper commentaries continued to frame their subjects in the context of a distinct American society. Immigration, for example, took on some editorial importance immediately following the war when editors proudly noted the attraction of this new nation to citizens from other countries. The *Washington Whig* of December 11, 1815, expressed a "peculiar glow of a patriotic affection" about the growing importance of the United States and its "thousand accumulated and accumulating blessings...and how must this admiration be increased when [the honest American] daily witnesses thousands of emigrants...attracted by the wholesomeness of our laws; the purity of our government; the humanity of our citizens, and the luxuriance of our soil."[33]

Tied to immigration was the theme of American expansion. As the nation's population grew through immigration and procreation, its people moved toward the Pacific, creating an ocean-to-ocean American culture. One editorial writer, in the April 24, 1819, *Columbian Register* of New Haven, Connecticut, discussed this phenomenon of manifest destiny, suggesting that in America, humanity was reaching its final and highest potential. This achievement, marked by American artistic, scientific, civil, and religious acumen, would represent "probably the last and broadest seat" of mankind in the American "empire."[34]

The fine arts also captured editorial attention, lending themselves to discussions of cultural distinction. "It was an accepted fact," wrote Pilant, "that what the Connecticut *Courant* called 'the encouragement of works of Literature and Genius, (had) in all great civilized nations been esteemed an object worthy the public attention.' With this went the idea that literary productions contributed to a foreigner's opinion about the high quality of an American character which would support the finer things of life."[35] Painting also served to strengthen loyalty and bonding, and it helped when positive reinforcement came from abroad, as discussed in an editorial published on December 11, 1824, in the *Nashville Republican*. "An Edinburgh writer, after giving his opinion of our more distinguished artists, holds the following language in respect to Mr. C. Harding of Ky," mused the editorial, referring to a Kentucky artist. "This extraordinary man is a fair specimen of the American character."[36]

The rise of the penny press in the 1830s, which formed the germ of the mass media as we have come to understand the term in the twenty-first century, helped carry many of these themes, along with some new ones, into an expanding number of American homes. The lower cost of the penny sheets, compared to the nickel that readers spent for the established daily newspapers, made them more accessible to a mass readership. This lent them greater appeal as daily reading fare for citizens and thus facilitated the self-appointed information-gathering and agenda-setting roles of their owners and editors. The rise of the penny press included the development of a new kind of "moral journalism," wrote Nevins, led by Horace Greeley and marked by editors "serious in their attitude toward all current problems."[37] This "respectable" new journalism led the way in forming public opinion:

> To Horace Greeley's great newspaper [the *New York Tribune*] we may unhesitatingly ascribe the development of the editorial page in its modern American character: that is a page treating a wide variety of topics in a variety of manners, though pursuing a consistent policy; achieving a level of genuine literary merit; produced by a body of editors, not by a single man, and representing their united judgment and information; and earnestly directed to the elevation and rectification of public opinion.[38]

Doctoral candidate Susan Annette Thompson argued in her 2002 dissertation that these mass circulation newspapers made daily newspaper reading culturally normal "in burgeoning cities throughout the United States, as tens of thousands of city dwellers came to rely upon their daily newspaper for information, instruction and entertainment, and tens of thousands more rural subscribers enjoyed the weekly versions of the penny dailies."[39] But the penny press not only reflected a changing society, wrote Thompson, it also was an active player in bringing about improvements that altered how the nation's citizens "lived, worked and did business....Contemporary historians such as James Parton believe that the penny press was stimulating an interest in reading among the masses and actually increasing literacy. They felt that it was empowering the middle and lower classes with useful information necessary for participation in a democratic government."[40]

The political issues of the penny presses were similar to those of their predecessors. They included slavery, which sparked a lengthy commentary in the *New York Plaindealer* in 1837 under a sarcastic headline, "The Blessings of Slavery." The editorial concluded that "slavery is indeed an evil of the most hideous and destructive kind; and it therefore becomes the duty of every wise and virtuous man to exert himself to put it down."[41]

Also on the editorial page agendas of the penny presses were economic matters, the annexation of Texas, and the war with Mexico, along with one other old-time issue: federalism, as evidenced by an 1840 editorial in the *Kennebec, Maine, Journal.* "It has for several years been apparent to us, as we see by General

Harrison's latest speech," the newspaper said in commenting on the administration of President Martin Van Buren, "that it has been to him, and as it has been to thousands of others, that the principle of monarchy in our federal government, so much dreaded by Patrick Henry, Luther Martin, and others, has been steadily developing itself under the present Administration."[42]

The editorialists also opined on cultural issues and matters of societal structure. Greeley's *Tribune* brought a number of exotic intellectual issues to the editorial plate, reflecting an American cultural menu that was moving into broader areas of thought. The editor offered opinions on various "isms," including transcendentalism, spiritualism, vegetarianism, and Fourierism,[43] with its belief in the socialist principles of Associationism. Such editorials marked a growing interest by editors in new areas that moved away from government, politics, and the economy. The publication in 1853 by S.S. Cox of his "A Great Old Sunset" editorial in the Columbus *Ohio Statesman* helped to liberate the American editorial from "domination by political subjects," according to Sloan, Wray, and Sloan. Cox described the sunset in remarkably poetic language that made of the editorial a work bordering on literary achievement in its portrait of a rain-washed scene in the aftermath of a "glorious storm":

> ...The sun, wearied of the elemental commotion, sank behind the green plains of the West. The "great eye of heaven," however, went not down without a dark brown hanging over its departed light. The rich flush of the unearthly light had passed, and the rain had ceased when the solemn church bells pealed, the laughter of children rang out loud and, joyous after the storm, was heard with the carol of birds; while the forked and purple weapon of the skies still darted illumination around the Starling College, trying to rival its angles and leap into its dark windows.[44]

"The sudden popularity of human interest editorials did not, however, mean that political editorials suddenly vanished," wrote Sloan, Wray, and Sloan. "Even today they are the staple of editorial pages; but after the 1850s, editorials on non-political subjects appeared more and more frequently."[45] Cox's editorial, which earned him the nickname "Sunset Cox," and others of a similar bent offered evidence of a rising interest in America of philosophical and artistic thought at the level of the common citizen. His sunset musings showed the influence not only of his religious beliefs but of Romanticism and its focus on the relationship of man to God and nature.[46]

Five years after Cox's sunset editorial, Walt Whitman wrote differently of a stormy night in a piece that presaged his masterpiece, "Leaves of Grass," in a *Brooklyn Times* commentary titled "Saturday Night—'Items' Makes a Tour" ("Items" being the pseudonym of the writer). The commentary portrayed an urban scene with "stores full of life." It depicted a citified American culture of the commoner (a trademark Whitman theme) out and about in the bustle of the city's streets. It also was evidence of opinion writers concerned not only with cultural topics that were apolitical but who also showed a care for the words, for the craft of writing, in creating their editorial visions.

The night was rainy. . . . Grant street on a Saturday evening presents quite a spectacle in the way of life and animation. On such occasions when good steady people or their servants are out "marketing" and when dissolute youths are busily squandering the week's earnings and making vigorous preparations for a "blue Monday," the swarms that fill the pave remind one more of Grand street in New York than of a thoroughfare of our own quiet 'Burgh. South 7th, with its hurrying crowds hastening from the ferry, and South 10th, with its procession of passengers on a smaller scale, also wear a busier aspect than usual.—People have the air of men who have finished the labors of the week and who are glad of it, and willing to let their contentedness be seen in their faces.[47]

Another kind of storm loomed in the next decade, one that would stir the editorialists once again to themes of national unity in a political context. The long-stewing controversy of slavery, combined with the issues of regionalism and secession, sparked the pre–Civil War editorial debate. The Fugitive Slave Act, the publication of "Uncle Tom's Cabin" by Harriet Beecher Stowe, the Kansas-Nebraska Act, the Missouri Compromise, and the nullification debate articulated by John Calhoun provided fodder for the editorialists, and all presaged the Civil War that would be fought over the issues of slavery and states' rights. An 1856 editorial in the *New York Evening Post* offered an example of the editorial demeanor of the day. "The truth is," wrote William Cullen Bryant,

that the pro-slavery party, which rules in the Senate, looks upon violence as the proper instrument of its designs. Violence reigns in the streets of Washington; violence has now found its way into the Senate chamber. Violence lies in wait on all the navigable rivers and all the railways of Missouri, to obstruct those who pass from the free States into Kansas. Violence overhangs the frontiers of that territory like a storm-cloud charged with hail and lightning. Violence has carried election after election in that territory. In short, violence is the order of the day; the North is to be pushed to the wall by it, and this plot will succeed if the people of the free States are as apathetic as the slaveholders are insolent.[48]

The editorialists took up their pens to battle over whether to preserve the union or to let the South go its way. This was a difference of opinion that the Philadelphia *Public Ledger* criticized in November 1860 for its divisiveness that inflamed both sides while doing little to settle the question for the good of the union, which was a common nationalist plea. The secession journals, the editorial argued, reprinted the northern editorials "for the purpose of inflaming them to still more desperate action. The violent declarations of the southern journals are then served up to northern readers by the northern press, and the people in both sections are thus deceived as to the true state of public feeling, and each supposes itself to be the special object of the other's enmity and hostility."[49]

The end of the Civil War inspired editorial language of nationalism and unity. Following Robert E. Lee's surrender to Grant, Bryant in the *New York Evening Post* on April 10, 1865, welcomed the peace in a tone of reconciliation in which he called on the nation to put aside "petty or insolent feeling of triumph over a prostrate enemy" and to get on with the business of the nation. His editorial invoked the spirit of reconstruction in an optimistic call for

> the return of industry to its wonted channels, of the establishment of our institutions on a basis more indestructible than ever before; of the elevation of the national heart to all the heights of heroism, of the diffusion of liberty to all races; and in the hope of a securer, broader nobler development of whatever is just and free in our society, until the example of the great republic shall purify and redeem all the nations of the earth.[50]

After the war, the press returned to more peaceful themes—and some not so peaceful but reflecting an American culture that included its negative aspects, such as tragedies and crime. The rise in mass transportation through railroads and steamboats led to increased incidents of disaster stories—railroad accidents and steamboat engines exploding that killed hundreds. The pressures of city life included petty larcenies and murder. "The penny papers did not invent crime and crisis stories," wrote Thompson, "but they certainly responded to them when they began to occur and their expansive treatment of them was a phenomenon new in American journalism."[51] Lafcadio Hearn of the *New Orleans Times-Democrat* explained this American fascination with crime as a natural fascination and almost morbid, at times, identification with criminals. In a July 27, 1887, editorial, Hearn wrote of a wife-murderer "who, perhaps, slaughtered his victim with pitiless ferocity, [and] is almost buried under a load of floral tributes from sentimental persons....It is not an uncommon thing for these sentimentalists to wish to link their destinies with that of the criminal. The mere fact that a man has been imprisoned seems to add some mysterious charm to his personality."[52] The editorialist suggested that another reason for this fascination with crime by readers and thus by the journalists who represented them might be simple escapism, a cultural phenomenon that the penny presses encouraged through their frequent, sensational emphasis on crime and tragedy: "a love of excitement and a desire to avoid the ordinary stagnation of domestic peace and happiness."[53]

Other broader social editorial topics included Bryant discussing the influence of Romanticism and the wonders of nature in an 1844 editorial urging creation of a new public park, and Francis P. Church showing a nurturing attitude toward children, an attitude that had arisen among middle-class citizens of Whig Culture, in his classic 1897 editorial in response to a letter to the editor from an eight-year-old questioning the existence of Santa Claus. The editorial is much more than a discussion of Santa Claus; it extols Romantic notions and hints at spiritualism in its metaphor of an infant's toy and its innards:

> You may tear apart the baby's rattle and see what makes the noise inside but there is a veil covering the unseen world which not the strongest men that ever lived could tear apart. Only fancy, poetry, love, romance can push aside that curtain and view and picture the supernatural beauty and glory behind. Is it all real? Ah, Virginia, in all the world there is nothing else real and abiding.

No Santa Claus. Thank God! He lives and he lives forever. A thousand years from now, Virginia, nay, ten times ten thousand years from now, he will continue to make glad the heart of childhood.[54]

U.S. editorials of the late 1700s, the 1800s, and throughout the 1900s offered discussions and debate ranging from Santa Claus to crime, from opinion writing espousing nationalism and patriotism during war with Britain to commentary condemning slavery and urging a setting-aside of animosities after the Civil War, from commentaries about literature and painting to alternative lifestyles and philosophies—all in the higher cause of American nationalism and culture. These editorials not only reflected American attitudes and culture from the post-Revolutionary era to that of post–Civil War America and the nation's emergence into world trade dominance and an age of imperialism, they also strove to set the union's cultural and political agenda. They did not only mirror the changing American society but also frequently led the charge. These editors provided a link between the masses of readers and common folks they represented and the elite ideologues and thinkers who expounded on the American economy, political framework, social structure, and philosophies. Some of these editors—Greeley, Bryant, E.L. Godkin, William Allen White, and Arthur Brisbane—belonged to that intelligentsia, and they shared its visions and musings with their readers. Others simply were workaday journalists. However, they all had a common vision of a nation that was different among nations, of an American culture that, with assistance from their editorial boosterism, criticism, and advice, had indeed become one unique from its European roots. It is a vision that has continued and that thrives today; the subjects of these early American editorialists, as will be seen in studies presented in this book, are some of the same ones that continue to dominate the editorials of modern-day newspapers. The one disappearing aspect for the most part in the modern day, however, is the competitive editorial voice, the subject of the next chapter.

CHAPTER 2

Dueling Editorial Pens

"The long agony is over," as the American says, and the new Administration, the strongest ever seen in this country since the days of Washington, has entered upon its career. Of the past we will not say much, since we can say no good. The country has been rendered contemptible abroad and distracted at home. Of Mr. Adams himself we must be permitted to state that his acts have all shown that we were not wide of the truth when we said, as may be seen in our files, that although not deficient in literary acquirements, he has certain defects of character that unfitted him for directing the affairs of a great empire; and that his prejudices against that nation, with which it more behooves us to be on good and amicable terms than with all Europe besides, were so blind and so inveterate that we ventured to predict that no satisfactory settlement could ever be effected with it during his Administration. The event has proved that our fears were not chimerical. As to his Cabinet friends and advisers, we shall dismiss them from our consideration at this time by congratulating the country on its escape from what was once called by an eminent English statesman "the worst of evils that could predominate in our country: men without popular confidence, public opinion, or general trust, invested with all the powers of government."

—*New York Evening Post*, March 5, 1829, on the administration of President John Quincy Adams[1]

At 6:00 p.m. on October 7, 1835, James Gordon Bennett, editor of the *New York Herald,* was walking up the north side of New York City's Wall Street. He had just left some Wall Street brokers, who were sources for his newspaper's money market column. As he neared the corner of William Street, a man appeared from behind the side of a building, struck him in the face, and then stood back and cursed the editor of New York's new, rising daily penny newspaper. Bennett recognized his assailant: Dr. Peter S. Townsend, associate editor of the *New York Evening Star*.

"Doctor Toonsen," said Bennett in his Scottish accent, stepping back from the man. "What d' ye mean b' this?" The men wrestled a bit before brokers and others stepped in to stop the fight. "This fellow is only a foreigner," Townsend told the crowd. "He comes to our shores to get his bread, and instead of behaving as he ought to do, he attacks and ridicules the editors of the *Star*—I am one— Mr. Noah is the other. He is a blackguard, and I hope, gentlemen, you will not permit him to come into the street hereafter."[2]

Indeed, Bennett had immigrated to the United States, had become a journalist and begun his own newspaper and did, on occasion, use it to ridicule the editors of the *Evening Star* and of other New York City sheets. Two days before, he had taken an editorial swipe at the *Evening Star* and its favorable review of an actor, written by Townsend, whom Bennett had dubbed in print "Peter Simple," the primary character in an English novel that depicted Americans unfavorably. It was that reference that angered Townsend. It was one of several such jibes aimed at Townsend and other New York City rivals—*Evening Star* editor Mordecai Noah, Benjamin Henry Day of the *New York Sun,* and James Watson Webb of the *New York Courier and Enquirer*.[3]

Physical encounters were not the normal means of expressing differences over editorial philosophies and ideologies in the penny press newspapers of these editors, nor of the editors of the political party newspaper organs before the penny press, nor of the editors of the so-called Golden Age of journalism newspapers of William Randolph Hearst, Joseph Pulitzer, E. W. Scripps, and Henry Raymond that grew out of the penny presses. What such encounters illustrated, however, was the combative spirit of journalism's past, when newspaper owners and editors saw their organs as means of communicating and arguing their political ideologies and when they conducted editorial battles not only in scurrying to beat the competition in obtaining hard news but also in their editorials. They represented a time when cities and communities had more than one daily newspaper and therefore offered a competition of opinions, ideas, and reportage.

The Federalist Papers were an early phenomenon of the newspaper editorial battles that arose in the wake of the American Revolution. After America won its independence from Britain, the young nation and its newspapers engaged in heated debate over the writing and adoption of its constitution. That argument was carried out in numerous newspaper articles, including the eighty-five essays comprising the Federalist Papers published in three New York newspapers by James Madison and Alexander Hamilton along with contributions from John Jay.

After the constitutional convention completed its work and the constitution was signed in mid-1787, the document was put before the states for ratification. The Federalists and Antifederalists and their party newspapers took up the debate over ratification, an editorial confrontation highlighted by charges of conspiracy and political intrigue. An editorial exchange in Boston offered an example of the sort of language and allegations that typified the editorial argument. That city's Federalist *Massachusetts Centinel* took up one side in the 1788 editorial debate, while the *American Herald* argued the other. The *Centinel* chastised the Antifederalists as "malignant, ignorant, and short-sighted triflers," marked by "the weakness of their heads, and the badness of their hearts." "But the *American Herald*," wrote historian Robert A. Rutland in his 1987 study of the ratification process,

> warned readers not to be stunned by the brilliance of names and told delegates of thirteen disadvantages in the new plan of government, which included the predic-tion that the "*Trade of Boston* (would be) transferred to *Philadelphia*" while "*Religion* (would be) *abolished*." The *Herald* advised delegates to postpone final action on the Constitution and await the call for a second convention, and this tactic became the emerging strategy of the Antifederalists in the New York and Virginia strong-holds.[4]

Massachusetts came through for the Federalists. New York followed suit, and by August 1, 1788—less than eleven months since the ratification process had begun, wrote Rutland—"that American must have been remote who had not learned the outcome of the struggle."[5] The United States had a constitution, and the new nation had established a tradition of robust, free political debate on the pages of its many, and competing, newspapers. As Rutland noted, these editors carried out this editorial dispute about the Constitution at a time when "Americans were accustomed to the airing of complaints more often than to the reading of facts in their weekly gazettes"[6] and when it sometimes was hard to differentiate between fact and opinion. That the debate was fostered by an unfettered press was important. "The overwhelming support of the newspapers in this first test of a national referendum was a key element in the successful rat-ification campaign and set the journalistic tone for political contests in America for generations to come," wrote Rutland.[7]

The rise of the penny press, beginning with the founding by Benjamin Day of the *New York Sun* in 1830, brought with it an increase in dissonant editorial voices, particularly in the center of American journalistic enterprise, New York City. This was where Day and his competitors, including Bennett, Noah, Webb, and Horace Greeley, waged a daily newspaper war, selling their sheets for one and two cents each, with the existing nickel dailies that continued well beyond the turn of the century. Bennett and his New York City rivals disagreed during the years of the penny press era over matters mundane and serious. Personal references to the opposition, by name and by newspaper, were frequent.

As in the partisan sheets of the post–Revolutionary War period, party politics stirred heated editorial debate in the penny newspapers. For example, in the Keystone State, Philadelphia's the *Pennsylvanian* and the *American Sentinel* dueled over the policies of President John Tyler. "No President has been more fiercely denounced by the rancor of party hatred than John Tyler," opined the *American Sentinel* in June of 1843 in an editorial headlined "A Defence Of President Tyler." "Professing Democratic principles, it is his misfortune to have been indebted for his election to 'Federal Whigs'—to have been the head of a party whose measures he was forced to negative, and he in turn be denounced as guilty of inconsistency, vacillation, ingratitude, and treachery." The editorial concluded that the "policy of Mr. Tyler's administration is developed and generally approved."[8] *Au contraire*, argued the *Pennsylvanian*, responding to its rival by name.

> The *Sentinel* insists upon it that at the time of his nomination to the Vice Presidency, Mr. Tyler was a conservative Democrat of the Rives school, hostile to the doctrines of Federal Whiggery, and that he was on this account selected to strengthen the Whig ticket, "without a why or a wherefore."...Mr. Tyler is made out, on the showing of his friends, to be a very paltry politician. But the *United States Gazette* denies the statements of the *Sentinel* in toto, and in the following terms declares that John Tyler received the nomination as a professor of Clay Whiggism.[9]

That identification with party, apparently, earned Tyler condemnation, judging from the editorial's selection of a quotation from the *United States Gazette*: "'He was selected by the Whigs. He declared himself to be a Whig, and a Clay man, and he was selected or rather nominated on these professions, as a compliment to the Clay men, who, though a *majority*, had given up their candidate—had given up against their better sense, and the *tears* of John Tyler.'"[10]

In the next year, the Washington *National Intelligencer* and the Washington *Globe* took up dueling editorial pens to argue the annexation by the United States of Texas. The *National Intelligencer* argued the prospect of annexation had been "sprung upon us without any regard whatever to the wishes of the country," and the proposed annexation treaty, which was about to be signed, "is the result of the mere individual will of the President, independent of any expression of the national will, such as ought to have preceded it." Further, the president, "entering upon this negotiation, appears to us to have acted upon a misconception of the nature and extent of the executive authority in reference to the treaty-making power."[11] The *Globe*, however, called for the immediate annexation of Texas, arguing that the newspaper had said before "that we looked upon Texas, in right, as a territory of the Union. The guardian who once had the disposal of this fair patrimony in his hands made way with it wrongfully by throwing it into the arms of the Spanish potentate. A revolution made it the possession of another power on this continent—Mexico; another revolution makes it the appanage of a young branch of our own family." The editorial invoked the image of empire in urging annexation. "The Roman citizens who gave new States to their country were indulged with a triumph at the seat of the empire. We should be glad to welcome, in the same way, the conquerors of Texas in the capital of the United States."[12]

Slavery was one of the more divisive issues of the penny press era. While most of these northern editors agreed in principle on its evils, they disagreed over whether it ought to be ended quickly or whether slavery should be phased out gradually to allow the southern economy an opportunity to adapt to the change and to lend the freed slaves time to be assimilated into the American society and economy. The *Sun*'s Day was an advocate of the latter policy, arguing in February 1834, "First, prepare the slaves for freedom, prepare an asylum where they can enjoy the blessing—and then bestow it."[13] But William Lloyd Garrison came out strongly for the immediate freeing of the slaves in his abolitionist sheet, the *Liberator,* which began publishing in Boston in 1829 but by the early 1830s was circulated throughout the nation, including in New York City. He set the tone with his first editorial, published on January 1, 1831, in which he expressed regret over his previous support of gradual emancipation and called instead for "the immediate enfranchisement of our slave population....I seize this opportunity to make a full and unequivocal recantation, and thus publicly to ask pardon of God, of my country, and of my brethren the poor slaves, for having uttered a sentiment so full of timidity, injustice, and absurdity."[14] Day took exception with Garrison, opining in December 1833 that the radical abolitionist is someone "whom we consider beneath the public notice," adding:

> he has not at heart the real interests of the African race. He would shrink from the thought that a daughter of his should marry a Negro—but still he is a violent advocate of their being put upon an equality with citizens of this Republic. Why recognize those as citizens with whom we are unwilling to associate as fellow men? We have already given our opinion of slavery—that it is an evil is the opinion of every honest man; but because it exists must we excite its victims to vengeance?[15]

As the United States moved toward the Civil War, newspaper editorialists took up their pens to battle over whether to preserve the union or to let the southern states go. After South Carolina seceded in 1860, followed by six more states, the *New York Daily Times* Raymond pushed for compromise and, after newly elected President Lincoln refused to publicly reassure the South, blasted the president in an editorial titled, "Wanted—a Policy." The editorial writer criticized Lincoln's inaction, arguing that the government "allows everything to drift, to float along without guidance or impulse to do anything....In a great crisis like this, there is no policy so fatal as having no policy at all."[16] But while Raymond's *Times* sought to keep the southern states, Greeley's *New York Tribune* said: "Let them go." While arguing against the rights of plantation owners to hold slaves, he wrote that 20 million should not hold five million Southerners by force. "We hold the right of Self-Government sacred, even when invoked in behalf of those who deny it to others," he said, citing the Declaration of Independence's clause giving governments their "just" powers through the consent of those who are governed.[17]

Greeley did not disagree with his fellow editors only on secession. He also engaged them in debate on other issues, ranging from the Mexican War, which he opposed, to matters of taste and lifestyle. The *Courier & Tribune*'s Webb chastised Greeley in 1844 for what he considered the *Tribune* editor's eccentricities, which included a diet of "bran-bread and sawdust." He also accused Greeley of sins that included "eccentricity of character," wearing a hat "double the size of his head" and "glorying in an unwashed and unshaved person."

> We look upon cleanliness of person as inseparable from purity of thought and benevolence of heart. In short, there is not the slightest resemblance between the editor of *The Tribune* and ourself, politically, morally, or socially; and it is only when his affectation and impudence are unbearable, that we condescend to notice him or his press.[18]

Greeley conceded on the next day that he chose to eat "mainly (not entirely) vegetable food," but why should that bother Webb? Regarding his personal appearance, Greeley denied affecting eccentricity, writing of himself in the third person, "and certainly no costume he ever appeared in, would create such a sensation in Broadway, as that James Watson Webb would have worn."[19]

A protracted 1846 editorial debate between Raymond, then of the *New York Courier and Enquirer,* and Greeley's *Tribune* argued the merits of Fourierism. Each writer contributed twelve articles to that debate, which took in a number of cultural issues, from marriage to religion. Wrote Thompson of the exchange:

> Raymond brought out the fact that the Fourierist or Associationist ideas on marriage were not as wholesome as Christians would like, and that Christianity itself did not occupy a foremost position among many adherents. Greeley countered with an adamant defense of the fidelity of Associationists such as himself to Christianity and the sanctity of marriage, but the debate was won by Raymond in the end. Greeley's remarks, genuine and sincere as they were, did little for the Association cause while the debate helped raise Raymond's stature as an editorialist.[20]

These sorts of editorial arguments over issues certainly less serious than slavery and war—Associationism, religion, diet, and fashion—demonstrated an awareness by the combatants of their roles as opinion leaders in society and were evidence of an intellectual climate that took such matters seriously.

Greeley and his rivals brought an equal fervor to the more compelling issues of the day, as shown by his reaction to the June 1845 death of former President Andrew Jackson. Greeley praised Jackson's patriotism while scorning him as a "jobber in human flesh," a "slave trader," guilty of "covert, rapacious treachery to Mexico." The *Evening Post* termed Greeley's remarks "ebullition of party spleen and impotent malignity."[21]

Those were harsh words, but they were indicative of the sort of heated editorial debate that often engaged a cadre of newspaper editors who saw themselves as keepers of the spirit of American liberalism—defined, of course, by each of them in terms of his own party and philosophy—and the flame of democracy. Whether commenting upon spiritualism, republicanism, federalism, or capitalism, these editorial writers established an agenda and style—heavy on politics, frequently strong in emotion and language—that would become standards of American press editorial and commentary writing that have been, and continue to be, a major contributor to this nation's shrinking marketplace of ideas.

MONOPOLY VERSUS COMPETITION

Patrick S. Korten and his youthful colleagues in 1969 decided they had had enough of the University of Wisconsin's official campus newspaper, the *Daily Cardinal*. In a spirit reminiscent of the founders of the partisan and then the penny presses of the preceding two centuries, they set up a competing newspaper. Invoking terminology that has become familiar to newspaper analysts and scholars—words such as "monopoly," "competition," "open marketplace"—Korten explained to readers in his 1969 editorial introducing the *Badger Herald* that the university community needed another voice.

"Seventy-seven years is enough," editor-in-chief Korten wrote in complaining of the monopoly status of the rival publication, which was founded in 1892. "It is time there was a truly 'independent' student newspaper at Wisconsin, one which competes in the open marketplace, and must make its editorial and business decisions on the basis of the competitive market." Citing what he termed the "liberal" or "radical" lines of the university's educational operation, Korten wrote that his newspaper, on its editorial page, "will give some attention to what are sometimes considered 'conservative,' but more accurately termed 'libertarian' approaches to attacking the many severe problems which plague our society. Perhaps in this way we can help stimulate some serious thought and careful introspection by those who consider themselves 'intellectual,' but to date have really only devoted their 'thought' to one set of alternatives."[22]

What Korten was writing about was the need for a variety of thought and opinion, or a marketplace of ideas. That this sort of competition arose in the arena of the college press and thus is a rare sort of competition, is significant; the college newspaper today is the only competing daily newspaper editorial voice in many U.S. communities that rely on one commercial press for their newspaper tidings. That Korten singled out the editorial page as an arena for debate is important; this is the section of the newspaper in which newspaper owners and editors through history have taken up their dueling editorial pens, and more recently their typewriters and computer keyboards, to do intellectual battle. So the issues of this "experiment," as Korten termed the *Badger Herald* in 1969, are some of the same ones as those in the larger media markets of the nation: monopoly voices, competing markets, liberal versus conservative ideologies vying for the attention of media audiences.

Newspaper industry observers and participants have identified this process of editorial debate, of diverse voices taking up differing sides of a political, social, or cultural issue, as an important ingredient of the American democratic experiment. It is a process that encourages ideas to be examined and issues decided from a pluralistic perspective that promotes differences and argument. As Rutland noted in his study cited above, it was no wonder that two centuries before, Thomas Jefferson said that given a choice "between 'a government without newspapers, or newspapers without a government,' he would unhesitatingly prefer the latter condition." Wrote Rutland of the national debate over ratification of the constitution:

> The example of free men arguing and trying to persuade, of losing and of winning, that was provided in the first great newspaper debates in 1787–88 set the nation on an unalterable course of freedom. Now, two hundred years later, we still find that the wholesomeness of full public debate is the best way to preserve our liberty.[23]

Rutland was writing of what has come to be known as a marketplace of ideas that, working through a competitive offering of newspapers (and other media in later American society), informs citizens about their communities and their political, cultural, and social institutions and nurtures a lively debate that helps the citizens formulate opinions and attitudes and thus to make more informed decisions about their elective government.

BENEFITS OF COMPETITION

The closure of hundreds of newspapers during the twentieth century brought about a decline in newspaper competition and an increase in monopoly newspaper communities, along with a rise of media consolidation through growing group ownership and, in the 1970s, the legalization of JOAs. Waning newspaper competition has sparked some debate among industry analysts and observers about the impact on the nation of this decreased competition. Factors in this disagreement range from the effects of competition on the process of democratic government to ownership patterns that are part of the process of media conglomeration and the role of these economic phenomena in the decline of media competition.

Writing in defense of the First Amendment, Theodore Glasser in 1984 argued on behalf of the importance of diverse ideas in media, particularly newspaper, markets. The amendment, he wrote,

> is desirable because it fosters a robust and uninhibited press; a robust and uninhibited press is desirable because it is a press able and presumably willing to accommodate divergent points of view; divergent points of view are desirable because they sustain

public debate; public debate is desirable because it nurtures an informed citizenry; and an informed citizenry is desirable because it brings about a more perfect polity and, in the end, legitimates the very idea of self government.[24]

Media analyst Ben Bagdikian in a 1985 paper concluded that economic changes in the media industries, including conglomeration, had negatively affected the nation through a homogenization of content. He linked this homogeneity to ownership traits. "The only reliable source of diversity and richness in U.S. mass media content is diversity of ownership of the media and a public attitude that accepts the legitimacy of a rich marketplace of ideas, including unconventional and anti-establishment ideas."[25]

Discussions of the benefits of media competition cite not only the Jeffersonian ideals put forth by researchers such as Glasser and Bagdikian but also *laissez-faire* economic theory, which argues that a free and competitive media market is one operating in classic capitalistic fashion and one that will foster a range of ideas, similar to products and goods, whose merits are decided by the consumers. The importance of media competition has been a subject of discussion not only among media workers, analysts, and scholars, it also has been an issue of importance to all three branches of the U.S. government. The U.S. Congress in 1970 enacted the Newspaper Preservation Act, signed into law by President Richard Nixon, enabling competing, separately owned participants in JOAs to circumvent antitrust laws by sharing sales, production, and circulation operations while maintaining separate, and competing, editorial operations. The act was upheld by a federal judge, who recognized it as being "designed to preserve independent [and thus competing] editorial voices."[26]

Because the loss of newspaper competition leaves communities with only one major daily, frequently group-owned, newspaper, analysis of newspaper competition necessarily takes in discussion of the effects of monopoly or chain ownership. Critics of media conglomeration cite the threat to local editorial autonomy of group ownership, particularly in monopoly situations. However, the literature on the subject, including some analysis of newspaper editorial commentary, offers mixed viewpoints.

Some studies have found negligible effects of competition and discernable benefits of group or chain, and sometimes monopoly, ownership. A study of two competing Pottsville, Pennsylvania, newspapers in 1946 and 1947 found only "slight" differences in editorial policy, with one newspaper publishing more editorials on local issues and showing somewhat less support than its competitor for the anthracite industry.[27] Gerard Borstel in a mid-1950s study found few consistent differences in comment along ownership or competition lines, but he did find a tendency for competition on political topics at one pair of the four pairs of competing dailies examined.[28] A 1956 study found no major differences in news and editorial content on monopoly newspapers due to a lack of local competition. However, this study cited another, by Ralph Nafziger and Thomas F. Barnhart, that found a twenty-year competitive battle between two Minnesota dailies produced highly diverse stands on various political issues until 1930, when the two papers' editorial stances became similar.[29]

Robert Entman in 1985 found little beneficial effect of competition in terms of opinion diversity in a comparison of the content of ninety-one newspapers representing cities with two competitive dailies, two papers with a single owner, or only one paper. The researcher concluded that news decisions of reporters and editors are based on journalistic rather than economic factors.[30] That same year, Benjamin Compaine argued that it is difficult to find convincing evidence that the trend toward group ownership has "ill served" newspaper readers. "There are at least as many documented cases in which a paper purchased by a group was substantially improved as there are cases in which a paper was weakened. ...As in any other business, owners have different styles and priorities. The good ones are not necessarily determined by chain ownership."[31]

Maxwell McCombs found little change in newspaper content when the Cleveland newspaper market switched from a competitive one to a monopoly with the closure of the *Press* in 1982.[32] John C. Busterna teamed with Kathleen Hansen in a 1990 study of presidential endorsements in the 1976–84 national elections that found chain-owned newspapers had more autonomy in these decisions than did other newspapers.[33] In their 1993 book, *Joint Operating Agreements: The Newspaper Preservation Act and Its Application*, Busterna and Robert Picard argued that U.S. newspapers have little editorial diversity and asked if JOAs can maintain a variety of editorial voices that the authors claimed did not exist in the first place.[34] David Demers in a 1993 study found little difference between chain-owned and independent newspapers regarding top editors' autonomy and ability to improve editorial content,[35] and in a 1996 study he concluded that corporate newspapers publish more local editorials, more letters to the editor, and more letters considered critical of mainstream groups.[36] A study of 258 newspaper editors a year earlier found that chain newspaper editors were more likely to see their role as activist.[37] Similarly, the American Society of Newspaper Editors found in 1980 that chain newspaper editors were more likely than their counterparts at independently owned papers to oppose their publishers and to enjoy more editorial freedom in national election endorsements.[38]

Other research has discovered opposite effects. Ralph Thrift Jr. found in a 1977 study of sixteen group-owned newspapers and eight control-group newspapers that group-owned papers tended to have fewer editorials of a controversial nature after purchase by a chain.[39] A 1975 analysis of endorsements in four election cycles (1960, 1964, 1968, and 1972) found a greater likelihood among chain newspapers to endorse presidential candidates, but the degree of homogeneity among the chain-owned newspapers was high for all four elections.[40] One of that study's authors replicated the finding regarding homogeneity in a study of election endorsements for 1976, 1980, 1984, and 1988.[41]

Other studies have found political and diversity effects in competitive newspaper situations and a correlating effect in the community. Dominic L. Lasorsa analyzed data from a 1988 American National Election Study (University of

Michigan Institute for Social Research) to conclude that newspaper competition was responsible for 4 percent of opinion diversity in the ninety-two counties studied, a level found by the author to be "significant."[42] Jan P. Vermeer in 1995 reported an effect on the public of newspaper competition in a study of gubernatorial and U.S. Senate races. "Specifically, the presence of more newspapers in a county leads to closer election outcomes in races for the U.S. Senate and for governor....The continuing decline in daily newspaper numbers may therefore have effects that go beyond convenience of access and competition for advertising."[43]

To examine the effects of daily newspaper competition on content, this chapter considers editorials of two sets of competing, non-JOA daily newspapers that were separately owned in Chicago, Illinois, and in Wilkes-Barre, Pennsylvania. The *Chicago Sun-Times*, with a weekday daily circulation of 479,508 in 2003, and the *Tribune*, which circulated 629,327,[44] were traditional newspaper rivals in a city noted for its robust political community. The Wilkes-Barre newspapers, with weekday 2003 daily circulation of 43,758 for the *Times Leader* and 32,335 for the *Citizens' Voice*, were analyzed for validation and comparison of findings in the Chicago market and to discern if any differences might exist in the two direct competition markets because of their circulation size differences. The research method, analyzing editorials based on geographical, topical, and political ideology differences, was defined in this book's Introduction.

THE CHICAGO MARKET FINDINGS

The *Tribune* published by far the greater number of editorials during the study period of the first month of 2001 and 2003, enjoying a more than twenty percentage point disparity. Part of the reason is that the *Sun-Times* published no editorials on Saturdays. But the *Sun-Times* offered a greater frequency of editorials on local subjects, also by a large percentage difference, nearly doubling the rate of local editorials of the *Tribune*. It also enjoyed a greater editorial frequency of editorials devoted to state and regional topics, but by less than a percentage point. The *Tribune*, though, had a large advantage in the frequency and percentages of editorials devoted to national and international categories. The *Sun-Times* published the sole editorial in the "other" category, a new year's editorial wish list covering issues and topics spanning several locales (see Table 2.1).

Politics and government topics dominated both newspapers' editorials, accounting for half of the *Tribune*'s commentary and nearly half, 45 percent, of the *Sun-Times*'. The two also offered similar frequency and rate of editorials on the second most dominant topic, economic matters. The newspapers parted ways on the third most dominant topic, with crime-related matters placing third in priority at the *Tribune* and subjects of general human interest claiming the third-place ranking at the *Sun-Times* (see Table 2.2).

Table 2.1   Geographic Concentration of Editorials in the *Chicago Tribune* and *Sun-Times* for January 2001 and January 2003

	Tribune	Sun-Times
Local	(4) 26 (15.4%)*	(2) 31 (30%)*
State/regional	(3) 31 (18.3%)*	(3) 18 (17.5%)*
National	(1) 78 (46.2%)*	(1) 42 (40.8%)*
International	(2) 34 (20.1%)*	(4) 11 (10.7%)*
Other	0	(5) 1 (1%)*
Total	169 (62%)**	103 (38%)**

*Percentages are of the total number of that newspaper's editorials only.
**Percentages are of the total number of editorials by both newspapers.
Preceding numbers in parenthesis are a ranking of that geographic listing by frequency.
Percentages are rounded to the nearest tenth of a percent.

The *Tribune* was responsible for more than half of the ninety-one editorials on forty common topics published by both newspapers, and the *Sun-Times* for just less than half. Nearly a third of all the editorials published by the newspapers were on common topics; so, the newspapers entered the same editorial realm often. About 40 percent of these editorials differed in their conclusions (see Table 2.3).

Political ideology differences accounted for the majority of editorial disagreement. For example, the two editorial boards differed on the governor's decision to commute death sentences of death-row inmates. Framing accounted for the remainder of the editorial disagreement. In their editorials on Israeli election, for example, both newspapers spoke favorably of the election, but one addressed

Table 2.2   Editorials by Topic Category in the *Chicago Tribune* and *Sun-Times* for January 2001 and January 2003

	Tribune	Sun-Times
Politics and government	(1) 86 (50.9%)*	(1) 45 (43.7%)*
Economic activity	(2) 17 (10.1%)*	(2) 13 (12.6%)*
Crime	(3) 16 (9.5%)*	(4) 10 (9.7%)*
General interest	(4) 11 (6.5%)*	(3) 12 (11.7%)*
Health and welfare	(4) 11 (6.5%)*	(5) 8 (7.8%)*
Popular amusements	(5) 8 (4.7%)*	(6) 5 (4.8%)*
Education and arts	(6) 6 (3.7%)*	(6) 5 (4.8%)*
Science and invention	(6) 6 (3.7%)*	0
War and defense	(7) 5 (3%)*	(7) 4 (3.9%)*
Public moral problems	(8) 2 (1.2%)*	(8) 1 (1%)*
Accident and disaster	(9) 1 (0.6%)*	0

*Percentages are of the total number of that newspaper's editorials only.
Preceding numbers in parenthesis are a ranking of that category by frequency.
Percentages are rounded to the nearest tenth of a percent.

Table 2.3 Editorials of Common Topics and Their Agreement and Disagreement in the *Chicago Tribune* and *Sun-Times* for January 2001 and January 2003

	Common topics	Agree	Disagree
Tribune	48 (28.4%)*	27 (56.3%)**	21 (43.7%)**
Sun-Times	43 (41.8%)*	26 (60.5%)**	17 (39.5%)**
Total	91 (33.5%)***	53 (19.5%)*** (58.2%)⁺	38 (14%)*** (41.8%)⁺

*Percentages are of the total number of that newspaper's editorials.
**Percentages are of that newspaper's total editorials on common topics.
***Percentages are of the overall total number of editorials.
+Percentages are of the total number of editorials on common subjects.
Percentages are rounded to the nearest tenth of a percent.

the wonders of a working democracy in the Middle East, while the other was an endorsement editorial for one of the candidates (see Table 2.4).

The newspapers published a combined total of fifty-seven editorials on local subjects, or 21 percent of all of their editorials. Seventeen of these, 29.8 percent of the local editorials, were on the same topic (nine by the *Tribune*, which editorialized twice on one of the local topics, and eight by the *Sun-Times*). Four of these editorials disagreed, two for ideological reasons. Sixteen of the newspapers' forty-nine state/regional editorials were on the same topic. The newspapers disagreed, either ideologically or in framing, on ten of them. Considering local, state, and regional editorials combined, the two newspapers published 106, nearly 39 percent of all their editorials, on subjects close to home. Nearly a third of these editorials, 31 percent, addressed common topics, and 13 percent of those differed in their conclusions or focus. So localism was relatively important to these newspapers, and local topics produced some diversity of opinion.

The newspapers offered a blatant difference in political ideology in the analysis of editorials on policies and initiatives of the President George W. Bush administration. The *Sun-Times'* ten editorials in January of 2001 on President Bush's policies welcomed the new Republican administration with a 90 percent

Table 2.4 Editorials of Common Topic Ideological Disagreement in the *Chicago Tribune* and *Sun-Times* for January 2001 and January 2003

	Ideological disagreement	Other disagreement
Tribune	13 (27.1%)*	8 (16.7%)*
Sun-Times	10 (23.2%)*	7 (16.3%)*
Total	23 (25.3%)** (8.5%)***	15 (16.5%)** (5.5%)***

*Percentages are of that newspaper's total editorials on common topics.
**Percentages are of the total number of editorials on common subjects.
***Percentage is of the overall total number of editorials.
Percentages are rounded to the nearest tenth of a percent.

support rate on issues that included the president's proposed tax cuts, problems surrounding the nomination of Linda Chavez as labor secretary, the appointment of John Ashcroft as attorney general, and the Leave No Child Behind education initiative. The *Tribune* offered one more editorial that year on domestic presidential policies than did the *Sun-Times*, but it divided nearly equally in support and opposition to administration policies. The *Tribune*'s editorials were a bit more far-ranging than those of the *Sun-Times*, discussing issues besides tax cuts, which the newspaper opposed, the Chavez controversy, in which the newspaper ended up siding with the Democratic opposition after initially adopting a wait-and-see attitude, and the Ashcroft nomination, which the newspaper ended up supporting, with some hesitations, after initially taking a wait-and-see attitude based on the confirmation hearings. The newspaper also supported Bush's education initiative.

Two years later, the number of editorials on administration policies by both newspapers declined, but the level of support and opposition to these policies changed little. The *Sun-Times* demonstrated 100 percent support for Bush administration policies, while the *Tribune* again split nearly equally between support and opposition.

During the two study periods, the newspapers frequently editorialized on different policies of the administration or on different aspects of certain policies or initiatives. For example, the *Tribune* published an editorial about the new president's proposal, in a State of the Union address, for development of hydrogen-powered automobiles, while the *Sun-Times* offered a more general piece on the address; and the *Tribune* editorialized on additional issues, ignored by the *Sun-Times*, that included increased tax expenditures on AIDS spending (support) (see Table 2.5).

In matters of national policies proposed or initiated by the Bush administration, the two newspapers offered their readers a variety and difference of opinion that, while not on opposite sides of the Republican–Democratic ideological fence in all instances, was evidence of an ideological rift between the two competing daily newspapers. One of the more apparent examples of this difference was found in the newspapers' reaction to the president's proposed tax cuts, which the *Tribune* opposed and the *Sun-Times* supported. The *Tribune* cited an economic expert and a member of Bush's cabinet in arguing against the

Table 2.5   Editorials of Support and Opposition to Policies and Decisions of the Administration of President George W. Bush in the *Chicago Tribune* and *Sun-Times* for January 2001 and January 2003

	Administration policy topics	Support	Oppose
Tribune	20	10 (50%)*	10 (50%)*
Sun-Times	14	13 (93%)*	1 (7%)*
Total	34	23	11

*Percentages are of that newspaper's total number of editorials on administration policies.

president's tax policy: "Paul O'Neill, the incoming Treasury secretary, stated a truth at his confirmation hearing last week that President George W. Bush has yet to acknowledge: That big tax cut package Bush made the centerpiece of his campaign won't do much to boost a slowing economy." The editorial concluded by referring to the state of the U.S. economy as further evidence in its argument. "But a slowing economy also jeopardizes the rosy government revenue estimates that have been used to predict future budget surpluses. The last thing President Bush should do is jerk the nation back into the dreary era of federal budgets scripted in red."[45] The *Sun-Times*, however, responded on the next day by hailing the chief executive as the ally of the taxpayers while dismissing the two primary arguments against the proposed tax reduction: It would take too long for the economy to feel its effects and the proposed amount of the tax cut was too big. The real issue, the editorial concluded, was not only economic factors but political philosophy.

> Some in Congress can't understand why Bush is so tenacious on this issue. It's not hard to figure out. Time and again during the campaign, Bush declared his belief in the benefit of tax reduction in general and in specific his commitment to the principle that the federal government should not take more than a third of a person's income in taxes. We guess it's going to take a little time for Washington to get used to a president who has principles other than self aggrandizement and self preservation.[46]

The newspapers also disagreed, but in more subtle ways having to do with framing and strength of argument, over President Bush's nomination of Ashcroft to be attorney general. The *Sun-Times* put forth a no-doubt-about-it opinion that dismissed Democratic Senator Edward Kennedy's "blusterings about Ashcroft's political views being 'so far out of the mainstream.'" The editorial mentioned one issue, abortion, on which it disagreed with Ashcroft. It then argued that as attorney general he would be sworn to uphold the law as it is, "not as I would have it." The bulk of the editorial listed issues on which the newspaper agreed with the nominee, concluding that the job of the Senate was not to ratify a nominee's political ideology. "Ashcroft is on record saying what he believes the responsibilities of the job are. Let him do it."[47] The *Tribune*, though, raised several questions about Ashcroft's political beliefs, suggesting that Bush could have found a better nominee, for a different office, to "appease Republicans from the rigid right.... Instead, Bush nominated an attorney general whose fiercely ideological past invites the fiercely ideological opposition that is massing against him." The newspaper, rather than concluding outright that Ashcroft should be confirmed, deferred to the confirmation process. "He'll be grilled, as he should be, on his thoughts and deeds. Then 100 senators—and the American people —will decide whether he is fit."[48] In a later editorial, the *Tribune* argued that Ashcroft "remains a flawed candidate" and said Bush would pay the price should Ashcroft fail to perform his job well. The newspaper made reference to

Ashcroft's treatment of Ronnie White, a black Missouri Supreme Court justice whom Ashcroft as a U.S. senator had kept off of the federal bench. "White was denied a federal judicial post because Ashcroft wanted to look tough on crime," said the editorial, which then concluded by advising the Senate to confirm Ashcroft while adding a final line that took this editorial in a decidedly different direction than the sole question of confirmation: "And Bush is now free to mitigate his man's biggest blunder. He could nominate Ronnie White for a federal judgeship."[49] That was a noticeably different take on this whole issue than the wholehearted support of Ashcroft by the *Sun-Times*.

One of the newspapers' disagreements on a state topic, the January 2003 decision by outgoing Illinois Governor George Ryan to commute the death sentences of all prisoners on death row, were part of a national debate. The *Tribune*, making note of the jubilation over the governor's announcement by defense attorneys and law students at Northwestern University Law School, where he made the announcement, also mentioned the "outrage and sheer anguish" of the relatives of murder victims. It voiced disagreement with the breadth of the governor's action but said nonetheless that it focused attention on the need of the state legislature to rectify the state's criminal justice system. "Death row will fill up soon enough," concluded the editorial, which was one of three by the newspaper on this subject, compared to one editorial by its rival. "Gov.-elect Rod Blagojevich has promised to retain the moratorium on capital punishment. Senate President Emil Jones has said criminal justice reform is his highest priority. Those are welcome words. Legislators must ensure that no future governor faces the kind of wrenching decisions Ryan made over the last two days."[50]

The *Sun-Times* in its editorial published on the same day also cited the need for reform of the state's criminal justice system, but it opined that Ryan had gone too far in dispensing "justice en masse, despite the cheers it may have received from the foes of the death penalty. The governor is merely reacting to wrongful conviction by issuing wrongful leniency." Adding that the governor had undone the work of "countless judges and juries" while "bringing comfort to the most ruthless criminals in our society and anguish to their victims' loved ones," the editorial dismissed the governor's decision in its conclusion as "theater aimed at activists. Even Ryan said Friday that the death sentence might be appropriate 'under the right conditions.' While national debate is certain to rage, the new governor and Legislature owe it to the people of Illinois to make sure those strict conditions are met."[51] Thus, this editorial came down in favor of the death sentence, its writer wishing to ensure that the proper legal conditions were set and met, while the *Tribune* appeared to leave open the debate over capital punishment. This was a stance the *Tribune* further defined in a subsequent editorial. "If legislators fail once again during their upcoming spring session to pass substantive reforms to the capital punishment system," the newspaper opined three days later, "then it will be time to rethink whether the state can responsibly have a death penalty at all."[52] This was an example of newspaper editorials engaging in an ideologically driven dispute over an issue of great importance, an issue of national and international concern. While such disagreements may be statistically rare in modern newspapering, they nonetheless demonstrate a marketplace of ideas in a newspaper competition that is functioning in a true Jeffersonian democratic sense.

THE WILKES-BARRE MARKET FINDINGS

One of the more striking differences between the findings of the Wilkes-Barre market analysis and those of the Chicago market analysis was the markedly heavier concentration, by both Wilkes-Barre newspapers, on local editorials. Also, not surprisingly considering the smaller circulations of the Wilkes-Barre newspapers and thus the relatively smaller size of their newsroom and editorial page staffs, the total number of editorials published by the two newspapers was much smaller: 145 editorials during the one-month, two-year study period. Another difference in the findings of this and of the Chicago market was the wide disparity in the frequency of staff-written editorials published by the newspapers studied, fifty-eight by the *Times Leader*, compared to eighty-seven by the *Citizens' Voice*. One other finding that deviated from those of the Chicago market was the lower percentage of editorials dealing with Bush administration proposals and policies. These numbered just two by the *Times Leader*, only 3.4 percent of its editorials, and three by the *Citizens' Voice*, also 3.4 percent. This rendered insignificant the ideological differences of the newspapers as measured by support of or opposition to administration policies.

Clearly, the newspapers in the Wilkes-Barre market were more concerned with subjects closer to home than were the newspapers in the larger Chicago market. More than 70 percent of the *Citizens' Voice*'s editorials and 60 percent of the *Times Leader*'s were on local topics. The two newspapers' 100 local editorials accounted for about 69 percent of all of their editorials. The *Times Leader* topped the *Citizens' Voice* in percentage frequency of editorials on state and regional topics, and the newspapers combined published slightly more than 10 percent of all their editorials on these subjects. Considering all editorials on topics closer to home (local plus state/regional concentration), the *Citizens' Voice* surpassed its competitor. In comparison to the Chicago market, nearly 80 percent of the newspapers' editorials were on local/state/regional topics, while the percentage for the Chicago market was 38.9 percent.

As for the other geographical categories, the *Times Leader* published about 20 percent of its total editorials on national topics and just one editorial on an international subject (1.7 percent of all of its editorials). The *Citizens' Voice* opined on national topics 14.9 percent of the time and, like its rival, only once on international subjects. It had one editorial in the "other" category, which was a beginning-of-the-year New Year's agenda-setting editorial that addressed subjects pertaining to more than one geographical category (see Table 2.6).

Table 2.6   Geographic Concentration of Editorials in the Wilkes-Barre *Times Leader* and *Citizens' Voice* for January 2001 and January 2003

	Times Leader	Citizens' Voice
Local	(1) 37 (63.8%)*	(1) 63 (72.4%)*
State/regional	(3) 8 (13.8%)*	(2) 9 (10.3%)*
National	(2) 12 (20.7%)*	(1) 13 (14.9%)*
International	(4) 1 (1.7%)*	(4) 1 (1.2%)*
Other	0	(5) 1 (1.2%)*
Total	58 (40%)**	87 (60%)**

*Percentages are of the total number of that newspaper's editorials only.
**Percentages are of the total number of editorials by both newspapers.
Preceding numbers in parenthesis are a ranking of that geographic listing by frequency.
Percentages are rounded to the nearest tenth of a percent.

A similarity in the findings of the Wilkes-Barre and Chicago markets was the domination of political and government topics in the editorials of both newspapers. The *Times Leader* published slightly less than half of its editorials on these subjects, while the *Citizens' Voice* published slightly more than half. The newspapers demonstrated noticeably different topical interests, based on percentage frequency, in four subject areas. The *Times Leader* offered more editorials on economic activity, which was a nearly triple percentage frequency to that of the *Citizens' Voice,* and it published more commentary on education and the classic arts, with an eight-to-one percentage frequency advantage. The *Citizens' Voice* showed greater interest in the subjects of public health and welfare as well as general human interest, besting the *Times Leader*'s percentage frequency in these categories by about three percentage points in each. Neither newspaper editorialized on the category of public moral problems (see Table 2.7); but as in the Chicago market analysis, the evidence of differing concentrations of emphasis on diverse topics indicates an important sort of editorial diversity other than ideological or framing differences: differing agendas.

The newspapers rarely published editorials on the same subjects, with common-topic editorials accounting for just 15.2 percent of their total number of editorials. About 17 percent of the *Times Leader*'s editorials were on the same subjects as its competitor, compared to just under 14 percent for the *Citizens' Voice*. The discrepancy in the total number of editorials on the same subjects by each of the newspapers is explained by the finding that each newspaper published different numbers of editorials on some of the same subjects.

The newspapers experienced a high rate of disagreement, about 68 percent, on same-subject editorials (see Table 2.8). Those that differed for ideological reasons accounted for two-thirds of all of the editorials of disagreement. The percentage of editorials of ideological disagreement for each newspaper's editorials on common topics was 50 percent for the *Times Leader* and 41.7 percent for the *Citizens' Voice* (see Table 2.9).

Table 2.7   Editorials by Topic Category in the Wilkes-Barre *Times Leader* and *Citizens' Voice* for January 2001 and January 2003

	Times Leader	Citizens' Voice
Politics and government	(1) 28 (48.3%)*	(1) 45 (51.7%)*
Economic activity	(3) 6 (10.3%)*	(5) 3 (3.4%)*
Crime	(2) 7 (12.2%)*	(2) 12 (13.8%)*
General interest	(4) 5 (8.6%)*	(3) 10 (11.5%)*
Health and welfare	(5) 3 (5.2%)*	(4) 7 (8%)*
Popular amusements	(6) 2 (3.4%)*	(5) 3 (3.4%)*
Education and arts	(4) 5 (8.6%)*	(7) 1 (1.2%)*
Science and invention	0	(6) 2 (2.3%)*
War and defense	(6) 2 (3.4%)*	(6) 2 (2.3%)*
Public moral problems	0	0
Accident and disaster	0	(7) 1 (1.2%)*
Other	0	(7) 1 (1.2%)*

*Percentages are of the total number of that newspaper's editorials only.
Preceding numbers in parenthesis are a ranking of that category by frequency.
Percentages are rounded to the nearest tenth of a percent.

Just fourteen of the newspapers' 100 local editorials in the two-year sampling were on common topics. Six of these were by the *Times Leader* and eight by the *Citizens' Voice*. The newspapers disagreed on eight of these, or better than half of all of their local common-topic commentaries. Six of these, three by each newspaper, differed because of ideology. That accounted for a 42.9 percent ideological disagreement rate for all local common-topic editorials. This was a marked difference in local ideological diversity compared to the Chicago market.

Of the newspapers' seventeen editorials on state/regional topics, only four were on common subjects, and the newspapers disagreed on all of them. Half of these disagreed for ideological reasons and half for framing. So, of the newspapers' 117 editorials on subjects closer to home (local and state/regional),

Table 2.8   Editorials of Common Topics and Their Agreement and Disagreement in the Wilkes-Barre *Times Leader* and *Citizens' Voice* for January 2001 and January 2003

	Common topics	Agree	Disagree
Times Leader	10 (17.2%)*	3 (30%)**	7 (70%)**
Citizens' Voice	12 (13.8%)*	4 (33.3%)**	8 (66.7%)**
Total	22 (15.2%)***	7 (4.8%)***	15 (10.3%)***
		(31.8%)+	(68.2%)+

*Percentages are of the total number of that newspaper's editorials.
**Percentages are of that newspaper's total editorials on common topics.
***Percentages are of the overall total number of editorials.
+Percentages are of the total number of editorials on common subjects.
Percentages are rounded to the nearest tenth of a percent.

Table 2.9   Editorials of Common Topic Ideological Disagreement in the Wilkes-Barre *Times Leader* and *Citizens' Voice* for January 2001 and January 2003

	Ideological disagreement	Other disagreement
Times Leader	5 (50%)*	2 (20%)*
Citizens' Voice	5 (41.7%)*	3 (25%)*
Total	10 (45.5%)** (6.9%)***	5 (22.7%)** (3.4%)***

*Percentages are of that newspaper's total editorials on common topics.
**Percentages are of the total number of editorials on common subjects.
***Percentage is of the overall total number of editorials.
Percentages are rounded to the nearest tenth of a percent.

eighteen were on common topics, and twelve of these disagreed for reasons of ideology or framing.

The newspapers' 2003 opinions regarding the legacy of Luzerne County Commissioner Tom Makowski, who had recently announced he would not be seeking a third term of office, provided an example of ideological editorial disagreement. The *Citizens' Voice* saw this decision as a major loss to the county's political scene. The newspaper's editorial listed some of the departing commissioner's accomplishments, which included creation of an emergency telephone system, steadfast support for the county's community college, development of walking paths and playing fields, and support of a safety net for the elderly. "The judgment, we are certain, will be that Tom Makowski was one of the best commissioners—hard-working, progressive, public-spirited, good natured, and with a record of real accomplishment," concluded the editorial.[53]

The *Times Leader*, though, a week later focused on the negative aspects of the commissioner's service, which included leaving the public out of the decision-making process, failing to give advance notice of meetings, refusing to adequately fund a county government study commission, opposing pension fund revisions that brought about savings, and tolerance of waste and incompetence. "We'll remember him," the editorial said. "Like a tick on the dog. The hair in the soup. The snow in the sock."[54]

Similarly, the newspapers quarreled over a proposal to house juvenile delinquents in a county nursing home. Such use of the Valley Crest home would be creative, argued the *Citizens' Voice*, pointing out that the county was experiencing budget difficulties.

> And the cost of re-doing the convention center would be big—$2.5 million for repairs and $5 million for a new building.
>   We don't want to see the taxpayers pay more. . . . When the budget crunch hit this past year, an editorial in this space said the commissioners should look for ways to save money creatively. The proposal to use Valley Crest space instead of building a $5 million detention center is indeed creative.[55]

The *Times Leader* disagreed. "Certain things in life just don't mix," said the newspaper four days later. "Such as oil and water. Or young criminals and the frail elderly." The editorialist questioned the decision by county officials to spend money on another project in his or her concluding remarks opposing this idea. "The commissioners' proposal only makes us wonder: If the county has all that extra room at Valley Crest, then why did it spend all that money—$4 million and counting—to purchase and renovate the Penn Place complex to create more office space?"[56]

Another area of editorial disagreement arose in the newspapers' comments on the loss of a state grant for a community crime prevention program. The *Times Leader* chastised the mayor for this, claiming it was the third time that the mayor had sought grant funding and failed to follow through. "A city whose crime problems are not negligible should not be looking any gift horse—let alone $600,000 worth—in the mouth," said the newspaper. "The mayor's willingness to go after government grant money and then fail to meet the requirements shows a lack of focus....His behavior is not only embarrassing, it's expensive."[57] The *Citizens' Voice*, though, in an editorial published six days later, associated the loss of this grant with the resignation of the city's Crime Watch coordinator. The editorial spoke to that resignation in the context of seven other recent resignations at city hall and called for "better attention" to the grant process. Citing the mayor's explanation that some of the vacant positions were not necessary for daily city operations, the editorial writer opined that the mayor "is right to keep a careful eye on staffing, and its associated costs," and then urged the mayor "to evaluate the administrative level. What work must it perform? What goals should it have? Are the people in place? Is there a solid mayoral/administrative team? If not, there should be."[58] This editorial, then, provided an example in which ideological and framing differences shared in producing editorial disagreement. One newspaper editorial blamed the mayor for losing a state grant; the other looked at the overall city administration and credited the mayor for keeping a sharp eye on staffing and costs while urging an evaluation of city administrative roles and functions.

COMPETITIVE MARKETS IN DIFFERENT WAYS

Clearly, a competitively diverse newspaper market existed in both of these direct competition markets. These markets demonstrated variance of ideas and of ideological viewpoints along with other differences, such as framing and agenda, on the editorial pages of their two major daily newspapers.

In Chicago, as noted earlier, nearly a third of the editorials published by the *Tribune* and *Sun-Times* in the two-year sampling were on common topics, and a substantial percentage of these, 41.8 percent, reached different conclusions. Of these differing viewpoints, 60.5 percent were based on ideological disagreements on subjects that ranged from capital punishment to the handling of surplus tax dollars. Of all editorials published by both newspapers, disagreement in conclusions comprised 14 percent and ideological disagreement comprised 8.5 percent. While both Chicago newspapers published most of their sampled 2001 and 2003 editorials on topics of politics and government and economic matters, they traveled different editorial priority routes in discussing other subjects. Crime was the third most dominant topic at the *Tribune,* for example, while at the *Sun-Times* it was general human interest. The *Tribune* published six editorials on science and invention, while the *Sun-Times* published none. The *Sun-Times,* on the other hand, offered a slightly higher percentage of editorials on public health and welfare.

The newspapers demonstrated different areas of emphasis on geographical editorial focus. The *Sun-Times* laid claim to the local editorial market, publishing nearly one-third of all of its editorials on local topics to the *Tribune*'s 15.4 percent, while the *Tribune* led the editorial count for state and regional topics. But based on the relative numbers of editorials on a combination of local, state, and regional topics, it could be argued that the editorial executives of the *Sun-Times* considered editorials on subjects closer to home to be of greater importance than, say, editorials on international topics. The *Tribune* published a greater frequency and percentage of editorials on national topics.

The newspapers' variance of editorial emphasis, both by topic and by geographic focus, provided evidence of a strongly diverse marketplace of ideas. One reason for the findings of ideological and topical editorial diversity in the Chicago market might be found in the history of these two newspapers and in a newspaper market known for its competitiveness. As the collegiate *Badger Herald* in Wisconsin was founded to provide an opposing ideological voice at the University of Wisconsin, the *Sun-Times*' forerunner, the *Chicago Sun,* was founded by Marshall Field in 1941 to counter the Republicanism of the *Tribune* (political leanings that have become reversed, based on the findings of this chapter's study, but they remain divided nonetheless).[59] The Chicago newspaper competition at times went beyond word exchanges; the city was the site of a violent battle during the Prohibition era of the 1920s in which *Tribune* circulation crews fought truck drivers for the rival *American.*[60] Also, the study was conducted on editorials during a time frame in which public issues were highly likely to invite diverse opinions. On the basis of these findings, the Chicago newspaper competition supports the argument that a pluralistic democracy thrives in a diverse marketplace of ideas and open exchange.

In Wilkes-Barre, meanwhile, newspaper executives demonstrated a kind of editorial difference and variety just as meaningful as the Chicago market's ideological and framing differences. It was a diversity that grew out of a newspaper strike when, in 1978, the editorial departments of the *Times Leader* and Wilkes-Barre *Record,* published by the Wilkes-Barre Publishing

Co., hit the picket lines. Some of the strikers formed the *Citizens' Voice*, which today is owned by Times Shamrock Communications, based in Scranton, Pennsylvania.[61]

One important way in which this market's ideological and framing differences were revealed was in the relatively scarce number of common editorial topics. Both Wilkes-Barre newspapers devoted considerable editorial space to local topics not taken up by the competing newspaper. These diverse topics all are important to a community; that the editorial boards of these competing newspapers deemed these separate topics worthy of comment while their rivals did not is evidence of agenda-setting priorities and perceptions clearly at odds.

Such topics included the following issues and stances, which sparked editorials from the *Times Leader* but not from its rival: the mayor's decision to purchase a $25,000 mobile crime prevention unit; the mayor's handling of a proposed movie theater for downtown; the need for a program to help recovering drug addicts in the county; the need to make permanent the loss of thirty-five county jobs due to streamlining; opposition to the mayor's goal of automating the parking ticket system; the local benefits of the Earth Conservancy program; the attendance by the mayor at a business/development series of meetings; the apparent conflict of interest of a school board member who wanted to start an alternative charter school within the public school district's boundaries; a proposal by a soft-drink bottling company to be a local school district's exclusive soda pop vendor; a controversy over a medical malpractice case involving a local hospital; possible election law violations by a campaign committee representing some local school board members; reassessment of county properties for tax purposes; the suggestion by the mayor that he might "crash" the inaugural parade for newly elected Governor Rendell; the need for county commissioners to eliminate job vacancies; and the loss of city and county revenues over failure to go after parking ticket scofflaws.

The *Citizens' Voice* editorialized exclusively on the following local subjects: the need to post county budget information on the Internet; the importance of evaluating neighboring cities' anticrime efforts in dealing with those of Wilkes-Barre; a local courtroom conflict involving a custody dispute between a mother and a grandmother; the cultural benefit of preserving a local historic coal breaker; a proposal calling for quarterly review of the county budget by county commissioners; the benefits of a proposal by an out-of-state company to construct a wind park to generate electricity; the positive aspects of a local effort to preserve and revive an historic hotel; the need for public involvement at a series of meetings on the future of the downtown neighborhood; the need to address the problem of a resident whose drinking water was contaminated with coliform waste; zoning of a meteorological tower in a local township; a criminal trial regarding the murder of two local residents who helped two men stranded on a roadside in 1999; progress on the cleanup of the Susquehanna River; strict punishment for property defacement; a study on changes needed in city government; an investigation into the case of a local school teacher accused of smoking marijuana and harassment; the proposed demolition of row houses in a northern city neighborhood; whether production of city calendars was a worthwhile endeavor for the city; a proposal to divide the city into five districts for city council representation; a call for negotiations between administrators and nurses threatening a strike at a local hospital; a proposed bond issue to pay for programs that included riverfront improvements and juvenile detention facilities; the need for criminal and credit background checks of rental housing applicants; and the need for a shelter for stray pets.

Each of these issues had an impact on local residents and taxpayers. Yet each is one that only one of the community's two newspapers took up editorially during the period of this study. If Wilkes-Barre had been a community with just one, monopoly newspaper, the chances are that one of the above lists of editorial subjects conceivably would have been ignored by that newspaper as the editors, publishers, and editorial boards offered opinions only on those subjects they found compelling enough for editorial attention. This range of local opinion, which was mirrored in the variety of opinions found in other geographical and topical categories, represented an important kind of diversity in editorial voices brought about by the existence of competing editorial voices. While it may be true that Wilkes-Barre residents would have had to read both newspapers to appreciate this diverse range of topics and agendas, the two newspapers nonetheless entered this varied menu of ideas into the public discourse; the ideas were there for the public to consume. Combined with the ideological differences cited earlier on issues on which both newspapers editorialized, the competitive newspaper market in Wilkes-Barre offers a robust marketplace of ideas. It is a marketplace that gives readers and policy makers diversity of opinion through competition, as envisioned by those who argue that newspaper and media competition help the democratic process by encouraging differing ideas and opinions.

The Chicago market analysis also found a large volume of editorials on unshared topics, including at the local level. Of the fifty-seven editorials that the two Chicago newspapers published on local issues in the sampling, just seventeen touched common ground. This means that forty local editorials, or 70.2 percent of all local editorials, dealt with separate issues. Though the Chicago newspapers demonstrated a lower percentage interest in local subjects than did the Wilkes-Barre newspapers, the relatively large number of editorials on separate local topics indicated an existence of independent agendas for the competing newspapers and their editorial boards similar to the agenda differences found in Wilkes-Barre.

Examples of local topics addressed by the *Tribune* included: attitudes toward gay teens in the public schools; Mayor Richard Daley's efforts to combat homicide and other serious crimes; the benefits of supportive housing programs for recovering alcoholics or people suffering from mental disabilities; the problem of obesity in Chicago; the decision by the mayor to refrain from challenging the petitions of four "underdog" candidates for mayor; the questionable awarding of a contract for advertising at city bus-stop shelters; the upcoming political agendas of local candidates running on a "reform" platform; a controversy over plans by the Salvation Army to renovate a substance-abuse facility in the city's Near West Side; and the need for a closed city road to be repaired and reopened.

Local topics claimed solely by the *Sun-Times* included: the race factor in promotion of city police; the mayor's pledge to end homelessness in Chicago within nine years; a proposed trolley line; a scandal involving a public school teacher accused of soliciting sex from a student; the decision by city officials not to use heavy-duty equipment for snow removal during two recent storms; the need for greater enforcement of traffic laws; the need for compromise in a dispute involving a suburban community's city officials requiring a building permit for a tree house; the closing of a longtime Chicago candy manufacturing plant; the urging by Mayor Daley that city businesses hire public housing residents; the need for moving forward on a redevelopment project on State Street; and plans by city police to more strongly enforce the proper use of designated bus lanes.

As in the Wilkes-Barre study, these separate issues identified as important by the particular newspapers were subjects that may not have been recognized or discussed in a newspaper market that did not include both of these newspapers. They represent a richness in diversity, one that takes in separate agendas that fill an opinion void. They represent a marketplace of ideas that would offer scanter ideological goods were it not for a lively newspaper competition.

Indeed, something other is at play here, in both of these markets, than a marketplace of ideas. Call it a market basket of ideas, an opinion and discussion shopping cart in which the consumers must not decide merely between beef and pork, skim or 2 percent milk, but that takes in other options as well, such as no meat or milk products, substituting vegetables or fish for beef and pork and soy products for milk. This is not exclusively a battle of truth and falsity; it also is a skirmish involving a mixture of unrelated or sometimes complementary ideas and agendas. What is occurring on these editorial pages, besides liberal versus conservative or Democratic versus Republican debates, is a promulgation of ideas about how society and culture ought to be shaped using frames of reference or perceptions and viewpoints that might not occur to the competing editorial board and that might not emerge at all if the second, competing, newspaper did not exist. A similar richness of agenda diversity was found in geographical concentrations other than local. This sort of idea abundance and variance, especially at the local level, cannot be supplied in a monopoly market.

To be sure, other factors besides competition, such as editorial department budgets and manpower, being part of group ownership, and ownership commitment to the concept of a vigorous editorial voice and to offering an editorial voice that differs from that of the competitor's, play a role in newspaper vitality and editorial strength. But, as numerous media analysts have noted, competition is a key ingredient to providing robust reportage and a variety of opinions and ideas. These findings of editorial diversity contradict the conclusions of previous research that found no or little effect of competition on newspaper editorials. Besides finding varying levels of ideological diversity in the editorials of independently owned city dailies, these analyses also found a broad range of editorial topics and framing in two-newspaper markets that simply could not exist in a monopoly market. The next chapter will explore the competitive nature of joint operating agreement markets.

CHAPTER 3

Wars Hot and Cold: The Seeds of JOA

We published on the 8th inst. an article compiled from Connolly's (alias Slippery Dick's) own books, showing the frauds which are perpetrated at the expense of the public in relation to the city armories alone. We gave the official lists of the armories, the rents paid for them, and the rents they were actually worth. We sent this article to Connolly, and we gave him the opportunity of correcting or denying it; but he could not do either.

Tomorrow morning we shall publish a still more important document, also compiled from Connolly's own books. We shall prove, and we challenge Connolly or any other of the city authorities to deny a single fact or figure in our statement, that the public are robbed of several millions a year under the head of armory accounts alone.

...These figures will convince any man beyond a doubt that Hall and Connolly, who signed the warrants, are SWINDLERS, and as such we once more arraign them before the bar of public opinion...

—New York Times, July 19, 1871, on its exposure of the public thefts
by the Boss Tweed political machine[1]

The world of George F. Babbitt verged on the cusp of technological and societal change. The 46-year-old fictional hero of Sinclair Lewis' 1922 novel, *Babbitt*, lived in a United States fresh from its victory in World War I, a nation anxious to discard the progressive politics of presidents Theodore Roosevelt and Woodrow Wilson. The country bustled on the economic upswing and happy days of the Roaring Twenties that preceded the Great Depression and World War II. Factories thrived, mass-producing automobiles and other technological marvels such as kitchen and bathroom appliances. It was a modern nation, an industrial leader that embraced the business-friendly politics of presidents Warren Harding, Calvin Coolidge, and Herbert Hoover. Babbitt's fictional city, Zenith, harbored an industrial class of men toting lunch boxes who "clumped toward the immensity of new factories, sheets of glass and hollow tile, glittering shops where five thousand men worked beneath one roof, pouring out the honest wares that would be sold up the Euphrates and across the veldt. The whistles rolled out in greeting a chorus cheerful as the April dawn; the song of labor in a city built— it seemed—for giants."[2] The city, Lewis wrote, "aspired among the morning mist; austere towers of steel and cement and limestone, sturdy as cliffs and delicate as silver rods. They were neither citadels nor churches, but frankly and beautifully office-buildings."[3]

It was an exciting world of commerce, conservative politics and a sophisticated cultural scene that included dancing and theater. A world in which a typical after-dinner discussion in the Babbitt household might center on Shakespeare, a topic he was willing to consider despite his scant knowledge of the bard and his themes. "I don't see why they give us this old-fashioned junk by Milton and Shakespeare and Wordsworth and all these has-beens," Babbitt says in reference to the high school homework of his son, busy studying in a corner of the living room. "Yes, I wonder why," responds his wife as she sits darning socks. "Of course, I don't want to fly in the face of the professors and everybody, but I do think there's things in Shakespeare—not that I read him much, but when I was young the girls used to show me passages that weren't really, they weren't at all nice."[4] On the subject of Shakespeare, Babbitt felt, "he wasn't really an authority. Neither the *Advocate-Times*, the *Evening Advocate*, nor the *Bulletin of the Zenith Chamber of Commerce* had ever had an editorial on the matter, and until one of them had spoken he found it hard to form an original opinion."[5]

Babbitt, of course, was not real. He was a fictional character, some might say a stereotype, a cliché, or a twentieth-century *Everyman*. Babbitt and his society, however, depict much that was factual about American culture in the second decade of the 1900s; it was an era of relative economic boom, of respite from war, of mistrust of foreigners, of the return to "normalcy" championed by Harding as a detour from the progressive politics of the turn of the century. Society, at least middle-class society represented by Babbitt and his fellow characters in Lewis' modern-day morality play, paid attention to editorial opinion even on aesthetic and artistic concerns such as Shakespeare, Milton, and Wordsworth. And in cities the size of Zenith, the powerbrokers and other citizens usually could rely on the sometimes differing opinions of at least two daily newspapers; it was an era in which nearly 300 American communities by the year 1930 experienced daily newspaper competition, unlike the American society of the early twenty-first century, in which just twenty-four American cities had daily newspaper competition.

Editorialists of Babbitt's day expounded on themes that ranged from presidential endorsements, war, capital punishment, and economic policy to cultural and societal issues. Though Babbitt's city of Zenith was fictional, it easily could have been any number of American cities enjoying an industrial boom in the early twentieth century. It could have been Pittsburgh, Pennsylvania, where the *Press* and *Gazette Times* (the forerunner of today's *Post-Gazette*) competed. Or Babbitt's Zenith might have been Tulsa, Oklahoma, where the *Tribune* waged editorial battle with the *Daily World*. Both of these sets of competing newspapers would later in the 1900s enter into JOAs, enabling them to continue competing editorially while sharing business and production operations. A brief analysis of their editorial page differences thus affords an opportunity to discern what these communities might be missing were they to become one-newspaper towns (as both did late in the twentieth century).

The early events of World War I, such as the sinking by the Germans of the British ocean liner the *Lusitania* in 1915, offered an opportunity for the *Pittsburgh Press* and the *Gazette Times* to put forward different takes on that foreign entanglement. The sinking, carried out without warning by a German U-boat on May 7 off the coast of Ireland, resulted in the drowning of 1,198 people, 114 of whom were Americans. The two newspapers shared anger over the situation, but their viewpoints diverged from there, as did the placement of their editorials.

Editorial position is one method, beyond political ideological or framing variations, that newspapers might show evidence of difference in their opinions. The lead editorial position, just like the lead story on the front page of the newspaper, commands the most attention, sending the message to readers that the newspaper editors consider this opinion to be the primary one of the day. The *Press*, an evening newspaper, made the *Lusitania* outrage the lead editorial of its May 8 edition. "The awfulness of a death struggle between great nations is never fully realized until we ourselves, or something belonging to us, happens to get into their way," began the editorial. "The thrill of horror with which the people of the United States learned yesterday afternoon of the sinking of the *Lusitania* with its great cargo of human freight is an example."[6] On that same morning, the *Gazette Times* rued the affront to international law. But the interesting aspect of the editorial was its position as the second editorial of the day, placed on the page below a commentary discussing the business climate in the United States. The editorial on the *Lusitania* began:

> Since international law and usage have been shot to pieces in the European war, their bearing upon the destruction of the *Lusitania* calls for no extended discussion. Hitherto, it is true it had been the practice of supposedly civilized nations, while exercising the right to sink merchant ships of enemy countries, to afford those on

board an opportunity to save their lives. The status of the *Lusitania* as an unarmed craft engaged in transporting passengers and cargo from a neutral to a belligerent port will not be questioned.[7]

In their differing conclusions, the *Press* urged that the president be given "the opportunity to deal with the situation unhampered by any explosions of jingoism or any partisan effort to 'force his hand,'"[8] while the *Gazette Times* called the incident "especially serious...since so many United States citizens were aboard the vessel—a score or more from our own city. Undoubtedly, some have perished. The situation cannot be ignored by our government. It is the gravest of the war to us."[9] The *Gazette Times*, though, had second thoughts about the situation. On the next day it published a lengthy editorial, this time in the lead position, that opened with a reference to partisans of Germany urging an "orderly process of diplomacy, and to keep cool and go slow." But, the editorial concluded, "there can be nothing but execration and condemnation for this frightful deed....Germany has committed an unpardonable offense for which, sooner or later, she will have to answer."[10]

Presidential campaigns often create disparate voices, and often similar opinions that differ in non-ideological ways such as framing, on competing editorial pages. Such was the case in the early twentieth century in Pittsburgh. The scrappy 1912 election saw former Republican President Theodore Roosevelt run for president on a third party, Progressive ticket, splitting the Republican vote and tossing the race to Democrat Woodrow Wilson. This election brought the two Pittsburgh dailies together in their support of the Republican candidate, William Howard Taft, on behalf of preserving a strong business and economic climate. But the *Gazette Times* then surpassed its rival in not only endorsing the Republican platform but by taking direct aim at Wilson in a separate editorial with a distinctly negative voice. This approach illustrates how newspaper editorialists can differ in ways other than political ideology through tone and framing; in this case, the *Gazette Times* focused on one candidate's negative aspects upon which the competing newspaper did not dwell. The following excerpt exemplifies the *Gazette Times'* anti-Wilson opinion. Besides its attack on Wilson's character, the editorial also offers an example of how editorialists might stamp their ideological position on other issues—trade protectionism in this case—as part of a political invective.

> From beginning to end of the campaign he has taken refuge in generalities and has resorted to mere phrasemaking. He has not discussed his platform comprehensively. He has not been frank nor explicit on the tariff plank. He has not explained how, if he removes the custom house barriers and invites an influx of foreign commodities in competitive lines, our manufacturers will escape injury and our workingmen the unwelcome penalty of reduced wages. This evasion—a studied and deliberate attempt to elude damaging criticism and avert adverse judgment—is self revealing of a weakness in Gov. Wilson's character which should cause every Republican and every conservative Democrat to "stop, look and listen."[11]

Twelve years later, the newspapers parted ways in their presidential candidate preferences. The *Press* lined up behind the Progressive Party, while the *Gazette Times* stood by the Republicans. The differing editorial opinions offered evidence of a political ideology variance that gave readers a clear option. The *Press*, in its support of Progressive Party candidate Robert M. La Follette on November 3, 1924, scolded the late Republican President Warren Harding and Vice President Calvin Coolidge for breaking their pledge on behalf of conservation, and it accused the incumbent administration and the Democrats of supporting "special privilege, the vested interests."

> The people should this year vote the two corrupt and untrustworthy old parties out and vote the new Independent party in. That party, with Senator La Follette as its leader, is the party of the people. It is the only party which is honest with its followers, and which can be depended on to restore the people to the control of their government.[12]

The *Gazette Times* on the next day offered an explanation for why the nation was Republican and why it ought to vote that way in the upcoming election. Opining that the Democrats offered little of worth to voters and that any radicalism in the campaign belonged to La Follette, the newspaper dismissed the Wisconsin senator as a man whose

> progressive principles have been picked from the junk heap of socialistic adventures in government that failed, and it is so un-American that it has boldly proposed, to knock off the cornerstone of the Constitution on which American liberties rest.... The Republican party, its candidates and the platform on which they stand, are soundly American. That is what has appealed to the people and will bring them to the polls today in greater numbers than ever before.[13]

Another example of editorial ideological disagreement came during one of the major criminal trials of the early twentieth century, that of Nicola Sacco and Bartolomeo Vanzetti, followed by their execution. The pages of the *Gazette Times*, which by now had become the *Post-Gazette,* and the *Press,* now owned by Scripps Howard, reflected those differences. This particular instance of editorial diversity offered a vivid example of how two newspapers, both supporters of the American democratic and capitalist system, judging by their previous presidential endorsement editorials, and both members of the American intellectual mainstream, furthered the democratic discussion by expounding opposing sides of this issue. Sacco and Vanzetti were put to death in Boston on August 23, 1927, having been convicted of the 1920 killing of a factory guard. Many believed they were victimized and wrongly executed because of their radical, socialist beliefs and associations. The *Press* in an impassioned editorial published on August 23, 1927, called the execution a mistake, despite the following of correct legal procedure that nonetheless was marked by a sorry "exhibition of judicial ineptitude."

> The work now to be done is to bring about a careful, calm, impartial inquiry into the Massachusetts judicial system. Good can be wrought out of this present mistake—for

we cannot recede from our conviction that this execution was a tragic mistake—if through this mistake the courts of justice in America can be protected against such mistakes in the future.[14]

The *Post-Gazette* countered on that same day with the argument that justice had been done, and the newspaper invoked the authority of society and the law. This editorial agreed with the *Press* position that every legal means had been exhausted on behalf of the two men, but it argued that "justice and authority stood firm. The case is ended. . . . The majesty of the law, the rights of society, will now be sustained by the united efforts of all justice-loving, God-fearing, law-revering citizens."[15]

Perhaps Babbitt's Zenith was Tulsa, where as a grandfather during the Cold War of the 1950s and 1960s and its accompanying anticommunist fervor he would have read two daily newspapers that offered the community little diversity in political ideology. Both Tulsa newspapers were conservative publications in a politically conservative state. But they nonetheless revealed some interesting differences in their editorial approach to some important subjects.

For example, the shooting down by the then-Soviet Union of a U-2 high-altitude spy plane piloted by Francis Powers in 1960 provided an example of how newspaper editorialists can agree, but in different ways and frames, on the generally negative outcome of a policy or event. The *Daily World* framed the incident as far less serious than did the *Tribune,* which viewed it as a major *faux pas* for which "heads ought to roll." Here, said the *Tribune* in its May 9 editorial, was an instance that Soviet leader Nikita Khrushchev could not have better created, "evidence of American war-mongering to impress the uncommitted masses of Asia and Africa. Here are pictures of a Russian anti-aircraft missile crew to swell Russian national pride and pump up anti-American anger. Here is the United States which counts heavily on moral suasion for strengths in its foreign policy now revealed as a red-handed invader." It was sheer folly, the newspaper opined, "to send an airplane deep into hostile territory on the shaky assumption that it can out-climb or out-run any pursuit."[16]

The *Daily World,* to the contrary, looked at the incident in a real-word frame of spies simply getting caught doing what spies do. "The British, in our opinion, see the situation in the full bloom of reality," the newspaper said in its commentary on the next day; "the free world has active spying apparatus, as does Russia, so what is there to get excited about?" In response to the *Tribune* editorial, the *Daily World* opined: "It is said in some high quarters that the U.S. should have taken care not to get caught spying immediately in advance of the summit conference next week. How so? Isn't it more probable that 'getting caught' was more a gambit of KHRUSHCHEV'S doing than it was a coincidental 'accident?'"

For what it is worth, might it not also be fair to point out that the case of pilot FRANCIS POWERS is the established "first" instance in which Americans have been caught spying in Russia? Isn't it fair to point out that Soviet spies long since infiltrated the American scene and in many instances not only were caught but executed?[17]

Neither newspaper had qualms three years later about dismissing President John F. Kennedy's "*Ich Bin Ein Berliner*" speech at the Berlin Wall as ineffective, in the eyes of the *Tribune*, but as a symbol of the U.S. shouldering a burden that ought to be taken on by the western Europeans, according to the framing of the speech by the *Daily World*. The two editorial approaches demonstrate how differences in framing sometimes can be just as meaningful as outright disagreement over political ideologies; both newspapers downplayed the speech, but for significantly different reasons.

The *Tribune* devoted the bulk of its June 27, 1963, editorial to contrasting Kennedy's speech with the Berlin airlift fifteen years before. The airlift, said the writer, "was a page in contemporary history that does credit to this country." The newspaper credited Kennedy with being at his "rhetorical best" in declaring that the wall "is an offense against history and an offense against humanity." But, it went on,

He could have said that The Wall was also an offense against the United States in addition to being a symbol of Communist failure.

Had the United States shown as much firmness in challenging the Soviets when it erected the wall separating West from East Berlin as it did 15 years ago, it is very likely that this barrier would not be standing today.

Today Berlin continues to remain a major point of contention between East and West. And, The Wall is a sore reminder that vacillation should have no part in our foreign policy.[18]

The *Daily World* praised Kennedy as "no mean propagandist" in using the wall "to twist the tail of the Bear and to rebuke Charles de Gaulle for his narrow European chauvinism. In doing so he committed the might of America more firmly than ever to the job of defending western Europe." But the danger in that stance, the editorial warned, was that if Europeans "think we are committed to our eyeballs they won't do much to help themselves."

That's why we wish President Kennedy hadn't laid it on quite so thick about our undeviating commitments to the security of western Europe whether our friends lend a hand or not. It is well to praise the defiance of West Berliners, but if it hadn't been for the determination of the Americans the Iron Curtain would be smack against the Irish Sea.

We're getting a little tired of reading how enthusiastic crowds turn out in Europe to watch U.S. Army maneuvers. We could use fewer cheerers and more marchers.[19]

The civil rights controversies of the 1950s and 1960s brought varied responses from the Tulsa newspapers. Both editorial boards, for example, grudgingly accepted the 1954 U.S. Supreme Court decision in *Brown v. Board of Education of Topeka* striking down school segregation, the *Tribune* a bit more so than the *Daily World*. And both cautiously greeted President Kennedy's 1963 proposed civil rights legislation aimed at ending racial discrimination. But the more conservative *Tribune*, the newspaper credited with sparking the 1921 Tulsa race riot, demonstrated a bit more reluctance than the *Daily World*. The *Tribune* in its lead editorial of May 18, 1954, on the Brown decision noted that despite the court ruling, "the same situation will continue to apply in most southern cities. For many years overwhelmingly Negro districts will continue to exist in all cities—north and south—where there are heavy concentrations of colored people. That will mean a continuation of schools that are almost entirely, if not wholly, colored." The editorial expressed "interest" in the intention of some southern states to eliminate public education and to subsidize segregated private schools with tax funding. This was a plan, the newspaper said, that "will mean new Supreme Court suits, although there certainly is nothing in the U.S. Constitution that says a state must maintain public schools." The newspaper urged acceptance of the fact "that compulsory public school segregation is on the way out—period." Finally, in bold face type, the newspaper called for recognition "that the obligation of good manners, patience and understanding applies equally to our white and colored citizens. In that spirit, we will accomplish this difficult thing."[20]

On the next day, in its lead editorial, the *Daily World* opined that the ruling "means the breakdown of a way of life. Further, it constitutes the next thing to a final blow to the doctrine of States' Rights." The newspaper made only passing reference to the intention by some states to abandon public schools, commenting that implementing such plans would be "not certain" and pointing out that Texas officials were "sullen but law-abiding." The newspaper agreed with its editorial rival that "it is likely there will remain many all-white or all-Negro schools." But it then went beyond the *Tribune* by declaring the ruling was not only the law of the land but correct as well, which was a distinction the *Tribune* had not made. "This is the United States of America. This is a nation of laws; it is a nation of law-abiding people. There can be no moral doubt of the rightness of the court's decision as it affects a nation of free people."[21]

The Tulsa newspapers offered their readers stark differences in their editorial reactions to the November 22, 1963, assassination of President Kennedy, beginning with an expression of grief by one and the lack of such emotion by the other. The *Daily World* opened its November 23 editorial with the observation that the "trivial affairs of the hour suddenly fade; the PRESIDENT has been shot to death." The newspaper, calling the "terrible act" a "calamity, a shame upon Dallas, upon Texas, upon our nation," made reference to the "load" that Lyndon B. Johnson must carry as he succeeded Kennedy. It noted the "tremors and dislocations still impossible to assess. For the moment, everything seems to come to a startled stop, but inevitably the nation must dry its eyes, shake off its shock and pull itself together." It concluded with condolences to First Lady Jacqueline Kennedy: "With the rest of the nation we feel the deepest sorrow for Mrs. KENNEDY and her family. May strength and wisdom go with PRESIDENT JOHNSON."[22]

The *Tribune*, however, framed the tragedy differently, offering evidence of how two newspapers might agree generally on the negative aspects of a news event while traveling different routes in their assessment of it. The *Tribune* began its day that afternoon without any display of shock or grief but with the observation that the murderer, whoever it was, "hoped to get away with it." From there, it differentiated between this killing and that done by "the vainglorious John Wilkes Booth, leaping from the Lincoln box to the stage and displaying himself to a theaterful of people," from the assault upon John Garfield by Charles Guiteau, and from Leon Czolgosz's attack on William McKinley. "The hideous thing in Dallas was the carefully-planned, cold-blooded elimination of a man. It was planned at long range with the help of a telescopic sight. It was planned in such a manner that the killer would have an excellent chance to descend from his sniper's loft and mingle in a crowd seething with confusion." The editorial then delved into conspiracy theorizing, noting that the man charged in connection with the shooting "once tried to take out Russian citizenship" and had been head of a "'Fair Play for Cuba' committee," and it found a "striking parallel between the current series of murders in Caracas, perpetrated by avowed pro-Castroites and designed to spread fear and confusion, and the assassination of the President yesterday." The conclusion, with no condolences or words of encouragement for Johnson, read: "As Uncle Sam bows his head in grief for his young President he should stiffen his back, as well. If the killing of John Kennedy is part of a pattern the world is in for some grim days."[23]

Newspaper editorialists frequently use presidential State of the Union messages along with other major presidential initiatives or decisions to put forth their political ideologies and philosophies and thus offer evidence of editorial variance. The Tulsa newspapers readily took advantage of the opportunity in 1965, when Johnson in his State of the Union message expanded on his Great Society goals with a renewed call for his war on poverty along with an anticrime initiative, assistance for small farmers, and a push for the arts, urban renewal, and antipollution efforts. "Something for everybody," claimed the *Tribune*. "And prosperity is going to soar so rapidly," asserted the newspaper in its acerbic commentary, "that federal tax collections will not only easily handle these new outlays but a further income tax may be called for. At least, that's the theory." As football linebackers pile on a quarterback in a blitz, the newspaper editorialist heaped sarcasm onto the president. "Maybe the old laws have been repealed," suggested the newspaper. "Maybe there has been a great breakthrough in economic theory in which perpetual deficits will no longer mean the ruination of the currency, as it has in all other nations that have been on this road. Maybe we can pump up a form of prosperity so overwhelming that the very lavishness of the expenditures will balance the budget and stave off inflation." The editorial concluded with a hint of linkage between the Great Society and the totalitarianism of Nazi Germany: "'The Great Society.' It's a wonderful slogan, like the 'Wave of the Future' or 'The Thousand Year Reich.' Jubilee! Jubilo! And let's hope we make the first turn."[24]

The *Daily World* on that same day joined its editorial rival in expressing some doubts about the president's aggressive agenda. However, the editorial board lent a more serious tone to the president's proposals, recognizing the political reality that Congress was likely to go along with Johnson. "He is a very practical man when it comes to putting bills through Congress," noted the newspaper, "and he has a touch of the magician as well as the strength of the arm-twister. There is also the matter of his Democratic majority in Congress. . . . Even allowing for some fallout Southerners and others, MR. JOHNSON'S party is usually going to have the votes when it needs them." For that matter, said the newspaper, "no one can quarrel with the idea of attacking poverty, disease, ignorance or water pollution." Perhaps, the newspaper suggested, showing an editorial attitude more accepting than the *Tribune*'s, "some first steps can be taken toward various goals listed in Monday night's speech."[25] This was a more thoughtful and reflective essay demonstrating a noticeable difference in depth and framing.

Finally, the opening act of the presidency of Richard Nixon, his 1969 inaugural speech, provided an agenda-setting stage upon which the two newspapers, both of which had endorsed the former vice president, tacked in different editorial directions. The speech, said the *Tribune*, "accurately reflects the mood of most Americans today." That mood, during this anti-Vietnam War, protest era, was one that had wearied of "riots and sit-ins" as a "road to social justice" and would no longer tolerate on college campuses "the tiny minority which seizes the administration building and tries to shut down the school until a foolscap full of impossible demands is met." Either the rule of law and conviction of criminals would win out, "or we are going to have a lot of blood in this country. . . . We're going to have to quit being so innocent. Disorder in American streets and on the campuses is not all spontaneous combustion." The editorial concluded that the American mood was one in which "most Americans are apparently seeking a breather from the flabbiness, the waste and the hysteria that were threatening to destroy us."[26]

Peace, at home and abroad, was the primary focus of the *Daily World* editorial on that same day. "The quest for peace was the dominant theme in MR. NIXON'S inaugural address," noted the newspaper, "a warm enunciation of the principles he intends to follow in the White House." This editorial spoke in broader verbal strokes, not of rioting in the streets, of college demonstrations and criminals run amok, but of "the swirling passions and often conflicting forces" of the world. These forces, the editorial writer suggested, would require the citizens of the nation to support the president. "If he is to make a new start in the search for peace, building on what has gone before but not bound by the past, he must work in an atmosphere of encouragement." The editorial concluded with a final word on behalf of peace: "MR. NIXON takes office at a time that cries out for a man of courage and strength, but also a determined peacemaker. We can ask no more than that—and let us pray to God that he will be no less."[27]

Nixon did end the Vietnam War. But of significance to the purpose here, his presidency helped bring about passage of the 1970 Newspaper Preservation Act and the legalization of JOAs. The competing newspapers discussed above had formed JOAs with their rivals before that landmark legislation, the Tulsa newspapers in 1943 and the Pittsburgh newspapers in 1961; the 1970 act codified these arrangements. Both of these JOAs eventually ended, first in Tulsa with the closing of the *Tribune* in 1992, followed by the closure of the *Press* in Pittsburgh in 1993.

The loss of these JOA competitions is meaningful in a discussion of the effects of competition on editorial diversity and vigor because of the resemblance of JOA editorial operations to competitive newspaper markets.[28] The silencing of these newspaper voices brought about a loss of editorial competition and the ideological and agenda-setting diversity it fosters.

MODERN-DAY JOA COMPETITION

The JOA newspaper management trend begun during the Great Depression was intended to preserve and foster newspaper competition, and diversity, while easing the financial stresses that had rendered some newspapers incapable of continuing robust head-to-head competition.[29] After the first formalized agreement in Albuquerque, New Mexico, in 1933, JOAs continued to be formed until 1969, when the U.S. Supreme Court ruled they were illegal. In the next year, Congress passed and President Nixon signed the Newspaper Preservation Act. The act allows competing newspapers in single communities, with the permission of the government, to create JOAs, in which separate newspaper companies share costs of production, business and circulation operations while maintaining independent, competing newsrooms.[30] However, for the federal government to approve establishment of a JOA, it must be demonstrated that one of the two newspapers is in "probable danger of failing."[31] A 1972 federal district court ruling, while pointing out that joint operating agreements were not intended to foster monopolies, said such agreements served to preserve editorial independence and the Newspaper Preservation Act met constitutional muster. In that ruling, Judge Oliver Carter wrote:

> Here the act was designed to preserve independent editorial voices. Regardless of the economic or social wisdom of such a course, it does not violate the freedom of the press. Rather, it is merely a selective repeal of the antitrust laws. It merely looses the same shady market forces which existed before the passage of the Sherman, Clayton and other antitrust laws. Such a repeal, even when applicable only to the newspaper industry, does not violate the First Amendment.[32]

Few studies deal explicitly with the effects of JOAs on the editorial diversity of the agreement's participating newspapers. The studies that have been done offer conflicting findings, as reported by Stephen Lacy in his review of the literature for a 1991 study on group ownership.[33] In a separate study, he found that JOA newspapers more closely resembled competitive newspapers in news and editorial content than they did monopoly newspapers.[34] Changing ownership and readership trends in newspaper markets lend importance to the study of the effects of newspaper ownership and competition on newspaper editorial independence and diversity. For example, the number of JOAs in the United States grew since the first formalized agreement in Albuquerque in 1933 to newspapers in twenty-two cities by the time of congressional adoption of the Newspaper Preservation Act in 1970.[35] As of 2003, this number had declined to thirteen cities, each with two JOA participants (see Table I.1). Meanwhile, the number of daily U.S. newspapers decreased over the last half of the twentieth century, from 1,772 in 1950 to 1,745 thirty years later despite a U.S. population increase from 150,000,000 to 220,000,000 during the same period.[36] As of 2003, the nation had 1,457 daily newspapers serving a population of 292,654,345.[37]

Analysts have offered conflicting conclusions on the success, or failure, of JOAs in fostering newspaper competition. Stephen R. Barnett of the University of California law faculty wrote in 1991 that JOAs were unconstitutional infringements of antitrust laws that the newspaper industry pressured President Nixon to sign and that there was some question about their value in preserving independent editorial voices and a vigorous marketplace of ideas. He argued in the *Columbia Journalism Review* that JOAs may have preserved some newspapers, but "it's likely that they kill more competition, and more papers, than they save." Barnett cited the Detroit market, "where the Gannett and Knight-Ridder chains plunged their previously profitable *Detroit News* and *Detroit Free-Press* into a ruinous price war in the belief, as the administrative law judge found, that 'failure too had its reward'—a belief borne out when Attorney General Edwin Meese overruled the judge and approved the JOA."[38]

> Further, it's increasingly clear that JOAs perversely produce the single-paper monopolies they are supposed to prevent. The JOA endgame, in which the owner of the weaker paper gets paid to kill it off, has rubbed out Newhouse's *St. Louis Globe-Democrat* and Cox's *Miami News*. The same fate now stalks Hearst's *San Francisco Examiner* and probably awaits, after a decent interval, Gannett's *Detroit News*— which was declared "dominant" for the purpose of gaining the JOA that now is doing it in.[39]

Newspapers' traditional watchdog function also has been adversely affected by JOAs, argued Barnett. Knight-Ridder's *Detroit Free-Press* protected Attorney General Meese, cited above for approving the Detroit JOA, from newspaper criticism. The chain, wrote Barnett,

> killed editorial cartoons and toned down editorials critical of Meese's conduct as attorney general, while its flagship paper, *The Miami Herald*, pitched in by telling its editorial cartoonist to lay off Meese. As columnist Jerry Knight wrote in *The Washington Post*: "It is a sad story, unworthy of a great newspaper chain, an embarrassment to the fine journalists who work for Knight-Ridder, such an embarrassment to the profession that few people in the news business want to write about it."[40]

Also, two 1985 studies indicated JOA newspapers charged higher rates to advertisers than did their competition, and JOA newspaper advertising rates increased four-and-a-half times faster than those of monopoly newspapers between 1972 and 1982.[41] Journalism educator David C. Coulson argued in 1988 that JOAs could inhibit editorial independence "in monopoly combinations" because participating papers avoided reporting on issues that could harm financial interests of one or both of the newspaper companies. "In short," he wrote, "the assumption that the Newspaper Preservation Act will save editorial competition is erroneous. It prohibits new entry in the newspaper market, decreases editorial independence in joint partnerships, and fails to curtail newspaper deaths."[42]

Lacy, however, in a 1988 study of JOA newspapers found that some goals of the Newspaper Preservation Act had been met. Conceding that JOA newspapers "may well charge monopoly prices for advertising" and "may well be a high barrier to entry in a market," he wrote: "While they are not exactly like competitive papers, the difference is less than the difference between JOA newspapers and monopoly newspapers." His study also suggested that, in at least four of the twenty-two JOA markets he analyzed, "the readers had a choice between two different editorial and op-ed sections and, occasionally, between two slightly different news sections."[43]

To study JOA newspaper editorial diversity and competition, this chapter analyzes editorials of four daily JOA newspapers in two metropolitan markets. One is Cincinnati, Ohio, where the morning *Enquirer* (daily weekday circulation in 2003 of 189,084) was published every day and the afternoon *Post* (46,061)[44] was published Monday through Saturday. The other market is Fort Wayne, Indiana, where the morning *Journal Gazette* (weekday daily circulation of 58,098 in 2003) published every day and the evening *News-Sentinel* (45,733) published Monday through Saturday.[45]

The purpose of this chapter's study is to examine whether two newspapers that are part of a JOA meet the Newspaper Preservation Act's goals of offering competing editorial voices. One additional research question for this analysis is whether these JOA markets resemble the direct competition markets in editorial diversity.

THE CINCINNATI MARKET

Between them, the *Enquirer* and *Post* published 262 editorials during the study period. The *Enquirer* published the majority of these, 150, or 57.25 percent. Part of the reason for this disparity is that the *Post* published no editorials on Sundays. The *Enquirer* offered a greater frequency and percentage of editorials on local subjects, more than doubling the *Post*'s local editorial output. The *Enquirer* also led its rival in the number of state/regional editorials, though by a much narrower margin. But the newspapers demonstrated an identical commitment to state and regional topics in terms of percentages of their total editorial output, 16 percent. Considering local, state, and regional editorials combined, these

Table 3.1 Geographic Concentration of Editorials in the *Cincinnati Enquirer* and *Post* for January 2001 and January 2003

	Enquirer	*Post*
Local	(1) 69 (46%)*	(2) 27 (24.1%)*
State/regional	(3) 24 (16%)*	(3) 18 (16.1%)*
National	(2) 52 (34.7%)*	(1) 56 (50%)*
International	(4) 5 (3.3%)*	(4) 10 (8.9%)*
Other	0	(5) 1 (0.9%)*
Total	150 (57.3%)**	112 (42.7%)**

*Percentages are of the total number of that newspaper's editorials only.
**Percentages are of the total number of editorials by both newspapers.
Preceding numbers in parenthesis are a ranking of that geographic listing by frequency.
Percentages are rounded to the nearest tenth of a percent.

topics accounted for the bulk of *Enquirer* editorials, 62 percent, compared to 40 percent for the *Post*. The *Post*, however, enjoyed an advantage in editorials devoted to national and international categories (see Table 3.1).

As in the direct competition markets of Chicago and Wilkes-Barre, political and government topics dominated the editorials of both Cincinnati newspapers. Crime was the second most-dominant topic of both newspapers. After those two topics, the newspapers traveled separate editorial routes in frequency and percentage of other topics (see Table 3.2).

The newspapers published seventy-seven editorials on common topics in the sampling, with the *Post* accounting for more of these same-subject editorials than

Table 3.2 Editorials by Topic Category in the *Cincinnati Enquirer* and *Post* for January 2001 and January 2003

	Enquirer	*Post*
Politics and government	(1) 60 (40%)*	(1) 63 (56.3%)*
Economic activity	(4) 12 (8%)*	(5) 6 (5.4%)*
Crime	(2) 18 (12%)*	(2) 9 (8%)*
General interest	(3) 15 (10%)*	(3) 8 (7.1%)*
Health and welfare	(5) 10 (6.7%)*	(6) 5 (4.5%)*
Popular amusements	(5) 10 (6.7%)*	(7) 3 (2.7%)*
Education and arts	(3) 15 (10%)*	(4) 7 (6.2%)*
Science and invention	(7) 1 (0.7%)*	(9) 1 (0.9%)*
War and defense	(6) 6 (4%)*	(3) 8 (7.1%)*
Public moral problems	(7) 1 (0.7%)*	0
Accident and disaster	(7) 1 (0.7%)*	0
Other	(7) 1 (0.7%)*	(8) 2 (1.8%)*

*Percentages are of the total number of that newspaper's editorials only.
Preceding numbers in parenthesis are a ranking of that category by frequency.
Percentages are rounded to the nearest tenth of a percent.

Table 3.3   Editorials of Common Topics and Their Agreement and Disagreement in the *Cincinnati Enquirer* and *Post* for January 2001 and January 2003

	Common topics	Agree	Disagree
Enquirer	38 (25.3%)*	19 (50%)**	19 (50%)**
Post	39 (34.8%)*	22 (56.4%)**	17 (43.6%)**
Total	77 (29.4%)***	41 (15.7%)*** (53.2%)⁺	36 (13.7%)*** (46.8%)⁺

*Percentages are of the total number of that newspaper's editorials.
**Percentages are of that newspaper's total editorials on common topics.
***Percentages are of the overall total number of editorials.
+Percentages are of the total number of editorials on common subjects.
Percentages are rounded to the nearest tenth of a percent.

the *Enquirer*. This discrepancy in totals is because one newspaper editorialized more than once on some of the same topics. More than a fourth of the two newspapers' editorials were on common topics. Slightly less than half of these common-topic editorials, about 47 percent, disagreed, either ideologically or in framing (see Table 3.3). More than 40 percent of these editorials of disagreement differed for reasons of ideology (see Table 3.4).

Of these newspapers' combined total of ninety-six editorials on local subjects, twenty-two were on the same topic, twelve by the *Enquirer* and ten by the *Post*. Seven of these local common-subject editorials disagreed, but none of this dispute was for ideological reasons. Of the newspapers' forty-two editorials on state/regional topics, fourteen were on common topics, six by the *Enquirer* and eight by the *Post*. The newspapers disagreed, for reasons of ideology or framing, in eight of these state/regional editorials. Local, state, and regional editorials combined accounted for just more than half (52.67 percent) of all the newspapers' editorials. Of these, more than a fourth (26.09 percent of all local, state, and regional editorials) addressed common subjects; and 15.22 percent of these disagreed in ideology or framing.

The 2003 results of state report cards designed to measure effectiveness of local school districts produced an example of framing differences in the

Table 3.4   Editorials of Common Topic Ideological Disagreement in the *Cincinnati Enquirer* and *Post* for January 2001 and January 2003

	Ideological disagreement	Other disagreement
Enquirer	8 (21.1%)*	11 (29%)*
Post	8 (21%)*	9 (23.1%)*
Total	16 (20.8%)** (6.1%)***	20 (26%)** (7.6%)***

*Percentages are of that newspaper's total editorials on common topics.
**Percentages are of the total number of editorials on common subjects.
***Percentage is of the overall total number of editorials.
Percentages are rounded to the nearest tenth of a percent.

newspapers' editorials. The *Enquirer* urged parents to learn how to interpret and use these report cards, which the newspaper called an "imperfect work in progress." The editorial noted that many parents did not know that states published school report cards. "Parents and other taxpayers ought to become very familiar with these report cards," the editorial advised. "Insist on reader-friendly, jargon-free information from schools. Learn to make sense of the data and then use the information to more wisely pressure schools to improve."[46] The *Post*, though, put a more local frame on the issue by criticizing the cards' findings regarding Cincinnati schools. It categorized the report cards as belonging to the "wacky, follow-the-bouncing-ball world of politically-mandated accountability." Rather than urging parents to use the report card to apply political pressure on the schools, the editorial warned of the possibility of "intervention down the road by the state and/or the federal government that in extreme cases could result in a superintendent or school board being replaced." Rather than place too much credibility on the cards, the editorial writer warned readers to "be wary of comparisons, too. After all, this year's Ohio report card is different than last year's. And next year's will change again."[47]

The newspapers' two editorials on the departure of the Clinton administration in the beginning of 2001 also offered examples of how newspapers can differ in ways other than ideology. The newspapers agreed that the manner in which the president and his staff left office was "tacky." But these commentaries criticized the outgoing president for substantively different reasons. The *Enquirer* chastised Clinton for what it viewed as his departures from precedent, the *Post* for vandalism in the White House. "Nothing epitomized his presidency as aptly as the way he left it," said the *Enquirer*, "hogging the spotlight in a tacky, dragged-out display of narcissism." The editorial complained that Clinton, ignoring the "graceful" departure of his predecessor, George Bush, had staged a "series of media stunts calculated to detract from the inauguration of George W. Bush." These stunts included a "long-winded farewell" at Andrews Air Force Base, followed by a last ride in Air Force One to New York to attend "another camera-hogging rally." Opined the newspaper: "It all showed an amazing lack of respect for the office he had just vacated and the traditions of Inauguration Day."[48] The *Post*, on the other hand, trashed the president's junior aides for preparing "a malicious welcome for their Bush replacements." This included disabling the "W" on computer keyboards and leaving "obscene voice mail messages, dirty pictures slipped among the blank sheets in the copying machines, graffiti in the bathrooms—to outright sabotage, such as cutting and misdirecting phone lines." The angst of staff members, who believed they were cheated out of an election victory, might be understandable, wrote the editorialist, "But this—destroying government property, defacing a national historic building—was a crime."[49] The difference between allegations of criminal activity and of narcissistic long-windedness is a marked sort of diversity beyond mere disagreement based on political ideology.

As noted, the number of local editorials published by the newspapers that disagreed was sparse, and none of these were for reasons of ideology. One example,
the newspapers' editorials in 2001 on the indictment of two city police officers in
connection with the death of a black man, offered evidence of editorials that,
with variances in tone and focus, framed a controversial differently while agreeing on the overall negative aspects of a local criminal proceeding. The headlines
set diverse tones: "A sad, senseless story" in the *Enquirer* and "A necessary prosecution" in the *Post*. The *Enquirer* editorial began with a reference to racial divisiveness in Cincinnati fueled by an "arrest gone wrong. A black man is dead and
two white cops are facing criminal charges." The newspaper gave some of the
particulars of the case, pointing out that the dead black man "resisted arrest
when confronted by police who wanted him for a previous escape from custody."
The rest of the facts, claimed the editorial, "are secret, sealed in grand jury
records." Reminding readers that the police officers "are innocent until proven
guilty," the editorial urged the city to "calm down and wait to hear the facts
before jumping to conclusions....If there is anything positive about what happened, it is that this case should reassure anyone who doubts that justice is
applied fairly."[50]

The *Post*, however, found other facts regarding this case that were not sealed
from public view. While refraining from mention of the dead man's previous
escape from custody, the editorial referenced the county coroner making public
his finding that the man died of "mechanical asphyxiation" while in the custody
of police and pointed out that the prosecutor, "himself a former police officer and
assisted by the Cincinnati Police Division's own internal affairs investigators,
took the case to the grand jury." The tone here, along with the inclusion of evidence more incriminating of the police officers than of the victim, suggested a
more skeptical attitude toward the police department than that of the *Enquirer*.
In its conclusion, the *Post* editorial agreed with its rival that the process, "so far
...has worked." But it then departed from the *Enquirer*'s assurances of fair justice
for all, calling for "a no-holds-barred, rigorous prosecution of these charges."[51]
The tone of this editorial clearly suggests a different frame, one more to the lik-
ing of those in the community who might be skeptical of police activity, than
that of the newspaper's JOA competitor.

The analysis of editorials supporting or opposing policies and initiatives of the
administration of President Bush revealed a clear political ideological difference.
The *Enquirer* published twelve editorials on the president's programs and policies. All of these supported the president on issues that included the president's
proposed tax cuts, his approach to dealing with North Korea's development of
nuclear weapons, his selection of Donald Rumsfeld as secretary of defense, and
his support of school vouchers. The *Post* offered two fewer editorials on presidential policies than did the *Enquirer* but with a significantly different rate of support
for the president: 50 percent. The newspaper opposed the president on policies
that included deficit spending, his proposed tax cuts, and faith-based initiatives

Table 3.5   Editorials of Support and Opposition to Policies and Decisions of the Administration of President George W. Bush in the *Cincinnati Enquirer* and *Post* for January 2001 and January 2003

	Administration policy topics	Support	Oppose
Enquirer	12	12 (100%)*	
Post	10	5 (50%)*	5 (50%)*
Total	22	17	5

*Percentages are of that newspaper's total number of editorials on administration policies.

to use tax dollars in support of private church-based welfare programs (see Table 3.5).

The *Enquirer* in January 2003 hailed the president's tax cuts as measures that would "help America's small businesses, which account for half of the nation's gross domestic product (GDP) and generate most of its new jobs."[52] The *Post* disagreed.

> The president can't have it both ways. He can't simultaneously fight one and maybe two wars, build up homeland security, provide a prescription drug benefit, shore up Medicare and put Social Security on a sound financial footing and at the same time enact a $670 billion tax cut (over 10 years) without taking on debilitating deficits.[53]

THE FORT WAYNE MARKET

The newspapers published 184 editorials during the sampling period, ninety-four by the *Journal Gazette* and ninety by the *News-Sentinel*. The *Journal Gazette* enjoyed a slight edge in local editorials and a larger one in editorials focusing on state and regional issues. About one-fourth of the *Journal Gazette*'s editorials dealt with national topics, and it published none in the sampling on international topics, compared to about 28 percent and 1 percent, respectively, for the *News-Sentinel* (see Table 3.6).

As in the other markets analyzed thus far, political and government subjects dominated the editorials of both newspapers, accounting for nearly half of each newspaper's editorials (see Table 3.7).

The newspapers published fifty-one editorials on the same subjects, or 27.7 percent of their combined total of 184 editorials. About one-fourth of the *Journal Gazette*'s editorials were on the same subject as its JOA rival, while common-subject editorials accounted for 30 percent of the *News-Sentinel*'s commentary. The discrepancy is because they published different numbers of editorials on the same subject. The newspapers disagreed either ideologically or in framing in more than half of these common-topic editorials (see Table 3.8). Ideological disagreement accounted for about 29 percent of the editorials of disagreement (see Table 3.9).

Table 3.6   Geographic Concentration of Editorials in the Fort Wayne *Journal Gazette* and *News-Sentinel* for January 2001 and January 2003

	Journal Gazette	News-Sentinel
Local	(2) 33 (35.1%)*	(1) 31 (34.4%)*
State/regional	(1) 37 (39.3%)*	(1) 31 (34.4%)*
National	(3) 23 (24.5%)*	(2) 25 (27.8%)*
International	0	(4) 1 (1.1%)*
Other	(4) 1 (1.1%)*	(3) 2 (2.2%)*
Total	94 (51.1%)**	90 (48.9%)**

*Percentages are of the total number of that newspaper's editorials only.
**Percentages are of the total number of editorials by both newspapers.
Preceding numbers in parenthesis are a ranking of that geographic listing by frequency.
Percentages are rounded to the nearest tenth of a percent.

Of the newspapers' sixty-four editorials on local subjects, fourteen were on the same topic, seven by each newspaper. They published five local editorials that disagreed either for ideological reasons or in framing, which is 35.71 percent of all of the common-subject editorials. Of the sixty-eight editorials published by the newspapers on state/regional topics, twenty were on the same topic. Eight of these were published by the *Journal Gazette* and twelve by the *News-Sentinel*, and the newspapers differed either ideologically or in framing in fifteen of these. That was a 75 percent disagreement rate for all of their common-subject editorials on state and regional topics.

So, the editorials on common subjects close to home, which accounted for nearly 72 percent of all the newspapers' editorials, offered strong evidence of

Table 3.7   Editorials by Topic Category in the Fort Wayne *Journal Gazette* and *News-Sentinel* for January 2001 and January 2003

	Journal Gazette	News-Sentinel
Politics and government	(1) 46 (49%)*	(1) 43 (47.8%)*
Economic activity	(3) 11 (11.7%)*	(2) 11 (12.2%)*
Crime	(2) 13 (13.8%)*	(4) 9 (10%)*
General interest	(5) 3 (3.2%)*	(3) 10 (11.1%)*
Health and welfare	(4) 4 (4.2%)*	(8) 1 (1.1%)*
Popular amusements	(6) 2 (2.1%)*	(6) 3 (3.3%)*
Education and arts	(2) 13 (13.8%)*	(5) 6 (6.7%)*
War and defense	0	(6) 3 (3.3%)*
Public moral problems	(7) 1 (1.1%)*	(7) 2 (2.2%)*
Accident and disaster	0	0
Science and invention	0	0
Other	(7) 1 (1.1%)*	(7) 2 (2.2%)*

*Percentages are of the total number of that newspaper's editorials only.
Preceding numbers in parenthesis are a ranking of that category by frequency.
Percentages are rounded to the nearest tenth of a percent.

Table 3.8   Editorials of Common Topics and Their Agreement and Disagreement in the Fort Wayne *Journal Gazette* and *News-Sentinel* for January 2001 and January 2003

	Common topics	Agree	Disagree
Journal Gazette	24 (25.5%)*	11 (45.8%)**	13 (54.2%)**
News-Sentinel	27 (30%)*	11 (40.7%)**	16 (59.3%)**
Total	51 (27.7%)***	22 (12%)*** (43.1%)$^+$	29 (15.8%)*** (56.9%)$^+$

*Percentages are of the total number of that newspaper's editorials.
**Percentages are of that newspaper's total editorials on common topics.
***Percentages are of the overall total number of editorials.
+Percentages are of the total number of editorials on common subjects.
Percentages are rounded to the nearest tenth of a percent.

both framing and ideological diversity. For example, though the newspapers agreed that Governor Frank O'Bannon's proposed budget in 2001 faced problems in its heavy reliance on funds raised from gambling to finance new education programs, they differed in how they framed their arguments. The *News-Sentinel* urged greater spending restraint by the governor and lawmakers, while the *Journal Gazette* suggested that the state's economic outlook might brighten, in which case the governor had properly targeted education spending. On the subject of downtown development, the *Journal Gazette* editorialized in 2001 that because of his strengths in planning and consensus-building, Fort Wayne Mayor Graham Richard should oversee a study of downtown development that would comprise representatives from at least twenty groups and organizations that had a stake in downtown development. The *News-Sentinel*, though, suggested that while the community apparently seemed unable to reach agreement on the composition of members to oversee a downtown development task force, it would be necessary to include voices from beyond downtown, in the outlying neighborhoods, and from a sector often overlooked in such endeavors, the arts community. The newspapers, then, showed disparity through their varying areas of focus.

The newspapers offered some sharp differences on regional issues in the 2003 editorial sampling. The *Journal Gazette*, for example, supported the posting on

Table 3.9   Editorials of Common Topic Ideological Disagreement in the Fort Wayne *Journal Gazette* and *News-Sentinel* for January 2001 and January 2003

	Ideological disagreement	Other disagreement
Journal Gazette	6 (25%)*	7 (29.2%)*
News-Sentinel	9 (33.3%)*	7 (25.9%)*
Total	15 (29.4%)** (8.2%)***	14 (27.5%)** (7.6%)***

*Percentages are of that newspaper's total editorials on common topics.
**Percentages are of the total number of editorials on common subjects.
***Percentage is of the overall total number of editorials.
Percentages are rounded to the nearest tenth of a percent.

the Internet of the names, photographs, and home addresses of convicted sex offenders. The newspaper argued that convicted child molesters should not be offered a shield of anonymity and urged the State Supreme Court to agree with that philosophy. The *News-Sentinel,* though, argued in a three-editorial series that the problems with such postings included, among other difficulties, unfairly punishing people beyond the legal penalties already determined by the normal workings of the criminal justice system.

The newspapers also offered opposing opinions on the governor's decision to move ahead on an interstate highway construction project, the *Journal Gazette* backing the governor and the *News-Sentinel* concluding that the governor chose the wrong route. "Gov. Frank O'Bannon made the tough but necessary call on Interstate 69 last week," argued the *Journal Gazette.* "Now it's time to finish a project that should have been completed decades ago."[54] The *News-Sentinel* countered five days later: "But Gov. Frank O'Bannon has picked the wrong route.... Environmentalists are likely to challenge the decision in federal court and press the state to reconsider the existing-roads route. Everyone who would see the state spend its money wisely ought to champion that legal fight *for at least another two years.*"[55]

The newspapers published twenty-six editorials on the policies of the Bush administration, which accounted for 14.1 percent of all of their editorials. While the newspapers published a similar frequency of editorials on Bush administration policies, they showed a clear distinction in their support of, or opposition to, those policies. The *News-Sentinel* supported the administration in seven of its twelve editorials on Bush's policies, a rate of 58.3 percent, while the *Journal Gazette* backed the administration policies just twice, for a support rate of only 14.3 percent of its fourteen editorials. And these two instances of support by the *Journal Gazette* offered only mixed backing of the administration; both editorials dealt with various aspects of these policies, with some receiving support and others not (see Table 3.10).

Commenting on the nomination by President Bush of John Ashcroft as U.S. attorney general, the *Journal Gazette* raised questions about this nominee's qualifications and criticized Ashcroft for what the editorialist called his "dismal record." The newspaper cited his "smear campaign" waged against Ronnie White, nominated by President Clinton to a seat on a federal court. White's

Table 3.10 Editorials of Support and Opposition to Policies and Decisions of the Administration of President George W. Bush in the Fort Wayne *Journal Gazette* and *News-Sentinel* for January 2001 and January 2003

	Administration policy topics	Support	Oppose
Journal Gazette	14	2 (14.3%)*	12 (85.7%)*
News-Sentinel	12	7 (58.3%)*	5 (41.7%)*
Total	26	9	17

*Percentages are of that newspaper's total number of editorials on administration policies.

nomination was "sunk by an onslaught of cheap shots by Ashcroft," said the newspaper, adding that Ashcroft had a lot of explaining to do. "If he is eventually confirmed, he can thank a Senate for showing more fairness and flexibility than Ronnie White ever received from him."[56] The News-Sentinel, though, supported Ashcroft's confirmation because of his qualifications. "We shouldn't worry or even care about that person's views on any particular issue," said the newspaper. "We should need to ask only this: Does this person have the integrity to carry out the duties of the office as specified by statute and tradition? By all accounts. . . Ashcroft has that integrity, and then some."[57]

President Bush's proposed education plan sparked ideological differences that also took in framing disparities. The Journal Gazette opposed the president's call for a voucher program, which would reimburse tuition costs for private schools, including parochial institutions. "The president's own daughters graduated from a fine public school system," the newspaper said. "He should focus on providing the same opportunity for all students, not on offering a voucher escape hatch that will sink the very schools that most need help."[58] The News-Sentinel also invoked the education of a political leader's children but in this case in its support of the voucher plan. Arguing that Indiana's U.S. Senator, Evan Bayh, could afford to "do right by his children," the newspaper said the senator, who opposed the voucher plan, "doesn't want his constituents to have the same options. How callous. . . . Vouchers would give the poorest parents what people such as Bayh already have."[59]

An interesting ideological difference arose in the News-Sentinel's two editorials on the Bush administration's policies leading up to the invasion of Iraq, editorials in which the newspaper reversed course, differing with itself ideologically. In the first editorial, the newspaper cited its recent story in which members of Veterans of Foreign Wars posts were interviewed about possible warfare with Iraq, leading the newspaper to question the Bush administration's case. Americans, the newspaper opined, "do have questions. Why this particular campaign against this particular villain at this particular time? If so many Americans aren't convinced by the answers, the administration has a lot of explaining to do before the first shot is fired."[60] Ten days later, the newspaper cited the war on terrorism, because it had been discussed recently by a couple of Fort Wayne political leaders, and it tied that war to the threat posed by Iraq and its leader, Saddam Hussein. The newspaper argued that President Bush had made a strong case in his recent State of the Union speech for attacking Iraq. "It might be harder than in past wars," the newspaper said, "to prove that we are acting in self-defense. But acting in self-defense will be ever more urgent."[61] In the end, then, the newspaper showed evidence of coming around to the Bush administration point of view on an issue that the Journal Gazette did not address during the sampling period.

Likewise, the Journal Gazette took on a couple of Bush administration policies that the News-Sentinel ignored. One was the administration's push to open the Arctic National Wildlife Refuge in Alaska to oil drilling. The newspaper accused the administration and Senate Republicans of using devious means on behalf of drilling. It claimed they used "a backward legislative ploy that distorts the budget process and Senate rules. Those opposed to more Alaskan oil must be prepared to cut off the maneuver, designed to reduce the number of votes needed for passage." Calling oil drilling in the refuge "one of the most visible and controversial environmental issues of the last few years," the editorial urged that pro-drilling legislation "be required to meet the same political tests faced by other bills before they are passed."[62]

As the editorials on Bush administration topics by the two newspapers suggest, commentary on subjects that both newspapers might not address editorially nonetheless can offer evidence of ideological leanings that contribute to the newspapers' respective philosophical bents, in this case conservative-leaning on the part of the *News-Sentinel* in comparison to the *Journal-Gazette*'s more liberal agenda. The Fort Wayne study found a pronounced ideological variance, with the *Journal Gazette* offering strong antiadministration commentaries in terms of editorial percentage (85.7 percent opposition rate) in comparison to the *News-Sentinel*'s (41.7 percent). Similarly, the Cincinnati analysis revealed noticeable diversity in ideology pertaining to Bush administration policies, with the *Enquirer* in total support of the president and the *Post* backing administration policies just half of the time. As was the case with the *News-Sentinel* in Fort Wayne, Cincinnati readers who leaned toward the policies of the Bush administration might have found more comfort in the *Enquirer*'s editorial philosophies.

The analysis of JOA editorials revealed a marked difference in editorials concentrating on issues close to home versus those of national or international concentration. On the basis of this analysis, it can be suggested that the *Enquirer* might be the newspaper of choice in Cincinnati for readers seeking opinions on local or state issues, while the *Post* might be the more appealing newspaper for those seeking commentary on national and international subjects. Similar conclusions can be drawn in Fort Wayne, where the *Journal Gazette* offered a greater percentage of editorials on subjects closer to home.

When the Cincinnati newspapers entered the same editorial neighborhood and commented on common subjects, they disagreed slightly less than half the time. The Fort Wayne newspapers had a slightly higher rate of disagreement, nearly 57 percent. However, just sixteen of the Cincinnati newspapers' thirty-six editorials of disagreement, about 21 percent, differed for reasons of ideology. The Fort Wayne market experienced greater variance in this statistic, nearly 30 percent. In either case, when newspapers in the JOA markets wrote on common subjects, they offered evidence of editorial diversity. That this evidence was a bit more pronounced in the Fort Wayne JOA perhaps speaks to ownership differences in the Cincinnati and Fort Wayne JOAs. Both Cincinnati newspapers are group-owned, the *Enquirer* by Gannett and the *Post* by Scripps Howard Newspapers, while in the Fort Wayne market one newspaper, the *News-Sentinel*, was a chain organ (then Knight Ridder, before that chain's 2006 sale to the McClatchy group), while the other was an independent operation owned locally. So, the Cincinnati market findings of relatively less ideological diversity than in Fort Wayne might provide evidence for those who argue that chain newspapers involved in JOAs can be more homogenous in their editorials and that group ownership could discourage criticism of institutions in which one or both JOA partners have financial interests.

Newspapers in both JOA markets showed marked variety in editorial topics. In Cincinnati, more than two-thirds of the two newspapers' editorials in the sampling were on subjects that the other newspaper did not address. In Fort Wayne, the newspapers editorialized on similar subjects just 27.7 percent of the time. While this disparity does not represent ideological diversity, it speaks to a diversity of subject matter that represents a noticeable variety of voices on a broad range of topics similar to that found in the direct competition markets of Chicago and Wilkes-Barre. That separate newspaper editorial boards in Fort Wayne selected numerous different topics deemed important enough to warrant comment demonstrates, as did the direct competition boards, a meaningful richness in editorial agendas, or a market basket of ideas that complements a marketplace of ideas.

This sort of diversity also arose at the local level in the JOA analysis. Of the Cincinnati newspapers' ninety-six local editorials analyzed, seventy four were on subjects that were discussed by just one of the two newspapers. Local subjects the *Enquirer* editorialized on exclusively included the fact that Cincinnati police had not killed or shot at anyone in 400 days; the decision by the Arts Consortium of Cincinnati to ignore a boycott against the city by several African-American groups; the need for the city and county to ease the property tax burden; the forming of a coalition to take action against black-on-black violence; the benefits to the local education community of Catholic schools; the need for a crackdown on local drug dealers; the failure of the city to bring code enforcement cases to court; the decision by a federal judge to stop construction of a cement loading facility on the riverfront; the decision by University of Cincinnati officials to keep secret the names of candidates for university president; county spending on building purchases; the reinstatement of Pete Rose to baseball; concentration of low-income residents in certain neighborhoods; the need to abide by the city's contract with police officers; the mayor's 2001 State of the City speech; the need to enforce safety standards at a teen drug-treatment center; the improving financial state of downtown; the educational benefits of a local charter school; and abandoned buildings in a city historic neighborhood.

Local subjects the *Post* editorialized on exclusively included the arrival of a new president of the chamber of commerce; the benefits of riverfront bike trails; installation of video surveillance cameras in two city neighborhoods; the need to invite the public to board meetings of the regional port authority; the financial state of city hospitals; the benefits of a city youth collaborative; the pay raise of the city manager; the mayor's 2003 State of the City speech; the need to overcome political differences to end litigation over a proposed juvenile jail; the need for a hearing regarding a proposed industrial project in a park; the hiring of ex-felons for city jobs; and a proposed expansion of the city's hate crime ordinance.

The Fort Wayne market analysis revealed a similar finding of local agenda richness. The following issues and stances sparked editorials from the *Journal Gazette* but not from its rival: the benefits of the decision by federal judges in the seventh circuit to encourage lawyers to perform more *pro bono* work; the wisdom of the city's decision to annex a growing neighborhood; the assets of a proposed merger of a local science and technology center with Indiana University–Purdue University Fort Wayne; the need to update a neighboring county's zoning plan; the need for consolidating fire districts within the county; the need for a review of policies and practices of the county's juvenile justice system; the wisdom of ethical standards set by the city for its employees; the financial irresponsibility of the city's overtime policies; the need for a crackdown on rules governing county and city employees; the need for the city to invoke the power of eminent domain to move a redevelopment project forward; the positive signal sent by the admonition of a county judge by the Indiana Commission on Judicial Qualifications; the environmental benefits of a hybrid automobile to be constructed by a local auto assembly plant; and the "welcome" steps taken by local legislators and law enforcement officials against dog fighting.

The *News-Sentinel* editorialized exclusively on the following local subjects: the worthiness of a decision by a neighboring county prosecuting attorney to refuse to plea bargain when serious crimes (such as murder or charges involving firearms) are involved; the proposed expansion of the local Memorial Coliseum; the need for data regarding the policy of passing low achievers to higher grades in public schools; the right of the city to regulate yard signs; the necessity of an updated and more detailed record of county septic systems; the benefits of the planned expansion of an after-school neighborhood facility run by Youth for Christ for neighborhood kids; the wisdom of Fort Wayne city officials in avoiding budgeting state gambling revenues that did not meet expectations; the positive recognition by the county prosecutor of the importance of trial work in the criminal justice system; and the value of a road project to link Fort Wayne to the city of Lafayette.

As in the direct competition markets of Chicago and Wilkes-Barre, if Cincinnati or Fort Wayne had been communities with just one, monopoly newspaper, chances are that one of the above lists conceivably could have been editorial subjects ignored by that newspaper. This range of local opinion represents consequential diversity in editorial voices brought about by the existence of competing editorial voices.

Political and government topics, as might be expected, have dominated all of the editorials in the markets analyzed thus far. Beyond that category, though, the newspapers have demonstrated sometimes marked differences in the priorities they set for editorial topics. Economic matters, crime, education, and public health concerns generally were popular subjects after politics and government, and the disparities among these other topics were not marked enough to demarcate trends that might speak to ideological or other kinds of editorial differences. But the wide variety of subject matter is distinctive, indicating a richness of agenda that is evidence of a competitive marketplace of ideas operating not in a manner so much of truth grappling with falsehood as it is of a vast menu of ideas mingling in a veritable stewpot of opinion.

Finally, the findings in this chapter of differences in editorial conclusions (ideological and framing variances); differing degrees of focus on localism, regionalism, national, and international topics; and the findings of agenda diversity all indicate that JOA market competition resembles direct market competition in terms of editorial content differences. A related question for the next chapter will be to discover if an evolving model of rivalry, that of metropolitan-area newspaper competition, can substitute for the competition offered by direct market and JOA markets.

CHAPTER 4

The New Deal and World War

The proposition of the crazy and reckless Republican managers, like Zachariah Chandler and Jay Gould, is that all three of the disputed States shall be declared to have voted for Hayes, and that he shall be declared elected President upon this basis. But can the Republican party afford this?

If Mr. Hayes should be declared elected in this way, by a majority of one electoral vote only, with the great majority of the popular vote against him, and with the almost universal conviction that the declaration was procured by fraud, would it be a situation such as the Republican party would desire? And would Mr. Hayes, under such circumstances, be able to perform the duties of the President effectively, successfully, and happily?

...The verdict, we think, would be that this once great party, having begun its career as the champion of freedom and the destroyer of negro slavery, had sunk through the depraving influence of the long possession of power, and had finally completed its history by bringing the whole people into a far baser kind of slavery by installing a President whom the people had not chosen. Can the Republican party afford this?

—*New York Sun*, November 12, 1876, on the election of
Rutherford Birchard Hayes as president[1]

Had Sinclair Lewis written a sequel to *Babbitt*, the novel might have found our hero in the throes of the Great Depression that would have ruined his real estate enterprise, as the non-fictional depression brought to ruin thousands of Americans at the end of the 1920s and through the next decade. The presidency of Franklin D. Roosevelt during the early 1930s through its culmination in World War II offered abundant opportunity for editorial commentary on issues ranging from war to an activist government policy aimed at economic recovery. Whether George Babbitt would have been one of those welcoming the Roosevelt administrations' economic experiments aimed at ending the depression, or whether he would have viewed the first Democratic president since Woodrow Wilson as a harbinger of evil socialism, the newspapers of the day provided ample editorial opinion to feed both the pro- and the anti-Roosevelt sentiments. Had Babbitt's Zenith been Cleveland, or the nation's capital, Washington, D.C., he would have found editorial diversity and disagreement on a wide selection of topics ranging from antidepression governmental action on the domestic front to American efforts against the Axis powers in World War II in foreign affairs.

For example, E. W. Scripps' *Cleveland Press*, in the spirit of its founder and his sympathies toward the common workers, editorialized for passage of the Wagner-Lewis Social Security Act of 1935. But the act, providing for a new tax with revenues to be set aside to supplement retirement savings of American citizens, drew a different sort of reaction from the *Cleveland Plain Dealer*. Besides offering opposing reactions to the measure, the newspapers also differed in the amount of space they gave to their editorials. These editorials thus offer evidence of another kind of measure of diversity: the length of opinion devoted to a topic.

The cool reception to the bill by the *Plain Dealer* indicated a reaction that, if not clearly against this popular legislation, suggested an editorial attitude of indifference compared to its red-carpet editorial welcome from the *Press*. "President Roosevelt's signature to the Wagner-Lewis social security act puts the United States, on paper at least, suddenly abreast a score of other civilized countries that for decades have provided against some of the hazards of the machine age," raved the *Cleveland Press* in an eight-paragraph editorial. "With all its faults, it may prove to be the greatest achievement of the New Deal."[2] The *Plain Dealer*, though, devoted just two paragraphs to the act, combined with two paragraphs on the president signing a bill establishing a forty-hour work week for postal employees. "The president's signature affixed Wednesday makes of the social security bill, using his own words, a 'corner stone in a structure which is being built, but is by no means complete,'" noted the newspaper.

> This social security act is an expression of the national interest in seeing justice done to the humblest citizen, to the helpless and friendless, the victims of a harsh industrial system which cares too little for its own casualties. "Historic for all time," Mr. Roosevelt says this session would be for having passed this measure, even if the session had done nothing else.[3]

Note that the opinions of the *Plain Dealer* editorial were not the newspaper's; they were attributed to others; the act was an "expression of national interest," and it was the president, not the newspaper, characterizing the legislation as "historic."

The entry of the United States into World War II and one of the events that brought about that war's end received interestingly diverse commentary from these newspapers. Both sets of reactions involved bombings and the Japanese: the December 7, 1941, attack by the Japanese on Pearl Harbor that led to the U.S. entry into the war, and the August 6, 1945, atomic bombing of Hiroshima by the United States. The newspapers reacted promptly, but differently, to the Pearl Harbor attack. Both editorialized on behalf of war and retaliation. The difference was found in their primary targets of retaliation—the Japanese for the *Press*, the Germans for the *Plain Dealer*.

"It came not by attack from Europe as so many feared," said the *Press* on December 8, 1941, "but in the Pacific, which many Americans believed impossible." The newspaper observed, with some prescience, that the Japanese, who had found the United States "slow to wrath," now would find a nation "mighty in wrath. They found us unwilling to strike the first blow. They will yet find us striking the last blow."[4] The *Plain Dealer*, however, began its editorial with a reference to World War I, telling readers that the nation faced a situation that was "the most serious" since then. The background of the two situations, it editorialized, was "much the same....The rights of our country had been shamefully disregarded by a nation with which we were at peace." That nation, in World War I, was Germany, not Japan,

> but the plot is the same and the course which this nation must choose is even clearer today than it was then. For to thinking people the consequences of an Axis victory are very much more certain. Hitler's technique is different from that employed by Kaiser Wilhelm, but the world he would build through complete military domination is even a poorer world and an unhappier world than the Kaiser ever contemplated.[5]

The word "Japan" or "Japanese" was used just once in the *Plain Dealer* editorial, while references to "Germany" numbered six. The *Press* editorial referenced Japan thirteen times, Germany once. So, while both newspapers expressed anger over the Japanese attack, there was a clear difference of framing in these editorials regarding which nation was seen to be the primary foe.

The "last blow" against the Japanese of which the *Press* warned came in the fiery, massive destruction of Hiroshima and then of Nagasaki. Following the dropping of the A-bomb on Hiroshima, both newspapers discussed the frightening and enormous power of this new weapon and its implications; they then concluded their editorial remarks in noticeably diverse ways that spoke to the differing attitudes toward nuclear weaponry that emerged following its first use. The *Press*, citing on August 7, 1945, a "new epoch" that compared to the first use of metal, the invention of gun powder and the use of electricity, discussed the weapon's ability to "save countless numbers of American lives." It urged that wise heads prevail in the development and use of this new energy. "Scientists have liberated an unbelievable force. Statesmen must use it for good instead of evil."[6] The *Plain Dealer*, discussing on the same day the "profound implications" of the bomb and atomic energy, observed that the United States had "not only devised a means of obliterating Japan but we have literally produced a monster capable of destroying all civilization." Like the rival commentary, this editorial pointed out the potential for good in the development of atomic energy, including the possibility of commercial uses. "Thus, it may be that the world is standing on the threshold of an economic revolution. The possibilities of the use of atomic energy to advance civilization or to alter the economic structure of a nation are limited only by the imagination." The *Plain Dealer* editorial writer then unleashed his own imagination in the concluding paragraphs of the editorial.

> For the superstitious Japanese, the atomic bomb contains an omen of doom. They think their emperor is descended from the sun and the rising sun is the emblem of their empire. But now the sun itself is destroying them and their empire, for the atomic bomb is composed of the same force from which the sun draws its power.
>
> If we may make a suggestion to the War Department, it is this; Why not drop a string of the atomic bombs in the crater of Fujiyama and see what happens? Perhaps—the greatest—explosive force ever devised by man would act as a trigger to release volcanic power, now dormant, to produce nature's most explosive demonstration.[7]

So, here was a remarkable difference in editorial opinion: one cautioning about future uses of the most destructive force ever created by humans and urging its use for good purposes, the other writing in the same vein until surrendering to jingoistic urgings that included an experimental and destructive use of the bomb with damages to the planet that can only be imagined.

Babbitt would have found in the editorials of the Washington, D.C., newspapers a more focused analysis of commentary on issues during the Franklin D. Roosevelt years. These editorials, along with later ones dealing with events of World War II, revealed a journalistic atmosphere not only of editorial difference but also of some editorial marvel over the president's daring political and legislative experiments. The now-defunct *Evening Star* of Washington, an anti-Roosevelt organ, and its morning rival, the *Washington Post*, published by Eugene Meyer, an influential Washington insider and close friend of Roosevelt Supreme Court appointee Felix Frankfurter,[8] offered the District of Columbia readership lively commentary on the antidepression war and later the military battle waged by the president and his brains trust. Some of these commentaries offered basic agreement but with nuances of difference in framing and tone; others displayed ideological departures that clearly identified one newspaper as being in the New Deal camp and the other on its periphery if not antagonistic.

Analysis of editorials dealing with some of Roosevelt's early programs that were designed to end the Great Depression reveals that the editorial writers of these competing capital-city dailies shared a mood of sacrifice in dealing with the hardships and severe economic woes of the crisis. They also shared a sense of respect and accommodation regarding the experimental and unprecedented nature of the president's and his administration's myriad attempts to deal with it. But ideological disagreements and differences in editorial framing often disrupted any spirit of harmony. For example, the newspapers traveled separate editorial roads in responding to the creation by Congress on May 18, 1933, of the TVA (Tennessee Valley Authority), a measure calling for the construction of a hydroelectric plant on the dammed Tennessee River in Alabama to produce cheap electricity and munitions plants and to promote regional economic development. It was legislation cautiously eyed by the *Star* as an experimental foray into the realm of socialism but that brought a warning of the need for government vigilance from the *Post*. Of "the great experiment," the *Star* said,

> The Congress and the President have finally determined to act upon the recommendations of the supporters of the Muscle Shoals bill. It marks a new departure for the Government. It will give hope to the friends of Government ownership and operation of public utilities. The experiment is under way. The next few years will provide the answer.[9]

The *Post*, avoiding discussion of the merits of the TVA, urged instead caution by those considering investing in the region. Warned the editorial:

> Doubtless thrifty speculators have already laid out miles of glamorous entrepots of commerce and culture to be vitalized by the Tennessee Valley Authority, with its power to issue bonds, build dams and power lines, plant forests, reclaim lands, and in all ways transform the region into a combination of the Garden of Eden and a Greater Pittsburgh.
>
> The real estate speculator is the serpent in the garden. Unless the innocent investor is on guard he will be bitten....It would be well for the Post Office Department to be on the lookout for mail frauds in connection with the booming of real estate ventures. The Tennessee Valley enterprise is an ideal vehicle for joy-riding by sharpers who seek to take advantage of gullible investors.[10]

These newspapers gave district readers an even stronger difference of opinion in their reactions in that same month to the Agricultural Adjustment Act, which was designed to establish parity of commodity prices and to cut production of crops to rid the country of commodity surpluses. The legislation called for meeting these goals by paying farmers to remove fields from production with funds raised through levies on processors. This was a notion that both newspapers described using the "experimental" terminology of the day, but with different conclusions about its merits. Note in the excerpts the use of descriptive adjectives and nouns that flavored the editorialists' descriptions of the legislation and thus set opposing tones—words such as "costly" and "agitating" versus "hope," "cooperation," and "practical." Such descriptives provide an example of the use of tone in establishing editorial differences. The *Star* alluded to imperial Rome in its discussion of the legislation, which, "signed yesterday by the President, like Gaul in the days of Caesar, is divided into three parts."

> Admittedly, the plan is an experiment. The country has had its fill of costly experiment with farm surpluses in the past....How far the President intends to go with this inflationary power is a question which is agitating a lot of people. If prices continue their advance; if business picks up and employment returns, these powers are likely to be used sparingly. On the other hand, should the hoped-for advance not materialize or lag, then it may be expected that the administration will go the full route in the matter of "controlled inflation" to which it has committed itself.[11]

The *Post*, noting the criticism the act attracted, cited the "serious economic conditions prevailing in agricultural districts" as justification for the legislation and as warranting support.

> Now that this measure is about to become law the whole country joins in the hope that it may succeed. It is clearly an experiment, and is recognized as such by President Roosevelt. A people that is accustomed to private initiative and reasonably free play of economic forces can not put aside apprehension over an innovation of such a momentous character....It is now time for cooperation from every source in the task of fitting this unprecedented measure to the practical needs of American farms.[12]

The next month, both newspapers hailed the passage of the NIRA (National Industrial Recovery Act), which called for industry cooperation in establishing codes to help control production and prices of goods and for presidential authority in establishing these codes and agreements. It also included a provision guaranteeing the right of workers to organize. But one of the newspaper's opinions of this piece of legislation changed markedly two years later, when the U.S. Supreme Court struck down the NIRA in 1935 on interstate commerce grounds in *Schechter Poultry v. U.S.* The *Star*, in an editorial that seemed to release the editorial board's long-building resentment of Roosevelt policies, gleefully welcomed the ruling, claiming that it "re-established the Constitution of the United States." This ruling, along with other recent court decisions, said the newspaper in language eerily prescient of the antigovernment pronouncements of President Ronald Reagan and fellow conservatives half a century later,

> turned back those who have sought to set Federal power above law. Granting the President and the New Dealers the fullest desire to improve conditions and to stamp out ills that undoubtedly have existed, a tendency toward governmental domination has developed that bordered on dictatorship.
>
> It was time to call a halt and to return to the basis of personal liberty of action. There is nothing that feeds on itself to such an extent and grows thereby as does power. Long steps have been taken toward the centralization of power in the Executive during the past three years. With each such step there has followed a reaching out for more power in other directions. Laws now in the making in Congress look to the further establishment of control by the Federal Government over the activities of the people.[13]

In pronouncing the apparent death of The New Deal, the editorial's conclusion framed the court decision in the context of the NIRA's potential long-term effects: "It may have changed the psychology of the Nation, if not of the administration."

The *Post* offered a more measured reaction, conceding the court had declared unconstitutional "the heart of the recovery act." But rather than praising the ruling, which the newspaper agreed brought an end to "the era of administrative law-making," the *Post* suggested—in a hopeful tone—that there might be legal and administrative wiggle room for the Roosevelt administration to yet play a strong role in economic policy-making. "In view of the uncompromising refusal to give the force of law to code provisions, it is clear that the structure of the recovery organization will have to be radically remodeled," said the *Post*.

> It looks as if very little room would be left under a revised law for code-making subject to enforcement by the Federal authorities in the manner now provided for. There would still be room for a type of voluntary industrial organization under a liberalized anti-trust law—a solution of our industrial problem that many business men would have originally preferred to the over-ambitious effort which took the form of the recovery law.[14]

As might be expected during a period of international crisis, the newspapers tended to stand united behind the president in foreign policy matters before and during the World War II years. But a glance at their editorials on a few of the key issues nonetheless revealed some interesting differences in tone and framing that attested to a vibrant editorial marketplace of opinion. For example, in one of the first acts of belligerency by one of the Axis powers toward the United States, the 1937 sinking by the Japanese of the U.S. gunboat *Panay* and three Standard Oil tankers in the Yangtze River above Nanking, both newspapers soundly chastised the Japanese, but with subtle differences. One of these was the focus on whether the act was deliberate. Japanese intent was an important factor in the incident, according to the *Star*, which said in its lead editorial that the emotions prompted by the sinking "are mitigated by Japanese official disavowals of any deliberate intent to violate American rights or do damage to our nationals or their interests." The editorial continued with a swipe at Great Britain, which the newspaper editorial board apparently believed gave weak response to Japanese provocation. "There will be little disposition in the United States to wait as long as Great Britain waited for an 'explanation' of a Japanese machine gun attack on her Ambassador, or to be content with as grudging and half-hearted an apology for that wanton act as London was willing to accept," said the newspaper, suggesting that the sinking of the vessel warranted a stronger response from Washington.

> The sinking of the Panay and the oil tankers can only have deplorable consequences if Japan, by failing adequately to atone for her misdemeanor, adds arrogance to injury. To tolerate such conduct by the marauders now putting China to the sword

and flame would be to stamp with approval Japan's whole campaign of brigandage and international lawlessness.[15]

The *Post*, in its third editorial of the next day, did not question whether the attack was intentional. "The deliberate Japanese attack on the gunboat Panay, which was at the time of her destruction virtually a floating embassy of the United States, is far too serious a matter for flag-waving or other heroics," said the newspaper, which continued the editorial with an attack on past appeasement. "For over six years repeated concessions made to Japan have resulted only in encouraging that country to become progressively more brazen in its attitude toward essential American interests. Such a course can only bring disaster, unless occasion is taken to check its trend in time."[16] Just what "occasion" the newspaper editorial board members had in mind is not made clear, but the *Post* clearly saw this incident as more serious than the "misdemeanor" description given it by the *Star*.

The issue of wartime neutrality came to the fore in September of 1939, following the entry of British and French forces into the European theater of World War II. The newspapers devoted lengthy editorial space to the declaration of war, particularly by Great Britain, with separate editorials on the issue of neutrality. A key difference between the two was in the placement of the editorials. The *Star* led its editorial page of September 4 with a discussion of the war activity in Europe and commented on the subject of neutrality in its second editorial. The *Post*, however, led its page on that same day with the neutrality issue, turning to England's decision to enter the war in its third editorial. Clearly, then, these newspaper editorial boards weighed the issue of neutrality differently, with the *Post*, on the evidence of its lead placement, putting more emphasis on maintaining neutrality. Other differences were found, primarily in framing. The *Star*, for example, concluded its editorial on the neutrality issue with a discussion of the president's intimation that he hoped to repeal the embargo, which was required by the proclamation of the neutrality law, on arms shipments to war participants.

> The *Star* shares that hope in the sincere belief that it is to our own selfish interests to withdraw even indirect support to the aggressor in this war, and to make our material resources, including fighting planes and other implements of war, available to those who are able to come here and purchase them—in this case France and Great Britain.[17]

But the *Post* avoided discussion of assistance to France or England, while noting that the side fighting in the war on behalf of the "spiritual values" of the United States "needs no identification to Americans." The newspaper concluded not with a plea for assistance to France and England to assure that the United States would not have to enter the war. Rather, it invoked a rather vague urging for diplomatic responses. "And both mind and conscience are stimulated by Mr. Roosevelt when he suggests that our influence should from this moment be thrown in the direction of a final peace which will make impossible continuation of such aggression as that for which the dictatorships have come to stand."[18]

Two of the major editorials the newspapers published in 1945 demonstrated a telling difference in attitudes toward the president. His death prompted similar editorial placement from both newspapers, which was a lead editorial discussing the challenge ahead for President Harry S. Truman in his ascendancy from the vice presidency followed by an editorial eulogy of Roosevelt. But analysis of the tonal differences in the two Roosevelt editorials reveals a distinct variance in the regard the separate editorial boards had for the dead president. The *Star* on April 13, 1945, praised him as a man of "courage born of faith and high conviction and a national leader who can scarcely be replaced." The newspaper credited Roosevelt with putting forth experimental policies, the merits of which "will be debated for years to come," that kept the nation's capitalistic economy "more or less intact." The editorial cited the political woes that beset the president in his second term, including the failed Supreme Court-packing proposal and the "ill-fated 'purge' of 1938," when the president intervened, largely unsuccessfully, in some U.S. Senate races, seeking the defeat of political opponents. "The most notable victories, from the New Deal's point of view, were won in the first term. In the realm of domestic affairs, the second term was distinguished principally by a falling-out among the victors." Also, the staging of a draft by the president's supporters, to bring him the Democratic nomination and a third presidential term, was "not among the brighter chapters of Mr. Roosevelt's career." History, said the editorial,

> will have to return its own verdict on the part which Franklin D. Roosevelt has played, and that which his influence will continue to play, on the world stage. It is enough for the moment to say that the hand which reached into the Pine Mountain cottage in Georgia has taken away a man of great stature. Those who opposed him on political grounds will be the first to say that he was the outstanding figure of his time.[19]

The president's death prompted an editorial of epic magnitude from the *Post*, however. The news of the passing, the newspaper proclaimed on the same day as the *Star*, "comes like a bolt from Jove, and the thunder is still echoing and reechoing through the diameter of our planet....It is as if a presence has been removed from the daily lives of all nations....The sepulcher of this man who has died is, indeed, the whole earth." The newspaper afforded the departed leader the stature of world hero who lifted the nation beyond the heights of historic empires. "No nation, not even ancient Rome, has ever attained such eminence, and the entire world looks to the United States for guidance in bringing the war in both oceans to a victorious end," sang the editorial, "and for aid in putting the world in the way of recovery from its awful travail. Franklin D. Roosevelt was the leader of this arbiter of the world's destinies." The editorial left no doubt of the high place he had carved for himself in world history. "So he grew to the Titan role which he filled at the day of his death. He will be

written of in years to come as the war's greatest casualty." The editorial concluded with a note of consolation to Roosevelt's wife, Eleanor, before invoking
supernatural stature on behalf of the dead president: "She deserves great honor
today, for it was she who organized her husband's life for the tasks that she felt,
in spite of the affliction which cut him down 20 years ago, were marked out for
him by Providence. In death he will reinforce the unity among nations which
he strove to achieve in his lifetime."[20] There was little doubt of the differing
esteem these two newspapers held for this president as a "man of great stature"
and a "national leader" in the eyes of the *Star,* and as a man chosen by God to
lead the United States to greatness, to be so noted by history, according to the
Post. Clearly, there was an ideological editorial dispute at work.

EMERGING MODELS OF COMPETITION

The closure of the *Cleveland Press* in 1982 and of the *Washington Star* in 1981
left both of these communities without competing dailies, though the establishment of the conservative *Washington Times* in 1982 rescued that city from being
a monopoly daily newspaper market. These closures reflect a widespread trend in
the American newspaper industry that has increasingly left communities that
traditionally have enjoyed daily newspaper competition with just one daily
newspaper serving the city proper but perhaps facing competition from daily suburban newspapers on their outskirts in a form of newspaper competition identified as "umbrella" competition in 1975 and 1978 by Stanford University
economics professor James N. Rosse. His model placed newspapers into four
layers, each constituting an "umbrella" that took in towns and cities in layers
beneath it. The layers are metropolitan dailies offering regional, national, and
international news; satellite-city dailies offering some regional, national, and
international coverage but more locally oriented than the metropolitan newspapers; suburban dailies focusing their coverage on their home communities but
carrying some national and international news; and weekly newspapers that
focus solely on local news.[21] Industry analysts have expanded upon Rosse's model
in their discussions of competition involving newspapers of different circulation
sizes in major metropolitan markets and in their suburbs and outlying areas.
Ensuing studies and analyses have supported the existence of competition among
these newspapers.

For example, Diana Stover Tillinghast in her 1988 study of the Los Angeles-
Orange County market identified a complex marketplace in which "vigorous
intercity competition has led to market consolidation and to shifts in circulation
and advertising." In this market, before the closure of the Los Angeles *Herald-
Examiner,* she found an adherence to competitive forces.

> Although there is extensive competition between layers...there is little direct com-
> petition within layers. In Los Angeles County, the competition is primarily between
> the *Times* and the suburban newspapers although there is within-layer competition

between the *Times* and the *Herald-Examiner*, particularly in city zones. In Orange County, the battle for circulation is primarily between the *Times* and the *Register*, a metropolitan layer paper and a satellite city layer paper.[22]

These studies, however, have tended to concentrate on circulation and advertising. Little analysis could be found of content competition involving umbrella newspapers, though Stephen Lacy in a 1988 study argued that content competition is important to an understanding of intercity newspaper advertising and that readership is a basis for advertising competition.[23] And no research could be found of editorial content relating to an emerging competitive market that is touched upon by analyses of umbrella competition but not fully developed. That market is what this book identifies as "metroplex" competition, in which two or more daily newspapers with separate ownership and business operations based in neighboring cities compete for advertisers and readers in a greater metropolitan area that comprises separate, independent communities.

Two such metroplex markets were selected for the modern-day editorial analysis for this chapter. One was the Pittsburgh, Pennsylvania, market in which the suburban *Tribune-Review* of Greensburg (weekday 2003 circulation of 119,338)[24] competed head-to-head with the *Pittsburgh Post-Gazette* (weekday 2003 circulation of 243,091) for readers and advertisers in the greater metropolitan area of Pittsburgh. Scripps Howard Newspapers sold its *Pittsburgh Press* to its JOA partner, the *Post-Gazette*, in 1992, and the *Post-Gazette* closed the *Press* in 1993. Subsequently, the *Tribune-Review* opened a Pittsburgh bureau and began competing with the *Post-Gazette* in a competitive situation that over the years has seen the *Tribune-Review* steadily increase its Pittsburgh presence. For the purpose of this chapter, however, this newspaper will be treated as a metroplex rival rather than the direct competition rival it had become by 2005.[25] The other is the Dallas/Fort Worth market, in which the *Dallas Morning News* (weekday 2003 circulation of 505,724) and the *Fort Worth Star-Telegram* (weekday 2003 circulation of 218,975) entered into a more active greater metropolitan area competition following the 1991 purchase and closure by the *Morning News* of its former direct competition rival, the Dallas *Times Herald*.

The purpose here is to analyze newspaper editorials to discern if metroplex newspapers serve as substitutes for direct competition newspapers or those that compete in a JOA in a way that promotes a marketplace of ideas. The method of analysis is the same as that used in previous chapters.

THE DALLAS/FORT WORTH MARKET

The Dallas metroplex newspapers published 297 editorials during the study period, 147 by the *Dallas Morning News* and 150 by the *Fort Worth Star-Telegram*. Differences were found in the number of editorials devoted to local topics, with the *Star-Telegram* publishing nearly 25 percent more than the *Morning News*. The Fort Worth newspaper, however, published fewer editorials, and a

Table 4.1   Geographic Concentration of Editorials in the *Dallas Morning News* and *Fort Worth Star-Telegram* for January 2001 and January 2003

	Morning News	*Star-Telegram*
Local	(3) 29 (19.7%)*	(1) 66 (44%)*
State/regional	(2) 36 (24.5%)*	(3) 31 (20.7%)*
National	(1) 61 (41.5%)*	(2) 47 (31.3%)*
International	(4) 20 (13.6%)*	(4) 5 (3.3%)*
Other	(5) 1 (0.7%)*	(5) 1 (0.7%)*
Total	147 (49.5%)**	150 (50.5%)**

*Percentages are of the total number of that newspaper's editorials only.
**Percentages are of the total number of editorials by both newspapers.
Preceding numbers in parenthesis are a ranking of that geographic listing by frequency.
Percentages are rounded to the nearest tenth of a percent.

lower percentage of them, on state and regional topics. The *Morning News* outpaced its competitor in the national editorial category by about ten percentage points and on international topics by a similar margin (see Table 4.1).

Political and government topics dominated the editorials of both newspapers, comprising more than half of each of their editorials. Differences were found in the frequencies of other topics, indicating that one newspaper's editorial board members may have placed more importance on these topics than the other board. Such topics included crime and health and welfare, which drew greater editorial attention from the *Morning News*, and economic activity, a subject dominated by the *Star-Telegram* (see Table 4.2).

Table 4.2   Editorials by Topic Category in the *Dallas Morning News* and *Fort Worth Star-Telegram* for January 2001 and January 2003

	Morning News	*Star-Telegram*
Politics and government	(1) 75 (51%)*	(1) 84 (56%)*
Economic activity	(7) 3 (2%)*	(5) 9 (6%)*
Crime	(2) 21 (14.3%)*	(2) 13 (8.7%)*
General interest	(5) 10 (6.8%)*	(4) 10 (6.7%)*
Health and welfare	(3) 12 (8.1%)*	(6) 6 (4%)*
Popular amusements	(6) 5 (3.4%)*	(7) 5 (3.3%)*
Education and arts	(4) 11 (7.5%)*	(3) 12 (8%)*
Science and invention	(9) 1 (0.7%)*	(8) 2 (1.3%)*
War and defense	(6) 5 (3.4%)*	(6) 6 (4%)*
Public moral problems	0	0
Accident and disaster	(8) 2 (1.4%)*	(8) 2 (1.3%)*
Other	(8) 2 (1.4%)*	(9) 1 (0.6%)*

*Percentages are of the total number of that newspaper's editorials only.
Preceding numbers in parenthesis are a ranking of that category by frequency.
Percentages are rounded to the nearest tenth of a percent.

Table 4.3   Editorials of Common Topics and Their Agreement and Disagreement in the *Dallas Morning News* and *Fort Worth Star-Telegram* for January 2001 and January 2003

	Common topics	Agree	Disagree
Morning News	29 (19.7%)*	10 (34.5%)**	19 (65.5%)**
Star-Telegram	26 (17.3%)*	10 (38.5%)**	16 (61.5%)**
Total	55 (18.5%)***	20 (6.7%)***	35 (11.8%)***
		(36.4%)$^+$	(63.6%)$^+$

*Percentages are of the total number of that newspaper's editorials.
**Percentages are of that newspaper's total editorials on common topics.
***Percentages are of the overall total number of editorials.
+Percentages are of the total number of editorials on common subjects.
Percentages are rounded to the nearest tenth of a percent.

The newspapers published fifty-five editorials on the same subjects, which was slightly less than a fifth of their total number of editorials. They disagreed either ideologically or in framing in nearly two-thirds of these common-subject editorials (see Table 4.3). But political ideological disagreement accounted for a minute number of these common-subject editorials, so the bulk of the newspapers' disagreement was found in areas other than political or ideological/philosophical differences (see Table 4.4).

In matters close to home, just two of the newspapers' fifty-five common-subject editorials were on local subjects. That was a mere 3.6 percent of all of their common-subject editorials. These two editorials disagreed, but for reasons of framing rather than ideology. Sixteen of the common-subject editorials, or 29.1 percent of all of the common-subject editorials, were on state/regional topics. Ten of these drew disagreement (6.3 percent of all same-topic state/regional editorials), but just two of these (1.3 percent of same-topic state/regional editorials) disagreed for reasons of ideology.

Only about 8 percent of all the newspapers' editorials dealt with Bush administration policies and decisions. Fifteen of these appeared in the *Morning News* and eight in the *Star-Telegram*. The analysis of Bush policy editorials provided only slight evidence of political ideological difference between the

Table 4.4   Editorials of Common Topic Ideological Disagreement in the *Dallas Morning News* and *Fort Worth Star-Telegram* for January 2001 and January 2003

	Ideological disagreement	Other disagreement
Morning News	2 (6.9%)*	17 (58.6%)*
Star-Telegram	2 (7.7%)*	14 (53.8%)*
Total	4 (7.3%)** (1.4%)***	31 (56.4%)** (10.4%)***

*Percentages are of that newspaper's total editorials on common topics.
**Percentages are of the total number of editorials on common subjects.
***Percentage is of the overall total number of editorials.
Percentages are rounded to the nearest tenth of a percent.

Table 4.5   Editorials of Support and Opposition to Policies and Decisions of the Administration of President George W. Bush in the *Dallas Morning News* and *Fort Worth Star-Telegram* for January 2001 and January 2003

	Administration policy topics	Support	Oppose
Morning News	15	7 (46.7%)*	8 (53.3%)*
Star-Telegram	8	4 (50%)*	4 (50%)*
Total	23	11	12

*Percentages are of the total number of that newspaper's editorials on administration policies.

newspapers. The *Morning News* disagreed with Bush administration policies in 53 percent of its editorials, the *Star-Telegram* in 50 percent (see Table 4.5).

THE PITTSBURGH/GREENSBURG MARKET

In the Pittsburgh/Greensburg market, the newspapers published 317 editorials, 169 by the *Post-Gazette* and 148 by the *Tribune-Review*. More than one-third of the *Post-Gazette*'s editorials were on local topics, compared to slightly more than one-fifth for the *Tribune-Review*. The newspapers published a similar percentage of editorials on state and regional topics. The *Tribune-Review* far outdistanced the *Post-Gazette*, by more than twenty percentage points, in editorials on national issues, while the *Post-Gazette* more than doubled the *Tribune-Review*'s editorial output for international topics (see Table 4.6).

As in all of the other analyses, political and government topics dominated the editorials of both newspapers, comprising more than half of their editorials. As was the case in other markets analyzed, the newspapers differed in the interest they showed in other subjects, with economic activity and subjects of general interest garnering greater editorial attention in the *Post-Gazette* and education

Table 4.6   Geographic Concentration of Editorials in the *Pittsburgh Post-Gazette* and Greensburg *Tribune-Review* for January 2001 and January 2003

	Post-Gazette	*Tribune-Review*
Local	(1) 63 (37.3%)*	(2) 32 (21.6%)*
State/regional	(4) 21 (12.4%)*	(3) 19 (12.8%)*
National	(2) 62 (36.7%)*	(1) 87 (58.8%)*
International	(3) 22 (13%)*	(4) 10 (6.8%)*
Other	(5) 1 (0.6%)*	0
Total	169 (53.3%)**	148 (46.7%)**

*Percentages are of the total number of that newspaper's editorials only.
**Percentages are of the total number of editorials by both newspapers.
Preceding numbers in parenthesis are a ranking of that geographic listing by frequency.
Percentages are rounded to the nearest tenth of a percent.

Table 4.7 Editorials by Topic Category in the *Pittsburgh Post-Gazette* and Greensburg *Tribune-Review* for January 2001 and January 2003

	Post-Gazette	Tribune-Review
Politics and government	(1) 93 (55%)*	(1) 89 (60.1%)*
Economic activity	(2) 15 (8.9%)*	(7) 4 (2.7%)*
Crime	(6) 9 (5.3%)*	(4) 10 (6.8%)*
General interest	(3) 12 (7.1%)*	(6) 7 (4.7%)*
Health and welfare	(7) 3 (1.8%)*	(8) 3 (2%)*
Popular amusements	(4) 11 (6.5%)*	(5) 8 (5.4%)*
Education and arts	(5) 10 (5.9%)*	(2) 13 (8.8%)*
Science and invention	(8) 2 (1.2%)*	(9) 2 (1.4%)*
War and defense	(3) 12 (7.1%)*	(3) 11 (7.4%)*
Public moral problems	0	(10) 1 (0.7%)*
Accident and disaster	(9) 1 (0.6%)*	0
Other	(9) 1 (0.6%)*	0

*Percentages are of the total number of that newspaper's editorials only.
Preceding numbers in parenthesis are a ranking of that category by frequency.
Percentages are rounded to the nearest tenth of a percent.

and the classical arts drawing somewhat greater percentages of editorials in the *Tribune-Review* (see Table 4.7).

More than one-fourth of the newspapers' editorials dealt with common subjects: nearly a fourth of the *Post-Gazette*'s editorial output and nearly a third of the *Tribune-Review*'s. The discrepancy in the total number of editorials on the same subjects derived from each newspaper publishing different numbers of editorials on the same subject. The newspapers had a disagreement rate of slightly more than 75 percent either ideologically or in framing on these same-subject editorials. Clearly there was some dispute under way in this market (see Table 4.8), and much of it was based on political philosophy; ideological disagreement accounted for more than half of the disagreeing same-subject editorials (see Table 4.9).

Table 4.8 Editorials of Common Topics and Their Agreement and Disagreement in the *Pittsburgh Post-Gazette* and Greensburg *Tribune-Review* for January 2001 and January 2003

	Common topics	Agree	Disagree
Post-Gazette	43 (25.4%)*	11 (25.6%)**	32 (74.4%)**
Tribune-Review	46 (31.1%)*	11 (23.9%)**	35 (76.1%)**
Total	89 (28.1%)***	22 (6.9%)***	67 (21.1%)***
		(24.7%)+	(75.3%)+

*Percentages are of the total number of that newspaper's editorials.
**Percentages are of that newspaper's total editorials on common topics.
***Percentages are of the overall total number of editorials.
+Percentages are of the total number of editorials on common subjects.
Percentages are rounded to the nearest tenth of a percent.

Table 4.9   Editorials of Common Topic Ideological Disagreement in the *Pittsburgh Post-Gazette* and Greensburg *Tribune-Review* for January 2001 and January 2003

	Ideological disagreement	Other disagreement
Post-Gazette	22 (51.2%)*	10 (23.3%)*
Tribune-Review	27 (58.7%)*	8 (17.4%)*
Total	49 (55.1%)** (15.5%)***	18 (20.2%)** (5.7%)***

*Percentages are of that newspaper's total editorials on common topics.
**Percentages are of the total number of editorials on common subjects.
***Percentage is of the overall total number of editorials.
Percentages are rounded to the nearest tenth of a percent.

Seventeen of the newspapers' eighty-nine common-subject editorials were on local subjects, which was 19.1 percent of all of their common-subject editorials. Thirteen of these—76.5 percent of the local common-subject editorials and 14.6 percent of all of their common-subject editorials—disagreed ideologically or in framing. Five of these editorials of disagreement, though, three by the *Tribune-Review* and two by the *Post-Gazette*, were on the same topic: the shooting by police of a crime suspect and the ensuing investigation. Eight, or 20 percent, of the newspapers' forty editorials on state/regional topics were on common subjects. Six of these editorials disagreed ideologically or in framing, which was 15 percent of all of their combined state/regional editorials and 75 percent of their common-subject state/regional editorials.

The analysis of editorials in support of or disagreeing with Bush administration policies revealed a stark ideological difference. The newspapers devoted more than one-tenth of their editorial output to Bush administration issues, with the *Tribune-Review* supporting the administration nearly 80 percent of the time compared to just 16.7 percent for the *Post-Gazette* (see Table 4.10).

DIFFERENCES OF OPINION AND OF FRAMING

The Dallas/Fort Worth metroplex newspapers more closely resembled separate publications in two distinct cities than they did competing daily newspapers in a

Table 4.10   Editorials of Support and Opposition to Policies and Decisions of the Administration of President George W. Bush in the *Pittsburgh Post-Gazette* and Greensburg *Tribune-Review* for January 2001 and January 2003

	Administration policy topics	Support	Oppose
Post-Gazette	18	3 (16.7%)*	15 (83.3%)*
Tribune-Review	24	19 (79.2%)*	5 (20.8%)*
Total	42	22	20

*Percentages are of that newspaper's total number of editorials on administration policies.
Percentages are rounded to the nearest tenth of a percent.

shared community. The strongest evidence for this conclusion was found in the local editorial sampling. Of the newspapers' ninety-five local editorials, just four of these, or 4.21 percent of all local editorials, were on a local subject of interest to both communities: the shared Dallas/Fort Worth Airport and local reaction to the escape of seven prisoners from a state prison. Both of the airport editorials were published by the *Star-Telegram*, so they were not editorial subjects addressed by both newspapers. The two editorials on the prison escape, one by each newspaper, differed in framing. One newspaper discussed local police department reaction and the other examined the differences in information coming from a myriad of government spokespeople on the issue. All other local editorials published by these newspapers dealt with subjects unique to their separate communities or to areas linked to these separate communities. So, the newspapers provided virtually no evidence of editorial agreement or disagreement at the local level.

Beyond this difference in localism, analysis of the Dallas/Fort Worth market found similarities to other markets, though the rate and range of editorial disagreement was markedly less. Of the editorials that took on like subject matter, twenty of them (36.4 percent) reached similar conclusions. Of those that reached dissimilar conclusions, only four—two by each newspaper—disagreed for reasons of ideology or philosophy. These focused on an international subject (human cloning) and on a state subject (state legislative committee appointments).

In their editorials on that second topic, the newspapers not only differed in their conclusions about acting Lieutenant Governor Bill Ratliff's appointments of committee leaders of the state Senate's twelve committees but also placed the editorials differently on the page. The *Morning News* made it a third editorial, while the *Star-Telegram* placed it in the lead position on the next day. The *Morning News* applauded the appointments, claiming the lieutenant governor "wisely continued Austin's bipartisan tradition Wednesday by appointing an equal number of Democrats and Republicans to lead the Texas Senate's 12 committees."[26] The *Star-Telegram*, however, criticized the appointments, saying that Ratliff "could hardly have started his tenure as acting lieutenant governor with a more unfortunate gaffe than omitting a Hispanic member on the committee that will draw new boundaries for the state's congressional and legislative districts." Though the editorial credited the lieutenant governor with rectifying this mistake by appointing a Laredo Democrat to the committee, it went on to say that he had "raised other questions by giving neither political party a majority on the redistricting committee—a panel that will grapple with the most combative issue facing the Legislature this year."[27]

These two editorials also provided evidence of a difference in framing. Besides disagreeing on the overall wisdom of the lieutenant governor's appointments, the editorials also differed in their attention to details of the appointment. The *Morning News* concentrated on the bipartisan equality found in appointing an equal number of state senators from the two main political parties; the *Star-*

Telegram discussed primarily one of those committees, the one responsible for redistricting. This sort of editorial diversity, that of framing, was the primary difference in these newspapers' thirty-five editorials of disagreement, accounting for thirty-one (nearly 89 percent) of all editorials of disagreement.

Commentary on President Bush's State of the Union speech in January 2003 provided an example of an editorial subject in which the editorialists framed their opinions differently. The *Morning News* in its lead editorial of January 29 began with a discussion of the president's comments about the "urgency to dismantle Saddam Hussein's regime" in Iraq, and the newspaper called on Secretary of State Colin Powell to "have pictures, details, specifics amidst his new intelligence. Regardless, Saddam Hussein continues to tease the world. The world should not let itself be mocked." The editorial then discussed the president's plans to fight AIDS in Africa, to rescue Medicare, and to cut taxes, which was a plan that the newspaper found "not convincing."[28] The *Star-Telegram* in its lead editorial on the same morning made passing reference, in the beginning of the editorial, to the Iraq situation, a subject on which it agreed with the *Morning News* that Powell needed to provide "more than just…hearsay." But the remainder of the first half of the editorial dealt with the domestic agenda, which was a portion of the speech that the *Morning News* had reserved for the second half of its editorial. And it included in its list more domestic-issue items than did the *Morning News* editorial, such as cracking down on "frivolous" lawsuits, development of hydrogen-powered vehicles, and expanded federal funding for faith-based initiatives. As for the president's proposed funding to fight AIDS in Africa, the newspaper, in disagreement with the *Morning News'* brief reference to this issue and with the president's stance, said: "The proposed $15 billion over five years—$10 billion in new money—for international HIV/AIDS treatment may sound noble, but it will ring hollow to the AIDS patients right here in Texas who are threatened with the loss of state-funded lifesaving medications because of the shortfall in the state's budget."[29]

Another editorial exchange on a national topic offered evidence of another sort of framing difference. In commenting on January 15, 2001, on the impact of Martin Luther King Jr. on the occasion of Martin Luther King Day, the *Morning News* used its lead editorial to point out progress that had been made in Dallas regarding the status of African-Americans: "The mayor and police chief are African-American. And so is the chairman of the Greater Dallas Chamber of Commerce board." But the editorialist went on to discuss work yet undone on behalf of racial equality. "The quest that eventually cost Martin Luther King Jr. his life is far from over.…With the surging growth of the Hispanic population in Texas, California, Florida and elsewhere, a new set of societal challenges has emerged that were not so apparent during Dr. King's days." The editorial concluded that the "promised land is within reach. And through his message that has touched the world for more than four decades, Dr. King is still on the mountain leading the way."[30] The *Star-Telegram*, in a bizarre commentary on King, published on the same day in its lead editorial position a likeness of the slain civil rights leader formed by the words from King's August 28, 1963, "I Have a Dream" speech. The words were, for the most part, tiny and thus illegible in the newspaper reproduction. The newspaper, which published the image with the permission of its originator, the *Detroit Free-Press*, added no commentary of its own other than King's birth date, his date of death, and the words, "May his dream be a dream for all Americans."[31] Beyond that, the newspaper offered no opinion on King and his vision, in contrast to the *Morning News'* commentary about the present-day situation regarding race relations in Dallas and the nation.

The editorials regarding Bush administration policies did offer some ideological diversity, but the number of editorials on Bush administration policies, totaling twenty-three, or just 7.7 percent of all of the newspapers' combined editorials, renders this measure somewhat meaningless.

The Pittsburgh/Greensburg metroplex, however, offered striking evidence of diversity of opinion that included not only clear political ideological differences but also meaningful disparities in geographical subject concentration and in conclusions reached in editorials on the same subjects.

The *Post-Gazette* enjoyed a marked superiority in attention to local topics, publishing 37.3 percent of its editorials on subjects in this arena compared to the *Tribune-Review*'s 21.6 percent. Considering the local editorials in combination with those focusing on regional and state issues, nearly half of the *Post-Gazette*'s editorials (49.7 percent) concentrated on subjects closer to home, while the *Tribune-Review* devoted slightly more than a third of its editorials (34.4 percent) to local, regional, and state issues. This disparity takes on additional meaning because, similar to the findings concerning localism in the Dallas/Fort Worth market, the *Tribune-Review*'s local editorials were for the most part limited to topics close to the then-home office of the newspaper—Westmoreland and Fayette counties—rather than to subjects dealing with the *Post-Gazette*'s home county, Allegheny County.

One of those local subjects concerned the local public television station WQED's attempt to sell the license of its sister station, WQEX, to a private broadcasting company. The *Post-Gazette* supported the proposed sale on the grounds that the money raised from the sale would help WQED "retire its $9.3 million debt, speed its digital conversion, build a programming fund and update its headquarters....On the way to FCC approval and beyond, the station must keep the public in public television."[32] The *Tribune-Review*, however, used this issue to render an opinion opposed to the concept of government-supported broadcasting. The newspaper endorsed the sale as making sense so long as "Pittsburgh is fated to have public broadcasting—a model that cable television certainly has rendered obsolete....Citizens for Independent Public Broadcasting should spend less time yammering at the government to assist it in pressing its views, and more time finding a way to *independently* prove its ideas for the airwaves have merit."[33]

The *Tribune-Review* published a greater frequency of editorials on national issues, by a difference of about twenty-two percentage points. Clearly, the

Tribune-Review's editorial board placed great importance on national topics. The *Post-Gazette*, though, nearly doubled the *Tribune-Review*'s percentage of editorials on international topics. As for subject categories, the newspapers were fairly close in their percentages of editorials on topics other than politics and government, though the *Post-Gazette* more than doubled the *Tribune-Review*'s percentage of editorials on economic activity, while the *Tribune-Review* offered a noticeable percentage advantage in editorials pertaining to education and classic arts.

The most apparent editorial difference between the two newspapers was in their agreement/disagreement with policies of the Bush administration. The *Tribune-Review* obviously was the more conservative, Republican-leaning, of the newspapers, supporting Bush-administration policies and decisions nearly 80 percent of the time. The *Post-Gazette*, on the other hand, backed the administration slightly less than 17 percent of the time. Several of the two newspapers' editorials of disagreement were on Bush policies (though they agreed on the subject of possible war with Iraq, both urging the Bush administration to avoid armed conflict). For example, on the issue of affirmative action as raised in the Bush administration's decision to become involved in a court case dealing with the University of Michigan graduate law school admission standards, the *Post-Gazette* argued that while race "can be a crude measure to include in the admissions process...the unfairness of it is not so simple as Mr. Bush suggests. Given historical racial discrimination, it doesn't make sense to ignore race as a factor among others when it may be the most significant of all." The editorial concluded that the Bush administration, by introducing an "ideologically motivated brief," endangered affirmative action "and thus the greater cause of social justice in America."[34] The *Tribune-Review* reasoned, however, that civil rights "aren't just for minorities; they're for *all* Americans. Kudos to the president for understanding this principle, and for having the fortitude to help fight for it in court [emphasis by the newspaper]."[35]

The newspapers differed in another matter of jurisprudence, one that other newspapers analyzed for this book also took up: the 2003 decision by lame duck Illinois Governor George Ryan to commute the death sentences of that state's death row inmates. The *Tribune-Review* accused the governor of overlooking the "difficult intellectual test" of

> distinguishing among the prisoners marked for death. When he said the system is arbitrary and capricious—he did not establish it was so in all cases—he then committed an act that was bluntly arbitrary and capricious. Ryan said, upon perpetrating this injustice, "I will sleep well knowing I made the right decision." Would that sleep come so easily to the families who again are drawn into the horror visited on their kin.[36]

The *Post-Gazette*, though, viewed the governor's action as "a call to conscience....The finality of the death penalty is the greatest argument against it.

In making his sweeping gesture, Mr. Ryan used his sovereign power in an unusual way, but it was not more capricious than the death penalty itself."[37]

The newspapers in 2001 engaged in an editorial disagreement over the issue of gun control. The *Post-Gazette* cited a fatal shooting spree by a forty-two-year-old Massachusetts man to argue against gun-related violence and on behalf of legislation to help control it. "Advocates of gun control argue (rightly) that American permissiveness toward firearms makes outrages like this more common," the newspaper said. "The real tragedy is in not sensing the urgency for action to prevent the likelihood of a fatal shooting spree coming to a school or workplace near you."[38]

Massachusetts came into play again when the *Tribune-Review* wrote later in that same month on the Senate Judicial Committee confirmation hearings of Attorney General-designate John Ashcroft. The newspaper chastised that state's U.S. senator, Edward Kennedy, for accusing Ashcroft of relying "on an extreme reading of the right to bear arms under the Second Amendment." The newspaper opined: "Excuse us, senator, but an armed citizenry that can protect itself against a tyrannical government is the *basis* for the Second Amendment if not liberty itself. When was the last time *you* read the Constitution, Mr. Kennedy?"[39]

That 28 percent of the two newspapers' editorials were on the same topic indicated that their editorial boards explored a large neighborhood of shared interests. That they disagreed on 75 percent of these issues, and on nearly three-fourths of those for reasons of ideology, was evidence of a lively intellectual debate on the editorial pages of the greater Pittsburgh community's two major newspapers.

So, the Pittsburgh area, by more than one gauge, offered evidence of a newspaper market with a distinctive difference and variety of editorials, a market of robust editorial competition offering readers a clear choice in ideological differences. The evidence was in the preponderance of opposing views on those editorials on the same topics and in the vast difference of support for policies of the Bush administration. Also, the newspapers offered readers a distinct choice in subject matter. They presented a marked variety of editorials, as shown by the finding that more than 70 percent of their editorials were on different topics even within such general categories as politics and government and popular amusements.

However, the Pittsburgh/Greensburg metroplex market differed from the JOA and direct competition markets of communities such as Fort Wayne and Chicago in one important way: focus on localism. Similar to the findings of the Dallas/Fort Worth metroplex, this market's editorials on local matters rarely discussed common topics or local subjects of concern to readers of the rival newspaper. Their local editorials were confined primarily to subjects nearer to their home base of either Greensburg and Westmoreland County or Fayette County or Pittsburgh and Allegheny County, whereas the JOA and direct competition markets offered greater relative focus on editorial interest in local matters that readers of both newspapers would find of interest. Of the *Post-Gazette*'s sixty-three local editorials in the 2001–03 sampling, just eight (12.7 percent) were on subjects of interest to readers of the home counties of both newspapers. The same trend was true for the *Tribune-Review*; of its thirty-two local editorials, only nine— 28.1 percent—were on subjects of interest to both home regions, and three of these were repeat-subject editorials, or subjects that already had been written on once by the newspaper's editorialists. So, when it came to localism, the two newspapers of the Pittsburgh/Greensburg market, like those in the Dallas/Fort Worth metroplex, more nearly resembled newspapers operating in separate, non-competing markets or even markets in separate cities or states. Thus, appeals that the Pittsburgh/Greensburg newspapers might make on behalf of editorial diversity would be based on competing ideas, both ideologically and in overall agenda and topic richness, found in state, national, and international subjects. And it should be noted that when these newspapers entered a local and state realm of interest to both sets of local readers, they demonstrated ideological and framing editorial disagreement; so, in this way, at least, they did offer a meaningful substitute for direct competition or JOA competition markets. Otherwise, they did not when it came to localism.

CHAPTER 5

2004 Presidential Campaign: A Split Editorial Decision

The Democratic papers, in resorting to various forms of apologetic causuistry for the offence, not only concede the substantial truth of the main charge, but also the necessity of making an apology for it, in order to break, as far as possible, its force as an objection to the candidacy of Governor Cleveland. We then assume as a fact, admitted and known to the people, that some ten years ago Mr. Cleveland, when he was about forty years of age, was guilty of the offence imputed to him, and that he is the reputed father of a bastard son, now living in Buffalo, and who, to the day of his death, will be stamped and humiliated with the disgrace of his illegitimacy.

. . . if the people of the United States who are in favor of sound morality follow our advice, they certainly will not bestow the honors of the Presidency upon Grover Cleveland. His election would argue a low state of morals among the people, and be a burning shame and never-to-be-forgotten disgrace to the nation. No man with such a private character as is shown in respect to him is fit to fill any office in the gift of the people.

—The *Independent*, September 4, 1884[1]

Presidential campaigns traditionally are a period of intense newspaper activity. They have produced coverage ranging from dispatches from the cities where the candidates made their daily stump speeches to in-depth analyses of social issues behind the political debates. On the editorial pages, campaigns spark extensive commentary that includes op-ed columns and newspaper editorials representing the official positions on issues and candidates by newspaper owners and editors. One of the most closely followed features of newspapers and their editorial pages during presidential campaigns is the newspaper endorsements of candidates for the nation's highest office. The 2004 presidential campaign, besides generating the largest voter turnout in three decades,[2] also produced a flurry of opinions on the nation's daily editorial pages. These included not only endorsements but commentary on related issues.

The final presidential election tally revealed a fairly evenly divided nation. Incumbent Republican President George W. Bush won re-election with just a 3 percent margin of victory in the popular vote—51 percent to 48 percent. He enjoyed a greater Electoral College vote margin, 53.2 percent to 46.8 percent. The nation's newspapers mirrored this split in their endorsement editorials. But they differed with the electoral majority, as the editorial endorsements favored Bush's challenger, Democratic U.S. Senator John Kerry of Massachusetts. By election day, Kerry had claimed the editorial support of 213 newspapers with a combined daily circulation of 20.88 million to Bush's 205 newspapers with a combined circulation of 15.74 million.[3]

The high level of interest in this race provided an opportunity not only to study differences in the editorial endorsements and campaign-related editorials of the nation's newspapers but to concentrate this study in the context of a marketplace of ideas. This analysis helped to determine not so much the power of editorials in swaying elections but rather whether daily newspapers involved in competitive markets offered their readers a political ideological choice in their opinions (i.e., Democratic versus Republican and liberal versus conservative) or in framing.

The marketplace metaphor expounded by Milton and Mill worked its way into the legal opinions of the U.S. Supreme Court early in the twentieth century. Justice Oliver Wendell Holmes in 1919 penned a noted dissent to the court's affirmation of the conviction of Jacob Abrams for violating the Espionage Act of 1917 by publishing a circular with Bolshevist leanings that criticized President Woodrow Wilson. The dissent put forward for the first time in American legal opinion the classic statement of a marketplace of ideas in its defense of contrary thinking and opinions: "The best test of truth is the power of the thought to get itself accepted in the competition of the market, and that truth is the only ground upon which their wishes safely can be carried out. That at any rate is the theory of our Constitution."[4]

Twenty-one years after the Abrams case the metaphor moved from the ranks of dissent to the court majority, as the court clearly enunciated the connection of robust discussion to democratic government. "Falsehoods," said the court on behalf of the right of the president of an AFL union to picket an Alabama company, "may be exposed through the process of education and discussion.... Those who won our independence had confidence in the power of free and fearless reasoning and communication of ideas to discover and spread political and economic truth." In language reminiscent of Milton's confrontation involving truth and falsehood, the court cited the "power of correcting error" through speech and education.[5]

The executive and legislative branches indicated agreement with the high court's endorsement of the marketplace concept when, in 1970, Congress passed and President Richard Nixon signed the Newspaper Preservation Act enabling JOAs. A federal district court, citing market forces, upheld the act two years later. The court noted JOAs would serve to preserve editorial independence and noted that the act "looses the same shady market forces which existed before the passage of the Sherman, Clayton and other antitrust laws."[6] Twenty-four years later, in the stated cause of encouraging competition and a diversity of voices on the electronic airwaves, Congress passed and President Bill Clinton signed the Telecommunications Act of 1996. Inclusion of electronic airways regulation in a discussion of the marketplace metaphor is apt because it reveals the importance of diversity, in the eyes of government officials as well as political, legal, and media analysts, to the democratic process.

The Telecommunications Act of 1996, noted American University communications professor Patricia Aufderheide in her 1999 book on the act, "boldly equated the public interest with a competitive environment, in which consumer and producer desires and needs can be matched efficiently in the marketplace, not structured by regulators."[7] Fordham University communications professor Philip M. Napoli two years later called the marketplace of ideas principle the "starting point for understanding" the relationships of two tangential principles beneath the umbrella of the Telecommunication Act's provisions for public service: competition and diversity. A "vigorous and robust marketplace of ideas," he wrote, "has long been a guiding principle in democratic theory and a prominent metaphor in the regulation of electronic media, from both political and economic perspectives."

> The central guiding assumptions underlying this metaphor have been: (a) that a robust marketplace of ideas creates an educated citizenry, thereby producing informed decision making and, hence, a well-functioning democracy; and (b) that a robust marketplace of ideas maximizes economic efficiency and consumer satisfaction.[8]

Media conglomeration critic and former newspaper journalist Ben Bagdikian invoked the marketplace metaphor in arguing similarly that the late twentieth-century trend of increasing concentration of media ownership led to a homogenization of media content that is damaging to the political system and to society. "The media may produce entertainment and sell merchandise," he argued in a 1985 journal article, "but if, in addition, they do not create a rich marketplace of ideas and serious information, they fail a prime function."[9]

While the purpose of the study reported in this chapter is not to analyze the power of editorials in helping to determine election outcomes, it nonetheless is important to note that some studies have found, if not a causal relationship of editorials to election outcomes, evidence that newspaper editorials appear to play an important role in the process. An increasing number of U.S. dailies do not endorse in campaigns and others have ceased the practice because they believe such editorials have little or no effect; and some studies have validated that sentiment.[10] Numerous other studies, though, have found some kind of editorial effect on elections. Fred Fedler, Tim Counts, and Lowndes F. Stephens observed in a 1982 study that editors who continue to endorse argued that "newspapers have a responsibility to endorse political candidates regardless of the endorsements' effect upon voters."[11] Their study of presidential endorsements of 188 daily newspapers published in the nation's 100 largest cities in the 1980 election found support for three of their hypotheses: "Citizens are more likely to vote for the presidential candidate endorsed by their city's only daily newspaper than for any of that candidate's opponents;" "If two daily newspapers are published in a city, and one remains uncommitted, citizens are more likely to vote for the candidate endorsed by the second daily than for any of that candidate's opponents;" and "Political candidates will receive a higher percentage of the votes cast in cities where all the daily newspapers endorse their candidates than in cities where the daily newspapers are divided, or in cities where all the daily newspapers endorse their opponents."[12] While other researchers also have found effects of editorials on elections,[13] the Fedler/Counts/Stephens findings are particularly appropriate for the current study's method and analysis of newspaper presidential campaign and endorsement editorials in a variety of competing newspaper markets.

Daily newspaper editorials, found through an Internet search of newspaper web sites, were analyzed on twelve 2004 presidential campaign-related subjects: whether Bush's secretary of defense, Donald Rumsfeld, should resign over abuses at Iraq's Abu Ghraib prison; Bush's May 24 speech defending his policies and decisions in the Iraq war; national energy policy in light of the rising price of gasoline during the spring of 2004; the Senate Intelligence Committee's July report on U.S. intelligence concerning prewar information on Iraq's weapons of mass destruction; Kerry's selection of North Carolina U.S. Senator John Edwards as a running mate; the Democratic and Republican national conventions; the three presidential debates; the controversy raised by Vietnam War veterans over Kerry's service during the war in Southeast Asia and his antiwar protest activity afterward; and the newspapers' editorial endorsements.

Two sets of competing newspapers were analyzed in three markets. One was direct competition markets as analyzed in Chapter 2, in which the newspapers in the same city are separately owned and are independent in all areas of operation. For these markets, the analyzed editorials were published by the *Boston*

Globe and the *Boston Herald* and the *Chicago Tribune* and the *Chicago Sun-Times*. The second was JOA markets as analyzed in Chapter 3. The JOA markets analyzed were Denver, where the *Denver Post* and the *Rocky Mountain News* competed, and Seattle, where the *Seattle Times* competed with its JOA partner, the *Seattle Post-Intelligencer*. The third market was metroplex competition newspapers as analyzed in Chapter 4. The analyzed editorials were published by the *Pittsburgh Post-Gazette* and the *Tribune-Review* and the *Dallas Morning News* and the *Fort Worth Star-Telegram*.

Coding for this analysis identified four categories of editorials: those that differed for reasons of political ideology, those that differed for reasons of framing, those that generally agreed in their analysis or conclusions, and those that did not appear (subjects for which no editorial could be found by one of the two competing newspapers). Also, this research drew on a tally of editorial endorsements conducted by *Editor & Publisher* magazine and published during the campaign on its web site, focusing on the markets identified in this book's Introduction as being either JOA or direct competition daily newspaper markets (see Table I.1). The six markets and twelve newspapers used for the analysis of the twelve election campaign issues were selected during the summer of 2004.

DIRECT MARKET COMPETITION NEWSPAPERS

Distinct diversity of editorial voice was found in the direct market competition. In the Boston market, nine of the twelve editorial subjects analyzed produced ideological differences, and three offered diverse voices for reasons of framing. Both newspapers editorialized on all twelve subjects. In Chicago, the newspapers disagreed ideologically on two issues, which included a key difference, their endorsements. They differed in framing in four editorials, one of them quite dramatically when the *Sun-Times* criticized its rival by name for its treatment of the Vietnam service controversy. Editorials in three categories—the Senate committee intelligence report, Kerry's selection of Edwards as his running mate, and the third presidential debate—could not be found in the *Sun-Times*. No ideological or framing differences were found in the Chicago editorials in three of the categories: whether Rumsfeld should resign because of the prison abuse scandal (both newspapers leaned against resignation), the president's speech on his Iraq war policies and decisions (both were generally supportive), and the second presidential debate (both saw it as beneficial to the voters). So, in the Boston market this analysis found 100 percent diversity, either ideologically (75 percent) or for framing (25 percent), and in the Chicago market it found 66.6 percent diversity, 22.2 percent for ideological reasons, 44.4 percent for reasons of framing, and three subject categories that did not produce editorials from both newspapers and thus offered no opportunity for analysis concerning differences or agreements.

Overall, the two direct competition markets produced agreement on three subjects, which accounted for 14.3 percent of the twenty-one editorial subjects addressed by all newspapers (of a possible twenty-four). Ideological disagreement was found for eleven subjects (52.4 percent), and seven subject areas revealed framing differences (33.3 percent). Thus, the total percentage for editorial subjects drawing diversity of opinion (ideology and framing combined) was 85.7 percent (see Table 5.1).

JOA MARKET NEWSPAPERS

The JOA markets also produced editorial diversity, though less marked than that of the direct competition market. In the Denver JOA, the *Post* and the *Rocky Mountain News* disagreed for reasons of ideology on just two of the twelve issues: the first presidential debate and the Kerry Vietnam controversy. The newspapers differed in framing on five subjects. These were the Rumsfeld/prison abuse controversy, gasoline prices, Kerry's selection of Edwards, the GOP convention, and the third presidential debate. They found general agreement on four topics: Bush's Iraq speech, the Senate intelligence report, the Democratic convention, and the presidential endorsement (Bush, but with a distinct difference of tone—see below). No editorial could be found in the *Rocky Mountain News* on the second presidential debate.

Table 5.1   Direct Competition Markets

	Chicago				Boston			
	A	D-I	D-F	NO	A	D-I	D-F	NO
Rumsfeld	x					x		
Iraq speech	x					x		
Gas prices		x					x	
Intelligence report				Sun-Times		x		
Edwards for VP				Sun-Times		x		
Democratic convention			x			x		
GOP convention			x			x		
Debate 1			x					x
Debate 2	x							x
Debate 3				Sun-Times		x		
Swift boat controversy			x			x		
Endorse		x				x		
Total (two editorials per item)	6	4	8	3		18	6	

A, agree; D-I, disagree ideology; D-F, disagree framing; NO, no opinion by one of the two papers.

The Seattle newspapers did not disagree once for ideological or philosophical reasons, but they produced framing differences on five subjects. These were Bush's Iraq speech, gas prices, the Democratic convention, the Republican convention, and the third presidential debate. They found common ground on five subjects: Rumsfeld/prison abuse, the Senate intelligence report, the selection of Edwards by Kerry, the first debate, and in their endorsements (both supported Kerry). Two subjects failed to draw editorials from the *Times,* and for one of these, the second presidential debate, the *Post-Intelligencer* chose this occasion to publish its endorsement editorial supporting Kerry rather than a commentary on the debate.

Considering the eleven total editorial subjects discussed by both newspapers, the Denver market produced 63.7 percent diversity, 18.2 percent of which was for ideological reasons and 45.5 percent for reasons of framing. The analysis of the Seattle market found 50 percent diversity, all for reasons of framing, with two subjects ignored by one of the newspapers and thus not counted in the total.

Overall, the two JOA markets produced agreement on nine subjects, which was 42.9 percent of the twenty-one editorial subjects addressed by all JOA newspapers (of a possible twenty-four total); two subjects on which they disagreed for reasons of ideology (9.5 percent); and ten subject areas on which they differed in framing (47.6 percent). Thus, the total percentage for editorial subjects drawing diversity of opinion (ideology and framing) was 57.1 percent (see Table 5.2).

Table 5.2   JOA Competition Markets

	Seattle				Denver			
	A	D-I	D-F	NO	A	D-I	D-F	NO
Rumsfeld	x						x	
Iraq speech			x		x			
Gas prices			x				x	
Intelligence report	x				x			
Edwards for VP	x						x	
Democratic convention			x		x			
GOP convention			x				x	
Debate 1	x					x		
Debate 2				Times				News
Debate 3			x				x	
Swift boat controversy				Times		x		
Endorse	x				x			
Total (two editorials per item)	10		10	2	8	4	10	1

A, agree; D-I, disagree ideology; D-F, disagree framing; NO, no opinion by one of the two papers.

METROPLEX MARKET NEWSPAPERS

The metroplex market produced marked editorial diversity in one set of competing newspapers and a unique finding in the other: a noticeable absence of editorial voice on the majority of the twelve issues by one of the competing newspapers in the Dallas/Fort Worth market. In the Pittsburgh/Greensburg market, the *Post-Gazette* and the *Tribune-Review* disagreed for reasons of ideology on three issues—whether Rumsfeld should resign, the president's Iraq speech, and in their endorsements. The newspapers produced framing difference on five subjects —gas prices, Kerry's selection of Edwards, the Democratic convention, and the first and third debates. Limiting the number of categories for comparison, no *Tribune-Review* editorials were found on the Senate intelligence report, the GOP convention, and the second presidential debate. None appeared in the *Post-Gazette* on the Vietnam service controversy.

The Dallas/Fort Worth newspapers disagreed ideologically on just one topic, the first presidential debate. They varied in framing on three topics. These were the president's Iraq speech, the GOP convention, and the Vietnam War controversy. They agreed on one topic, the endorsement of Bush. The most remarkable finding for this market was the high number of issues that did not draw editorials (commentary that could be found within a week of the event) from the *Star-Telegram*. The newspaper failed to editorialize on seven topics, which accounted for more than half of the total number of subjects analyzed. The ignored topics were the Rumsfeld/prison scandal issue, the high gasoline prices, the Senate intelligence report, Kerry's selection of Edwards as his running mate, the Democratic convention, and the second and third presidential debates.

Considering the eight editorial subjects discussed by both newspapers, the Pittsburgh/Greensburg market produced 100 percent diversity, 37.5 percent for reasons of ideology and 62.5 percent for reasons of framing. Of the five subjects on which both newspapers editorialized, the Dallas/Fort Worth market produced 80 percent diversity, 20 percent for ideology and 60 percent for framing. But the lack of editorials for comparison in this market was important; the subjects that failed to draw any editorials from both newspapers accounted for 58.3 percent of the twelve editorial subjects.

The two metroplex markets produced agreement on one subject. This accounted for 7.7 percent of the thirteen editorial subjects addressed by all newspapers (of a possible twenty-four). The analysis found four subjects on which the newspapers disagreed for reasons of ideology or philosophy (30.8 percent), and eight subject areas in which they differed in framing (61.5 percent). Thus, the total percentage for editorial subjects drawing diversity of opinion (ideology and framing) was 92.3 percent. But the significance of this finding is diminished by the high rate of subjects, 45.8 percent, that produced no opinion in both markets (see Table 5.3).

The endorsement record of the twelve newspapers analyzed throughout the campaign found complete disagreement in both of the direct competition

Table 5.3   Metroplex Competition Markets

	Pittsburgh/Greensburg				Dallas/Fort Worth			
	A	D-I	D-F	NO	A	D-I	D-F	NO
Rumsfeld		x						Star-Telegram
Iraq speech		x					x	
Gas prices			x					Star-Telegram
Intelligence report				Tribune-Review				Star-Telegram
Edwards for VP			x					Star-Telegram
Democratic convention			x					Star-Telegram
GOP convention				Tribune-Review			x	
Debate 1			x		x			
Debate 2				Tribune-Review				Star-Telegram
Debate 3			x					Star-Telegram
Swift boat controversy				Post-Gazette			x	
Endorse	x				x			
Total (two editorials per item)		6	10	4	2	2	6	7

A, agree; D-I, disagree ideology; D-F, disagree framing; NO, no opinion by one of the two papers.

markets (100 percent, with the *Chicago Tribune* and the *Boston Herald* supporting Bush and the *Chicago Sun-Times* and the *Boston Globe* supporting Kerry). It found complete agreement in the JOA markets (100 percent, with the *Denver Post* and the *Rocky Mountain News* both supporting Bush and the *Seattle Times* and the *Post-Intelligencer* coming out for Kerry). The metroplex markets split [50 percent, with both newspapers in the Dallas/Fort Worth market supporting Bush and the two newspapers in the Pittsburgh/Greensburg market dividing over Bush (*Tribune-Review*) and Kerry (*Post-Gazette*)].

EDITOR & PUBLISHER TALLY

The *Editor & Publisher* summary produced similar results as the twelve-subject analysis for the direct market competition, but it revealed greater ideological diversity in the JOA markets. Of the separate newspaper cities (direct competition markets) listed in Table I.1, five produced split, or opposing, endorsements: Washington, D.C. (*Post* for Kerry and *Times* for Bush); Chicago (*Sun-Times* for Kerry and *Tribune* for Bush); Boston (the *Globe* backed Kerry and the *Herald* supported Bush); Trenton, NJ (*Times* for Kerry and the *Trentonian* for Bush); and

New York City (*Times* for Kerry and *Daily News, Post,* and *Sun* for Bush). Two of these markets supported the same candidate: Honolulu (the *Advertiser* and the *Star-Bulletin* both backed Kerry) and Wilkes-Barre (the *Citizens' Voice* and the *Times Leader* both supported Kerry). And *Editor & Publisher* found that one of the competing newspapers failed to endorse in four markets: San Francisco (the *Chronicle* supported Kerry); Columbia, Missouri (the *Daily Tribune* endorsed Kerry); Green Bay, Wisconsin (the *News-Chronicle* backed Kerry); and Kingsport, Tennessee (the *Times-News* liked Bush). So of the eleven direct competition markets, seven of them offered endorsement editorials from the competing newspapers. Of these seven, five of the competitors differed in their endorsements, which was a diversity percentage of 71.4 percent. Two supported the same candidate, for an agreement percentage of 28.6 percent. The four markets that did not produce editorials from the competing newspapers accounted for 36.4 percent of the eleven direct competition markets. The direct competition newspapers thus offered a marked difference of ideological opinion.

In the JOA tally, *Editor & Publisher* found opposing endorsements in five of the thirteen markets: Fort Wayne, Indiana, (the *Journal Gazette* supported Kerry and the *News-Sentinel* Bush); Las Vegas, Nevada, (the *Sun* backed Kerry and the *Review-Journal* endorsed Bush); Albuquerque, New Mexico, (the *Tribune* backed Kerry and the *Journal* Bush); Charleston, West Virginia, (the *Gazette* came out for Kerry and the *Daily Mail* for Bush); and Madison, Wisconsin, (the *Capital Times* liked Kerry and the *State Journal* Bush). Four of the JOA market newspapers backed the same candidate. They were Birmingham, Alabama, (Bush); Denver (Bush); Cincinnati (Bush); and Seattle (Kerry). Four JOA markets did not produce endorsement editorials from both participants. These were Tucson (the *Daily Star* endorsed Kerry); Salt Lake City (the *Tribune* backed Bush); Detroit (the *Free Press* endorsed Kerry); and York, Pennsylvania (the *Daily Record* endorsed Bush). So, of the nine JOA markets that offered endorsement editorials, 55.6 percent of them differed in their endorsements, and 44.4 percent of them supported the same candidate. The four markets that did not produce editorials from one of the competing newspapers accounted for 30.8 percent of the thirteen JOA newspaper markets. The JOA newspapers thus offered a less pronounced difference of ideological opinion in their endorsement editorials than did the direct competition markets.

The metroplex markets were less clearly defined than the direct competition and JOA markets, but some other communities that lend themselves to this sort of market analysis would include Saint Paul/Minneapolis, Minnesota (*Pioneer Press* and *Star Tribune*) and the Los Angeles metroplex (*Times, Daily News, Orange County Register*). These markets, in addition to the Pittsburgh/Greensburg and Dallas/Fort Worth markets, produced no clear divisions or trends: the Saint Paul/Minneapolis newspapers split, with the *Saint Paul Pioneer Press* backing Bush; and *Editor & Publisher* found only one endorsement among the three Los Angeles newspapers, with the *Daily News* backing Kerry. The Pittsburgh market, as noted, split.

EVIDENCE OF DIVERSITY

The direct competition newspapers in both sets of data (the twelve campaign issues analysis and the *Editor & Publisher* scorecard) offered strong evidence of markets providing their readers two distinct kinds of editorial diversity. In the *Editor & Publisher* tally, these newspapers offered an ideological diversity rating of 71.4 percent. The magazine analysis produced no evidence of the other kind of diversity—framing—as it considered only support for or opposition to the Democratic and Republican candidates.

The analysis of newspaper editorials on campaign issues produced a similar finding as the *Editor & Publisher* tally for the direct competition market. Considering editorials that differed for reasons of ideology and framing combined, this market produced a diversity rating of 85.7 percent. A slight majority of this diversity, 52.4 percent, was political ideology disagreement. An example of ideological variance was found in the editorials of the *Chicago Tribune* and its rival on the gasoline price spike of the spring of 2004. The *Tribune*, adopting a policy of the presidential candidate it ended up opposing (Kerry), called for higher gasoline taxes. "In order to force U.S. drivers into a leaner gasoline diet and lessen our reliance on foreign oil, the federal government should sharply increase taxes at the pump," urged the newspaper. It then went on to differ with its eventual presidential candidate of choice, Bush, over increased drilling. "Bush's idea to drill our way out of the problem—with little effort to conserve fuel—would also do little to help. Drilling cannot keep up with America's growing appetite for oil."[14] The *Sun-Times* took the opposite stance, siding with the philosophy of the incumbent president it ended up opposing in its endorsement editorial. "If we want to drive the cost of gas down, we're going to have to drill for more oil or consume less fuel."[15] The editorial also called for a switch by consumers to more fuel-efficient transportation through increased fuel-efficiency standards or through voluntary purchase of more gas-efficient automobiles. It did not suggest, though, tax hikes to encourage this.

In Boston, the *Globe* and *Herald* offered ideological differences in their observations of the Democratic National Convention. The *Globe* editorialist wrote of the image that Kerry put forth during his acceptance speech. The writer opined that the "importance of image—that elusive combination of looks, likeability, and values—may frustrate political and policy experts. But even delegates, in informal conversations this week, agree that Kerry must continue to demonstrate his passion for leadership as well as his sense of duty. To paraphrase former President Bill Clinton: Emotion and wisdom are not opposing values."[16] But whereas the *Globe* suggested that Kerry's military credentials were sound, the *Herald* argued otherwise. The newspaper criticized Kerry for his voting record on defense appropriations and intelligence service funding, concluding that he had not provided enough reason for the nation to oust a wartime president: "The Kerry vision for this nation remains a work in progress. The rhetoric of hope and optimism is surely uplifting, but a nation needs to hear more than catchy phrases to oust an incumbent president."[17]

The Chicago newspapers produced one of the sharper disagreements found in this study in their editorials on the allegations by Swift Boat veterans of the Vietnam War that Kerry had not earned his war medals. The *Tribune*, concluding that the debate "resolves in Kerry's favor," argued that Bush's distancing himself from the accusations against Kerry "should be the end of the debate about John Kerry's experience in Vietnam."[18] The *Sun-Times* opined that much of the debate "is Kerry's own fault" because he "held up his service as iconic, emphasizing his few months in Vietnam over his many years in the U.S. Senate." The newspaper concluded that the allegations on this issue "are childish squabbles, not worthy of the great democratic traditions of this country, and can only be remedied by restraint and candor on both sides." In a sidebar editorial, however, in language reminiscent of penny press-era newspaper attacks on rival sheets, the newspaper took aim at its competitor for a column written by a *Tribune* editor, William B. Rood, who had served in Vietnam with Kerry. The Tribune column defended Kerry and other Vietnam combat veterans.

> There is something disquieting in the silence of *Chicago Tribune* editor William B. Rood, who says he knew of facts supporting the beleaguered Democratic candidate and his account of events, but said nothing and did nothing until the campaign came looking for him and asked for his support.
>
> Only then did he come forward with his story. That makes one wonder. As does Rood's telling the story only once, for his newspaper, and then refusing to answer the legitimate questions about his account. This is a matter of both political and historical importance, too vital to be allowed to be influenced by selfish motives.[19]

The JOA market newspapers in both sets of analyses produced similar overall percentages of diversity. In the *Editor & Publisher* listing of presidential endorsements, the JOA newspapers produced a diversity rate of 55.6 percent. In the analysis of the twelve presidential campaign issues, this market produced an overall (ideology plus framing) diversity of opinion rate of 57.1 percent. Much of this difference, though, 47.6 percent, was for framing rather than ideology. So, the JOA market was much less ideologically diverse in the twelve-issue analysis than it was in the *Editor & Publisher* endorsement analysis.

The Denver JOA market offered an example of framing diversity in the editorials on Kerry's selection of Edwards as a running mate. While neither newspaper hailed or criticized the selection, they differed in how it might have helped Kerry's candidacy. The *Denver Post* suggested that Dick Gephardt, the U.S. representative from Missouri, may have been a better choice but that Edwards might help Kerry in some regions of the country. "His style and message could serve Democrats well in the industrialized swing states of Ohio, Missouri and Pennsylvania. If so, the Bush-Cheney ticket could be in serious trouble," the newspaper said.[20] The *Rocky Mountain News* said the selection "confirms a bold strategy" by Kerry to try to compete, not in the industrialized swing states, as the *Post* had suggested, but in the South. And it added an opinion, on domestic policy issues, that the *Post* editorial had not. "Edwards is undeniably intelligent and energetic, and does not seem the least bit mean-spirited," said the *News*. "If he lacks foreign policy gravitas, so did George W. Bush before his election. We just wish the North Carolina senator's vision of the economy involved more prescriptions for growth and fewer calls for class warfare."[21]

The Seattle JOA market provided evidence of framing differences in the *Times'* and *Post-Intelligencer's* commentaries on the Democratic National Convention. The *Times* questioned how Kerry would make his budget numbers add up to his campaign promises of creating jobs and undoing President Bush's tax cuts for the wealthy before concluding that Kerry and Edwards "have started to make the case for new leadership."[22] The *Post-Intelligencer* also questioned the Democratic candidate, but for different reasons that suggested, if not an ideological parting with its rival, a difference in agenda and topic (war) instead. "It's one thing to say the United States 'never goes to war because we want to,'" the newspaper said, quoting Kerry. "It's quite another matter to bring our troops home quickly—without leaving a toxic trail behind." Also, the *Post-Intelligencer* concluded its editorial with a different frame; instead of suggesting that the Democrats had begun the process of changing leadership, it simply noted noncommittally that "elections are about choices. The time for such consideration about the country's future has begun."[23]

One of the more remarkable findings of the JOA study was in the analysis of the Denver newspapers' endorsement editorials. This finding suggests that while two rival newspapers might agree in their conclusions (and they did, both endorsing Bush for re-election), marked differences can be found in editorials in their tone and reasoning. In its ten-paragraph editorial supporting the incumbent, the *Rocky Mountain News* put forth a positive assessment of its candidate of choice, citing the Bush doctrine of preemptive strikes against potential enemies in response to the September 11, 2001, terrorist attacks against the United States and supporting the goals of the president's domestic agenda. It concluded: "America is a huge, energetic, resourceful nation whose fate does not hinge on the politics of one man. The question is which candidate's vision is more likely to make us safer, freer and more prosperous than his rival's. For us, the answer is George W. Bush."[24]

About a week later, the *Post* responded with a thirty-one paragraph editorial that seemed almost as much an argument with itself as with the rival newspaper. The editorial, apparently written by a committee and evidence of a divided editorial board, opened with an indictment of the Bush presidency. It observed that one of the key questions regarding an incumbent is, "Are we, as Coloradoans, better off today than we were four years ago? In a word, no." The editorial observed that household and medical costs had gone up, and 90,000 state residents had lost health coverage, "Washington is ringing up record deficits and sticking the next generation with the bill. In Iraq, Colorado-based military units and reserves are deployed in a hostile environment for questionable purposes and an uncertain result." The editorial found both candidates qualified, "and we don't think the world will come to an end if voters turn to the Democrat." The newspaper then switched its attention to Kerry, questioning his decisions in Congress, his "willingness to consider firm military options when American strength is being tested," and his "emphasis on putting U.S. policy to a global test." Back to Bush, the editorial said its support for the incumbent "is tempered by unease over the poor choices and results of his first term. To succeed in his second-term, Bush must begin by taking responsibility for U.S. failures in Iraq, admit his mistakes and adjust U.S. strategy. Big time, as his running mate might say." The editorial continued in that spirit until the conclusion, when it arrived back where it began, citing the September 11, 2001, terrorist attack and then citing former President Ronald Reagan's hard line toward the Soviet Union. "That's the kind of leadership the United States should offer. We believe George W. Bush is up to the challenge."[25] This was a remarkable difference in tone, if not framing, in two editorials that agreed ideologically in their conclusions.

The metroplex market analysis provided abundant evidence of differences in framing and in ideology, and, as in the Denver JOA market, of strong differences of tone in endorsement editorials. The Pittsburgh/Greensburg market offered marked ideological and framing differences, whereas the Dallas/Fort Worth market revealed a different kind of editorial competitive relationship. The Texas market not only provided some difference in editorial framing but also demonstrated somewhat of a monopoly voice by one of the metroplex rivals, the *Dallas Morning News*, through an absence of editorial voice by the *Fort Worth Star-Telegram* on several of the analyzed issues. Absence of an editorial voice on a topic can have meaning, just as a decision by the U.S. Supreme Court not to hear a case has legal significance because it upholds a lower court ruling and it affirms the *status quo*. As suggested by the Fedler, Counts, and Stephens study cited above, failure by a competing newspaper to editorialize on a subject lends more weight to the opinion of the newspaper that editorializes on that subject. Also, it raises several questions about the reason that a newspaper's editorial board chooses not to discuss a particular subject. These reasons can range from the perceived importance placed on a topic by the editorial board to the board's lack of knowledge about it.

Nonetheless, this market analysis did find some revealing differences. The Pittsburgh/Greensburg market offered a distinct difference of opinion, based on ideology, in the newspapers' commentaries on the Rumsfeld/prison abuse controversy. The *Post-Gazette* called for the departure of the defense secretary to set an example and send a message to the American forces, "who are truly disgusted at what has taken place. It is also the American forces, who are Mr. Rumsfeld's responsibility, who will see what happened to him and will not repeat those acts in Iraq, or anywhere else."[26] The *Tribune-Review*, though, offered a list of Americans who would not want to see Rumsfeld go. The list included the president, "reasonable people," and "us.... Those few who perpetuated the heinous acts against the Iraqi detainees are being brought to justice. *They* should pay the price for *their* illegalities. We need Don Rumsfeld to get on with prosecuting the war [emphasis by the newspaper]."[27]

The Pittsburgh/Greensburg market offered a stark difference in framing in the editorials on the Democratic National Convention. The *Post-Gazette* put forth a rather tepid summary of the proceedings. "In any case, last week gave Americans a chance to get to know Mr. Kerry and other Democratic leaders, and to consider what difference it would make to the country if they, rather than Mr. Bush and the Republicans, occupied the White House and the majority in Congress."[28] But the *Tribune-Review* chose to ignore the Kerry message and instead set an agenda for President Bush to address at his party's convention in the context of issues he had promised to take on in his first term.

> School choice? Social Security reform? Tort reform? Less government? These and so many other promises for "best days" have fallen by the wayside. Instead, political capital is squandered on such nonstarters as the federal marriage amendment.
>
> If, in fact, the Bush campaign kowtows to moderates and liberals, assuming that core supporters who came out four years ago will do so again, Nov. 2 will be a grim day of reckoning."[29]

In one of the few editorial subjects addressed by both newspapers in the Dallas/Fort Worth market, the Swift Boat Vietnam service controversy, the newspapers offered an example of framing differences. They addressed the issue from different sides, the *Star-Telegram* questioning at length the credibility of the Swift Boat Veterans for Truth in the group's criticism of Kerry's war service, and the *Dallas Morning News* questioning Kerry's believability. Their framing also differed in their conclusions. Opining that reasonable people would disagree about Kerry's antiwar statements, the *Star-Telegram* said the election should be about "health care, the economy, education, energy, the environment, national security and America's role in the world."[30] The *Morning News* in its final paragraph offered a similar sentiment regarding the relevance of this issue; but rather than citing the importance of the domestic agenda, as its rival did, it focused on the war. "Frankly, we care less about what John Kerry did in a war 35 years ago—and what George W. Bush did not do there—than we care about what both men would do in the war America's fighting today. Each day spent disputing Vietnam is a day not spent talking about the countries that matter most to America's present and immediate future: Iraq, Iran and North Korea."[31]

Both of these metroplex markets produced editorial endorsement variations similar to that found in Denver. The Dallas and Fort Worth newspapers agreed that Bush should be re-elected. But the *Star-Telegram*, in contrast to the *Morning News'* staunch, positive endorsement of Bush, criticized the president's handling of the Iraq war and of some domestic issues, including Social Security, Medicare, health care and environmental standards. The editorial concluded with a plea for the "old" Bush: "In short, we expect to see the George W. Bush whom we sent to Washington in the first place."[32] And in the Pittsburgh/Greensburg market, in contrast to the *Post-Gazette*'s forthright endorsement of Kerry, the *Tribune-Review* offered a list of faults of the president. These included the Medicare prescription drug plan, "runaway domestic spending," immigration policy, and the handling of the Iraq war. The newspaper then swallowed hard and came out for Bush's re-election, opining that "even this president's worst failures are preferable to John Kerry's best plans."[33]

This market, then, offered evidence of editorial diversity, both framing and ideological; but these differences may depend, in part, on regional influences and those of ownership. The *Tribune-Review* in the Pittsburgh market, for example, has an owner with strong conservative credentials, while the *Post-Gazette* ownership has a more moderate reputation. The Dallas market is known historically for its cultural and political conservatism. The emerging metroplex market phenomenon, which is a type of market that could be on the rise as the process of newspaper closure and consolidation continues, is one that warrants continued study.

These findings suggest many factors and influences upon editorials: Ownership can play a role in editorial decisions, as shown in the generally conservative bents of papers such as the *Boston Herald* and Greensburg *Tribune-Review*; the dominant cultures of certain geographical areas might influence editorial and public opinion, as shown in the Dallas/Fort Worth, Denver, and Seattle regions; and communities with a history of pluralistic cultures and diverse journalistic enterprise and opinion might produce political and cultural splits, as shown in the Chicago and Boston markets.

What these findings do not support, however, is that newspaper editorials play a decisive role in setting political agendas. Considering *Editor & Publisher*'s finding that more newspapers of greater circulation supported Kerry, Bush would not have been re-elected president of the United States had the dominant editorial opinion held sway.

These findings strongly suggest, though, the existence—even in those communities that did not split in their editorial endorsements—of a lively marketplace of ideas and of diverse opinion when two or more newspapers battle not only for advertising revenue and circulation, but for ideas and thought. Indeed, even when both newspapers in some markets agreed upon who ought to lead the country in the White House, they sometimes found different reasons for their conclusions. They often presented diverse explanations and justification, and they sometimes found themselves in opposition over framing and agenda-setting issues such as why and how leadership ought to be carried out.

In those communities where newspapers disagreed over leadership, even more evidence was found of diversity. This evidence frequently was seen in unequivocal, unyielding language that demonstrated the existence of *bona fide* political, and cultural, disagreement. The diversity found in these analyses simply does not exist in monopoly newspaper markets, which now are the dominant markets in the United States.

The editorial variances found, ranging from subtle differences in tone and framing to outright ideological battling, is evidence of the kind of discussion, difference, divergence, and dualism that the builders of this democracy and its advocates have insisted is vital to maintaining a democracy. The disappearance of this kind of diversity is a symptom of a changing American economic and political climate that threatens the maintenance of a democracy that depends on pluralism and multiculturalism. It is a system of government that even those who have opposed each other on the bench of the nation's highest court have recognized requires an availability of opposing and different thoughts, ideas, and ideals in the public forum.

CHAPTER 6

The Good Fight: Editorialists Enjoy Competition

Few who consider the matter seriously will justify such a war. Men who would not hesitate a moment, if their country was invaded or its honor and good name were at stake, to offer their lives to save it, have not been able to see any justification for this war of sympathy with Cuba. They fail to see why they should sacrifice their lives and those of their sons for such sympathy. They fail to understand why it is necessary to fill this land with widows and orphans out of sympathy to the Cubans. . . . The first hostile gun fired at an American ship by the Spaniards compels every patriot in the United States to range himself under its flag and against its foes, and he will fight with the best and bravest; but he will know all the time that he has been driven into an unjust and unnecessary war, to satisfy the demands of men who, for political purposes solely, have desired to plunge the republic into foreign war.

—New Orleans Times-Democrat, April 15, 1898,
on the looming Spanish-American War[1]

Editorial page editors of daily newspapers in competing markets believe that communities benefit from editorial competition, but they do not believe the format of editorials that they are writing today will be around a half century from now. These are two findings of a survey of the daily newspaper editorial page editors in competing daily newspaper markets conducted through the Internet and through telephone interviews for this book.

In other findings, these editors consider their commentaries to be important contributors to American culture and political dialogue, but they believe that the public, business community, and politicians tend to place less importance on editorials today than they have historically. None of these editors, though, views Internet web sites or cable television as significant threats to or competitors of the daily newspaper editorial page.

These findings were gleaned from a questionnaire sent by e-mail in October 2004 to editorial page editors of eighteen newspapers whose editorials were analyzed in the previous chapters of this book. The editors responded to the survey over a three-month period (from October through December). While the selection of these newspapers was not random because of the limited number of competing newspaper markets in existence today, fourteen of them belonged to the small number of daily newspapers that continued to operate in the nation's twenty-four competing editorial markets as of 2003 (see Table I.1). Six of these newspapers were in direct competition markets. They are the *Boston Globe* and *Herald*, *Chicago Tribune* and *Sun-Times*, and Wilkes-Barre, Pennsylvania, *Times Leader* and *Citizens' Voice*. Eight of them were part of JOA markets. They are the *Seattle Times* and *Post-Intelligencer*, the *Denver Post* and *Rocky Mountain News*, the Fort Wayne, Indiana, *Journal Gazette* and *News-Sentinel*, and the *Cincinnati Enquirer* and *Post*. Four of them belonged to what has been identified in this book as metroplex markets. They are the *Pittsburgh Post-Gazette* and Greensburg, Pennsylvania, *Tribune-Review*, and the *Dallas Morning News* and *Fort Worth Star-Telegram*.

Twelve of the eighteen editors participated in the survey, a response rate of 66.7 percent. However, the author does not claim statistical validity for this percentage because of the small pool of participants; the importance of this survey is anecdotal. All but one of the respondents were editorial page editors; the managing editor of the Wilkes-Barre *Citizens' Voice* responded for his newspaper. The editorial page editor of the *Cincinnati Post* filled out the survey but chose not to elaborate on the answers because of disagreement with the method. All but one of the surveys were completed by e-mail; the editorial page editor of the *Dallas Morning News* answered the questions during a telephone interview. The editors were presented eleven statements requiring one of five responses: Strongly Agree, Agree, No Opinion, Disagree, Strongly Disagree. Responses that did not indicate one of these five answers were listed under "No Opinion." Participants were invited to elaborate on each response. They also were asked four open-ended questions, and respondents in the metroplex markets were asked one additional question. Editors from the following newspapers did not participate: JOA newspapers the *Cincinnati Enquirer*, the *Denver Post* and the *Rocky Mountain News*, and direct competition newspapers the *Chicago Sun-Times*, the *Boston Herald*, and the Wilkes-Barre *Times Leader*. Following are the statements.

1. It is important that a community has more than one daily editorial voice.
2. Members of my community view one of its two dominant daily newspapers as being liberal, or Democratic, and the other as being conservative, or Republican.
3. Conglomeration and monopoly ownership in the American newspaper industry has affected editorial diversity and competitiveness.
4. Newspaper editorials are important contributors to the American cultural and political dialogue.
5. Editorial competition and diversity in cities that have more than one daily newspaper is as vigorous as it once was.
6. The newspaper editorial as I have known it in my career and lifetime will still be with us fifty years from now.
7. Publishers today, whether of chain-owned or independent daily newspapers, place as much importance on editorials as publishers did in the past.
8. Historically, American politicians, business and community officials, and the reading public regarded newspaper editorials as important.
9. Today, American politicians, business and community officials, and the reading public place as much importance on newspaper editorials as they did in the past.
10. The increase of opinions made available by cable television and the Internet has made daily newspaper editorials less important or meaningful.
11. Cable television and the Internet serve as adequate replacements for daily newspapers lost because of a newspaper's closure.

Following are the open-ended questions.

1. Can you cite any examples of issues or controversies over which you and your competition have disagreed in editorials?
2. Are there ways in which competing editorials can differ other than ideologically?
3. Why is the newspaper editorial important?
4. Any additional comments you wish to make?

The following question was asked only of newspapers in the metroplex markets.

1. Do you consider your newspaper and the (name of metroplex rival newspaper) to be in competition, both in your newsrooms and on your editorial pages?

All editors were told at the beginning of the survey that any comments they made were subject to quotation and that they would be identified in the discussion of the findings by name, by title, and by the names of their newspapers. Also, three newspaper editorial page editors were asked follow-up questions for the purpose of explanation of some findings.

EDITORIALS THROUGH TIME AND TECHNOLOGY

Two-thirds of the survey respondents, 66.7 percent, believed the editorial as they know it today will not be in existence fifty years from 2004; and slightly more than half, 58.3 percent, said publishers today place as much importance on editorials as did publishers of the past (see Table 6.1). As for editorial roles and perceptions in the past, half of the respondents had no opinion on whether editorial competition and diversity in cities with more than one daily newspaper is as vigorous as it once was. This finding offers at least two interpretations: that the editors have no great understanding or appreciation of American editorial history, or that they do not believe historical editorial diversity and competition has much relevance in the analysis of the modern editorial marketplace. In their responses to questions eight and nine, all of the respondents agreed strongly (41.7 percent) or agreed (58.3 percent) that American politicians, business and community leaders, and the reading public historically have regarded newspaper editorials as important; but these numbers decreased when the same question was

Table 6.1   Editorial Editors' Attitudes on Editorial Issues

	Strongly agree	Agree	No opinion	Disagree	Strongly disagree
Competition is beneficial	8	2		2	
Conservative versus liberal	2	4	3	3	
Conglomeration effects	3	5	1	3	
Newspaper editorials important	7	5			
Editorial diversity still vigorous	1	1	6	4	
Editorials 50 years from now	2	1	1	8	
Publishers see editorials as important	2	5	3	2	
Editorials historically important	5	7			
Level of importance today	3	4	1	4	
Cable, internet effect on editorials		4	2	2	4
Cable, internet as substitutes for newspapers			2	4	6

asked about modern attitudes involving this same reading audience. The number of editors who strongly agreed with the statement declined to 25 percent, while the number of those who agreed with the statement declined to 33.3 percent. Four respondents, 33.3 percent, disagreed with the statement, and one (8.3 percent) had no opinion. So, editorial page editors were less sure about reader esteem of their product in modern times in relation to how they believed that readers viewed editorials historically.

For example, James Vesely of the *Seattle Times* believed that editorials today "are too often written for and about the power structure rather than the reader. It's easy to connect with the politically and academically powerful and write either in support or criticism of them. I worry we are too often out of touch with folks working on the loading dock, or teaching a class or going into the Navy. Elitism is an easy thing to fall into."

He cited the increasing number of sources for commentary as a reason that editorials are seen as less important today. "Politicians respond to their advocacy base, and that base often bypasses newspapers for talk radio, the Internet and direct mail. Newspapers are still seen as the biggest blog on the block in local communities, but increasingly historical figures rather than dynamic agents of change." As for the Internet and cable television serving as adequate substitutes for daily newspapers, he said not yet. "The trick will be for newspapers to move into cyber rather than staying in fiber. The newspaper can live if it transforms itself into a different delivery system, keeping the news and opinion product but going online all the time."

These reasons are the same ones for which Vesely saw daily newspaper editorials as less important or meaningful and why he believed the newspaper editorial he knows will not be around in another fifty years. "The structural changes within newspapers are fundamentally changing methods of delivery and response times to the point where editorials may flow as blogs throughout the day."

Vesely's rival, *Post-Intelligencer* editorial page editor Mark Trahant, wrote that he saw no important change in readers' perceptions of editorial roles over time. "One way to gauge this is by endorsements. We don't have the resources to interview and endorse every elected office—yet folks are always calling and seeking us out. Even when they know we're not likely to agree."

Trahant agreed with Vesely that the newspaper editorial likely will be different fifty years hence. "However, what won't change is the need for discourse in a democratic society. Different groups need to talk to one another—and editorial pages can help bring about that conversation."

Half of the responding editors disagreed (two) or strongly disagreed (four) that the increase of opinions made available by the Internet or cable television has rendered daily newspaper editorials less important or meaningful, while ten of them (83.3 percent) registered disagreement (four) or strong disagreement (six) that the Internet or cable television serve as an adequate substitute for newspapers lost because of closure.

Some editors argued that newspaper editorials offer greater context and rely more on research than do opinions found on the Internet and cable television. The *Boston Globe*'s Renee Loth cited professional standards. "The web is in its infancy and has not yet developed the professional journalistic standards to be a truly informed addition to the media landscape," she wrote, adding that editorial opinions in newspapers are more than "tossed-off blogs or 'talk-radio' rants. There is so much rumor, conspiracy and other uninformed junk on 'alternative' cable and websites. This makes well-respected, time-tested, traditional media 'guides' even more important to readers trying to find their way through the media clutter."

Bruce Dold of the *Chicago Tribune* cited localism in his discussion of the effects of Internet and cable on newspaper editorials. "Cable television shows and Internet dialogue deal with national issues," he wrote. "They also tend to dissolve into incoherent shout-fests. I have seen nothing in new media that has lessened the influence of the editorial page, particularly on local issues."

Fort Worth Star-Telegram editorial page editor Paul Harral agreed on the localism aspect, and he expanded on the credibility issue raised by Loth. "Most users of the Internet are aware that much of the information they can find is unreliable, and when the issue is important, they will turn to trusted sources," he wrote. "The original reporting in the United States is still primarily done by newspaper reporters. That won't change until and unless other forms are willing to invest the kind of resources necessary—and that isn't going to happen."

The *Dallas Morning News*'s Keven Ann Willey, though, argued that these media alternatives have brought a challenge to the newspaper editorial writer: to be more persuasive and timely. Editorial writers, she said, "certainly can still be persuasive, but they can't do it the way they used to do it, you can't wait two or three days to pontificate on it. Cable and Internet have required us to step it up and be more agile at what we do, and if we rise to that challenge I think we can be as influential, but a lot of editorialists are struggling with how to meet that challenge." However, she welcomed the competition of the new media. "I just think the more the merrier. I just think that it's best to have a variety of voices, Internet, cable, newspaper, everything, and sometimes the newspaper can be the most local."

In the Pittsburgh metroplex market, the *Tribune-Review*'s Colin McNickle wrote that while readers find "respite, sanity and comfort in newspaper editorials," the Internet and cable should be viewed less as substitutes and more as "adjuncts to the newspaper. To wit, the Internet search engines often are employed by our readers to further educate themselves about a position we've taken." McNickle's competitor, the *Post-Gazette*'s Tom Waseleski, wrote that while these alternative sources for news and opinion do not offer much when it comes to local issues, they provide a "higher entertainment quality to opinions than newspaper editorials," and most of the sources on the Internet are "by and large, just people who think what they think. That's fine if you just want to talk across the fence to your neighbor, but if you want an educated opinion about an important subject confronting the community, there is no substitute for a good editorial."

OWNERSHIP, GROUP EFFECTS

The subjects of the Internet and cable television arose in the discussion by the *Dallas Morning News*' Willey of the effects of media conglomeration and monopoly newspaper ownership on editorial diversity and competitiveness. "I think people tend to think of these issues through one platform, newspapers," she said, "and when you're talking about diversity and competitiveness and those issues, that overlooks the explosion of news coverage and opinion on the Internet and cable TV, so there's more diversity of opinion even though there's more consolidation of newspapers."

Willey was in the minority on this issue, however. This question prompted considerable discussion about the negative aspects of newspaper group ownership. For example, Vesely of the *Seattle Times* wrote that group ownership demands for 20 percent profit margins "is automatically going to deplete competitiveness because resources are withdrawn for the high-expense items—travel, investigations, attorney counsel, specialized staff." Harral of the then-Knight Ridder-owned *Star-Telegram* said, "consolidation of ownership in publicly held companies has to be at least questionably beneficial if not negative to the industry. Maximizing return on investment can be counter-intuitive to the constitutional duties of newspapers. By its nature, good journalism is expensive."

The *Post-Intelligencer*'s Trahant interpreted the question as applied to pressure from group owners to conform in editorial ideology. That is a pressure Trahant, and Dold of the *Chicago Tribune*, said they have not experienced. The *Boston Globe*'s Loth pointed to recent news reports of self-censorship within group-owned television and radio outlets in the broadcast media. Citing one broadcast group's decision to order its members not to air a film documentary critical of President George Bush during the 2004 election campaign, she wrote: "One needs only look at the Sinclair broadcasting flap (or Clear Channel radio's aggressive advocacy of the war in Iraq) to demonstrate how media conglomeration narrows the range of permissible editorial content." Waseleski of the *Post-Gazette* in Pittsburgh applied the same anti-competition rationale to newspapers. "Particularly as readership declines and newspapers fold, more communities become one-newspaper towns. That costs the readers that second voice and also reduces competition toward a better news product."

The *Tribune-Review*'s McNickle wrote negatively of the effect of conglomeration on news quality. "Chain newspapers—especially in smaller markets—tend to, as I like to say, say everything in their editorials without saying anything. They're afraid to take a stand. That's not what an editorial page is supposed to do. It's supposed to take a position. Readers look to newspaper editorial pages for guidance, not weasel words."

Leo Morris, editorial page editor of the then-Knight Ridder-owned Fort Wayne *News-Sentinel*, made reference to the rare nature of the two-newspaper market of his community. "Many cities much larger have only one newspaper, which results in a lot of 'on the other hand' wishy-washy editorials." Across the hallway, Tracy Warner of the family-owned *Journal Gazette* argued that the effects of conglomeration depend on the chain. "Some offer the individual newspapers much more independence than others. Those that dictate a certain position on a certain issue hurt diversity and competitiveness."

Dold of the *Chicago Tribune* agreed, arguing that his company offered an example of "how large newspapers companies have not reduced editorial diversity. Newspapers in the [Tribune] company make their own decisions on editorial policy. This was reflected in presidential endorsements. Some Tribune Co. papers endorsed John Kerry, some endorsed George Bush. All those decisions were made at the local level." Similarly, Harral in Fort Worth wrote that his chain, Knight Ridder, "has increased diversity and competitiveness in most ways."

IMPORTANCE OF COMPETITION, EDITORIAL VOICE

As noted above, a large majority of the editors, 83.3 percent, agreed or strongly agreed it is important for a community to have more than one daily editorial voice. They believed even more strongly, 100 percent (seven strongly agreed, five agreed), that newspaper editorials are important contributors to the nation's cultural and political dialogue. The editors cited the marketplace of ideas concept and reader expectations as benefits of multiple editorial voices, while one worried about the effects of media ownership. All of these editors worked in competitive environments at the time of the survey.

"The robust functioning of a democracy depends on an informed electorate," argued the *Boston Globe*'s Loth. "That can only be achieved by a great diversity of information and opinion. Two newspapers are required to keep each other honest; in the case of the *Globe* and the *Herald*, which agree on very few things editorially, this is especially crucial."

In the metroplex markets, the *Post-Gazette*'s Waseleski observed that "readers want choice. They get suspicious when there is only one news outlet or one daily editorial voice conveying its world view." His rival, McNickle, cited the need to avoid a dominant voice. "Discourse is incredibly important in civic life. If there's only one voice, it's far too easy for the public to think the sole voice is the 'right' voice."

The *Dallas Morning News*' Willey suggested it is wrong to consider this question only in terms of newspaper editorials. "I'd interpret editorial voices to include online, TV, multiple platforms, not just newspapers." Her Fort Worth competitor, Harral, cited the benefits of competition, which he said "tends to make both parties better and more attentive to the customers—or, in the case of newspapers, the audience. But there needs to be a caveat: the opinion needs to be informed."

In the JOA markets, the *Journal Gazette*'s Warner cited the assets of diverse thought, and his competitor, Morris, argued on behalf of the benefits to a democratic form of government of "all points of view." The *Seattle Post-Intelligencer*'s Trahant pointed out that the two dominant Seattle newspapers offer different points of view, citing his newspaper's opposition to the war in Iraq while, he said, the *Times* called it a just war. "Some readers like to identify with a newspaper they regularly agree (or disagree with)." Vesely of the *Times*, though, took the argument beyond differing ideologies. "The world is now awash in information and competing voices. While it is nice, and nostalgic, to think of the two-daily town or the competition among reporters, who owns the dailies and what level of profit margin they are expected to produce have a far more lasting effect on the community."

Some editors readily identified their newspapers as belonging to one philosophical camp as opposed to their competitors, in language at times reminiscent of editorial battles of yore, which offers evidence that editorial page editors view their pages as ideological arenas of robust competition.

In the Pittsburgh metroplex market, for example, Waseleski of the *Post-Gazette* discussed by name the owner of the competing *Tribune-Review*, Richard Scaife, identifying him as "a well-known financier of conservative Republican causes....The *Pittsburgh Post-Gazette* is generally seen as liberal, sometimes Democratic. But a close reader would find it endorsing Republican as well as Democratic candidates." A careful reading of its editorials would reveal the *Post-Gazette* as a "moderate" voice, Waseleski argued. "But we'll accept the l-word; it's part of our history." Rival McNickle agreed with the "liberal" tag for the *Post-Gazette* and the "conservative" label for his newspaper, adding: "I would actually go a step further and argue that the [*Post-Gazette*] isn't so much liberal as it is socialist." The Dallas metroplex rivalry was a bit less distinctive, tending away from clear-cut editorial differences. Willey claimed that her newspaper is the dominant one in a market of many voices. Harral wrote that his newspaper would be considered the more moderate of the two, arguing that moderation, conservatism, and liberalism are defined by particular issues.

As in the more conservative Dallas, regional cultures and histories come into play in JOA market Seattle, according to that city's editorial page editors. "This is Seattle," wrote the *Post-Intelligencer*'s Trahant. "It's a progressive town (even more liberal than most Democrats). That results in the P-I—a left-centrist voice—being more conservative than many of its readers. The *Times* is probably center-right. This community doesn't really have a conservative Republican voice, except for talk radio." Vesely of the *Times* argued that the difference between the newspapers, rather than being a split of political ideologies, "is closer to being differences between being city-centric or suburban-regional. The labels flow, not from politics but from geography and landscape."

The Fort Wayne editors cited traditional differences. "In the beginning, the morning *Journal Gazette* was the Democratic paper, the evening *News-Sentinel* the Republican one," wrote the *News-Sentinel*'s Morris. "We've evolved over the years into a liberal editorial page and a conservative one, but many people still identify us with our former party labels." The *Journal Gazette*'s Warner answered similarly. "From strictly an editorial page perspective, the *Journal Gazette* is and has long been liberal....From numerous calls, letters and conversations over the years, I believe many readers view the pages this way."

In the direct competition markets, the *Globe*'s Loth said the ideological distinctions in her city are clear to the readers. "Ask anyone with a passing knowledge of both newspapers this question and they will agree 99 percent that the *Globe* is a liberal paper and the *Herald* is conservative. And if one is looking just at editorial positions of the two newspapers (not the news coverage) they would be right." But the difference is a bit less clear in Chicago, argued the *Tribune*'s Dold. "The second major newspaper in my community has shifted its philosophical direction several times in the past twenty years, so it is difficult to say there has been a clear distinction between the two major papers."

The editors' responses to the open-ended question asking them to recall editorial battles involving them and their rivals indicated a debate that, if not frequent, is evidence nonetheless of a lively difference of opinion. In Fort Wayne, Warner cited his newspaper's endorsement of the Democratic governor, as opposed to the *News-Sentinel*'s backing of the Republican candidate. He added: "Our newspaper was a strong supporter of a local ordinance to prohibit discrimination based on sexual orientation; the other newspaper was equivocal, raising issues but neither supporting or opposing it. Our newspaper has favored a direct route, new terrain extension of Interstate 69 from Indianapolis to Evansville; the other newspaper wants to use existing routes." Rival Morris cited broader differentiation, one that speaks to general political ideologies but that also takes in a different kind of disagreement: progressivism versus traditionalism. "We almost always disagree on national politics," he wrote. "We disagree less often on local politics. There isn't a 'liberal' or 'conservative' way to fill potholes. But we do disagree on many community issues, with the J-G emphasizing 'progress,' us 'tradition'."

In Seattle the *Times*' Vesely cited endorsement editorials, pointing out that his newspaper backed Bush over Al Gore in 2000, while the *Post-Intelligencer* backed Gore. The newspapers agreed on Kerry in 2004 but differed on gubernatorial candidates. Rival Trahant cited one other issue of disagreement besides the presidential and gubernatorial election endorsements: government subsidies for the Boeing Corporation. "Even though we're a hometown paper, we said the European Union was right to keep this fight out of the World Trade Organization. The *Times* supported Boeing. We take opposite stands on a regular basis —say, once a week or so."

As suggested by the findings cited earlier in this book, Harral of the *Fort Worth Star-Telegram* offered more evidence of agreement than of disagreement in the

Dallas/Fort Worth market; and he cited a sort of disagreement that the research in this book has identified as framing differences. "Interestingly, the *Morning News* and the *Star-Telegram* are remarkably in sync on many major issues, although we may arrive at those decisions from different directions. We've actually cooperated to a great extent on regional transit issues and hosted jointly sponsored meetings of decision-makers to discuss that issue." Willey cited only one difference editorially, the endorsement of a long-time Republican U.S. representative, whom her newspaper opposed.

The editorial lines of battle, though, were much more clearly drawn in the Pittsburgh metroplex market. The *Post-Gazette*'s Waseleski said the newspapers disagreed on political endorsements, arguing that his newspaper endorses candidates from both major parties "while they endorse conservative Republicans almost religiously. We disagree on the proper use of public funds. We support using public funds as a way to leverage development and improvement in a region like ours, which can be described as recovering Rust Belt. The other paper in town would rather see the money returned to the taxpayers." He also cited his newspaper's backing of taxpayer support for the construction of two new sports complexes that were a "catalyst for development on Pittsburgh's North Shore. They fought the plan tooth and nail, saying it was a waste of public money." The *Tribune-Review*'s McNickle cited that same issue, arguing that in 1997 its rival joined with the "corporate elite" in promoting the use of taxes for the stadium construction. "The P-G even had a stake in one of the teams [the Pittsburgh Pirates], yet it shilled for the tax usually without revealing the conflict."

In the direct competition markets, the *Citizens' Voice* in Wilkes-Barre, Pennsylvania, wrote managing editor Paul Golias, disagreed with the *Times Leader* over a home rule initiative for county government, which his newspaper supported. Dold offered no examples of editorial differences, though some were cited in earlier portions of this book. In Boston, Loth offered several examples of issue differences with the *Herald*. "We are pro-choice, they are pro-life. We oppose the death penalty, they support. We support affirmative action in hiring and education, they oppose. We support gay marriage (NOT the watered down civil unions); they oppose," she wrote. "Oh yes, we supported freezing a planned state income tax rollback when the state faced a three-billion-dollar shortfall; they opposed, saying there was waste in government programs. (We won)."

THE IMPORTANCE OF NEWSPAPER EDITORIALS

Not surprisingly, while these editors frequently disagreed ideologically and on such issues as the effects of converging media and media ownership, the future of the editorials (and of newspapers), and the vigor of modern-day editorial diversity, they found common ground on the importance of editorials—but with a few caveats. Golias of the *Citizens' Voice* in Wilkes-Barre, Pennsylvania, for example, wrote that his belief in the newspaper editorial's contribution to society might not be as strong as it was twenty years ago. "There are so many other sources of information now that I believe the influence of newspapers has been diluted. We have anecdotal evidence that more people are willing to admit that the newspaper's position means little." Nonetheless, he believed that the newspaper editorial "is a living, breathing part of the community, and it is in position to sift through competing and conflicting stances on issues." In Boston, the *Globe*'s Loth wrote about the public interest of the newspaper editorial board, as opposed to the varied interests of special-interest and advocacy groups. In this era of complex and fast-paced lives, "we on the editorial board have the great advantage of spending our working hours immersed in the issues of the day, taking advantage of the terrific academic and other resources in this city," she wrote. "The newspaper editorial is an opportunity for the editorial board to share with the readers the wealth of that valued knowledge—of course distilled through our analysis and opinion."

In the metroplex markets, Waseleski of the *Pittsburgh Post-Gazette* wrote that he has experienced strong reaction to the newspaper's editorials, and he cited the democratic nature of his readership. "I have a keen sense that all sorts of readers follow them, regardless of income level, education and other demographics. They want us to weigh in on important subjects, and they relish the chance to debate with us and their fellow readers in our letters section." The importance of the editorial, he wrote, is its public guidance: "It explains an issue, an action or a person in the public eye in a way that readers do not have the time or the ability to discern themselves." His rival cited the role of editorials in the nation's history, and he noted how a newspaper editorial differs from the output of cable television and Internet pundits. "A public bombarded with opinions needs a respite from the talking heads and the blogs," wrote McNickle. "It [the newspaper editorial] is a well-thought-out persuasive piece of writing designed to expose shibboleths and say something with some meat. It is, and will remain, an American institution."

In Dallas, Willey said newspaper editorials are "part of the community dialogue and an important contributor to that dialogue." She argued that editorial endorsements become more significant "the further down the ballot you go—the more local you get. I don't think too many people decide who to vote for president based on newspaper recommendations, but I do think people look to newspaper recommendations on issues like the legislature, ballot propositions, the school boards and so on. That's where the newspaper editorial is quite significant." Harral up the road in Fort Worth cited the marketplace of ideas concept. "I deeply believe that editorials are a central point of that marketplace. Reasoned commentary by informed writers can help frame the parameter of debate —and should."

The *Post-Intelligencer*'s Trahant in the Seattle JOA market viewed the importance of the editorial in terms of public dialogue and pragmatist-flavored experimentation. "Wordsworth says the most noble human trait is discourse. The back and forth tug over ideas. Newspaper editorials are an extension of discourse.

They help democracies sort out things, testing ideas and hopefully helping citizens reach a logical conclusion at some point." Vesely of the *Times* also invoked the metaphor of dialogue, calling an endorsement editorial a "conversation with the reader about what the paper stands for, not the candidate....Unlike all the other devices of modern journalism—civic reporting, focus groups, redesign—the editorial remains the most direct connection with readers so far devised."

Morris in Fort Wayne wrote that editorials force thought and encourage readers to organize facts and to come to conclusions. "A good editorial is an argument, and argument brings out both strengths and weaknesses in propositions. Many plans fail simply because their proponents have skipped the step of a good, healthy argument." Argued his competitor, the *Journal Gazette*'s Warner: The editorial's contribution to the American cultural and political dialogue "is in many ways the mission and soul of the editorial page, to raise issues of importance and/or interest to readers and to offer opinions. Editorial pages bring injustices and inequalities to the attention of the public and offer possible solutions—and they do so using logic and fact rather than the shouting that passes for opinion on many talk shows."

TONE, THE UNIQUE METROPLEX MARKET, FOLLOW-UP, AND THE UNASKED QUESTION

Besides their agreement regarding the importance of editorials, the editors also concurred in the notion that editorials need not disagree ideologically or philosophically to be different. Several editors cited tone or style of writing or length of an editorial as differences that can convey meaning. Editorials can range from "sharp criticism to equivocal recognition of an issue," wrote Fort Wayne's Warner. "Some will cite a wrongdoing with no recommended course of action; others will emphasize necessary action."

In Seattle, Trahant wrote about editorial length and style. Arguing that many newspaper readers avoid the editorials, he said this is one reason to write them shorter. "The P-I wants readers to get a variety of opinions every day. We write them as quick hits—250 words—in a conversational style. When we want to say something is really important (and it's not often) then we go longer on topic. We like edits to be conversational, sometimes fun."

Loth argued that editorials can differ in the research that goes into them. "We pride ourselves on the *Globe* ed page of always reporting out our editorials—and not just by doing web research. ('Research' is not reporting!) We get OUT of the ivory tower and into the community, go to lots of night meetings, interview many experts before reaching our conclusions and writing what I believe are better informed and thus more persuasive editorials."

Harral of the metroplex Fort Worth market also cited style in arguing that an editorial's reasoning can set it apart from the competing argument. "The *Star-Telegram* tends not to take itself overly seriously, which, interestingly, seems to have a sort of reverse effect on interested parties. Our positions are often viewed as very honest simply because they are not intended to be overly heavy-handed." Willey at the *Morning News*, though, invoked editorial voice. "I think that an editorial voice can be as important in how persuasive it is as its position can be. There's sort of the *Wall Street Journal* or the *New York Times* voice, a very institutional voice, and there's a conversational kind of voice." The voice of an editorial, she argued, can be just as weighty as the editorial's stance on an issue. "We spend a lot of time in editorial meetings talking about the voice of an editorial—is this a whack-them-about-the-head-and-ears kind of editorial or is this a calm, rational, reasoned editorial? Is this a time for outrage, or is this a time for solemn-as-ice?"

In Pittsburgh, the *Post-Gazette*'s Waseleski also cited the reasoned approach "with a solid argument woven throughout" versus "smackdowns of talk-show rhetoric that have less steak and more sizzle. Despite the temptation, print journalists should not emulate the Rush Limbaughs and Michael Moores of our day. A good editorial needs to be well researched in addition to well written."

In response to the final question regarding metroplex market editorialists' attitudes regarding rivals, these editors were generally dismissive of their competition while conceding that some competitive fires do burn. In the Dallas metroplex, Fort Worth's Harral said the competition is stronger in some circulation areas than others; but he said he pays little attention to the rival newspaper. Willey at the *Morning News* said reporters at her newspaper want to beat the *Star-Telegram* even though there is not a large cross readership. In Pittsburgh, Waseleski, while claiming to seldom read the *Tribune-Review*'s editorial page, noted that the *Tribune-Review* refers to his newspaper "disparagingly in occasional editorials, which I find flattering. We never refer to them or their viewpoints." He wrote that his newspaper's Sunday editorial page offers a "smorgasbord of opinions, while theirs is mostly, though not entirely, one ideology." McNickle, though, left no doubt as to whether this is a competition. "Indeed. . . . We often beat them on important stories. And we often are quicker to comment on breaking news events. To wit, I wrote 'live' after each of the three presidential debates; the P-G chose to wait a day. In my mind, that's stale by then. And readers see the difference."

McNickle also offered an explanation, in a follow-up question to the e-mail survey, regarding doubts that might have been raised by the *Tribune-Review*'s editorial endorsing the re-election of President Bush in 2004. As discussed previously, the editorial raised questions about Bush before settling on the incumbent as preferable to Kerry, raising the possibility of a divided editorial board. "The *Trib* considered not endorsing anyone for president in 2004," he wrote in an e-mail sent on February 28, 2005. "We had/have significant differences with Mr. Bush. While we favored regime change in Iraq, we thought containment was a better option. And, prior to the war, we questioned how good the post-war plan was, if there was one at all." Pointing out that the *Tribune-Review* had praised the recent Iraqi elections, he wrote that the newspaper also disagreed with the president on the prescription drug and the guest-worker programs. "The president aided and abetted congressional profligacy by keeping his veto pen capped. But in the final analysis, we decided to endorse the president for re-election, given the alternative of Mr. Kerry. While we have 'issues' with Mr. Bush, John Kerry was wholly unacceptable."

The *Fort Worth Star-Telegram*'s Harral also offered an explanation on his newspaper's endorsement of Bush. It was an endorsement editorial that, similar to the *Tribune-Review*'s, raised doubts about Bush's policies and aims and that wished for a reincarnation of the Bush the newspaper had known in the past, including as governor of Texas, before backing the president for re-election. Harral's written explanation conceded the existence of a split editorial board.

"We seldom actually vote on issues before the board, but in this case we took a vote at the start of the meeting to reach the final decision," Harral wrote in his explanatory e-mail of February 23, 2005.

> The vote went in favor of Bush. The results I consider private, but there was dissention. The editorial was an honest reflection of the global opinion of the board. We were, in fact, disappointed that the harmony demonstrated in the Texas capitol during Bush's time as governor did not translate to Washington. We also realize that it probably couldn't, because the players were different. But we thought there could be less conflict at the national level, and we believe that George Bush, given his credentials, was best equipped to deal with that issue.

Harral also was asked about his board's decision not to editorialize on some subjects, analyzed here, during the 2004 presidential campaign. His answer suggested that some of the issues, such as whether Defense Secretary Donald Rumsfeld should resign as a result of the abuse scandal at Iraq's Abu Ghraib prison, the spike in gasoline prices during the spring of 2004, and the Senate Intelligence Committee's July 2004 report on U.S. intelligence concerning prewar information on Iraq's weapons of mass destruction, had been addressed in some form over a period of time. (These subjects had not appeared in editorials within a week of the reporting of the event, a parameter set in this research; and they produced no results in Internet searches of the newspaper's editorial archives.)

As for other issues for which no editorial could be found, Harral wrote the following:

> We generally do not comment on presidential debates in specific. We don't like knee-jerk next-morning reactions. We've been burned too many times in those kinds of editorials. And we don't like "horse race" political coverage and think that falls into that category. We said little about either convention, partly on the basis cited above. We don't follow this slavishly, but we also seldom comment on internal political party decisions. There are exceptions—but selection of a running mate would not be one.

In Denver, *Post* editorial page editor Jon Wolman, who did not participate in the survey, explained in an e-mail of February 24, 2005, that his editorial board also had split on the endorsement issue. "We took extraordinary steps to ensure that the full range of views was represented in our pages," he said, quoting from an open letter to the readers that his newspaper had published.

Finally, as referenced above, one of the editors who participated in this survey refused to offer any explanation beyond filling out the survey because, as he told the author in his e-mail explanation, he disagreed with this research's failure to investigate certain aspects of the editorial page editor's job having to do with staffing and budgets.

Robert White, editorial page editor of the *Cincinnati Post*, wrote that he believed the author should have included information about staffing and other matters in a published study regarding the Cincinnati market, in a different forum, and presented in a different version in Chapter 2 of this book. Specifically, the finding that his competitor, the *Enquirer*, was found to offer more editorials on local subjects troubled White (both newspapers were group-owned, the *Post* by Scripps Howard and the *Enquirer* by Gannett).

The reason for this finding, White wrote, "is that they have more warm bodies working on the editorial page. They're a far larger paper. They had then [the research's study period], and have now, about five or six full-time writers and editors. That gives them the luxury of assigning a greater variety of local editorials." He added that he, the sole editorial writer for his newspaper, was required to place two editorials per day on his editorial page. "I have access to the Scripps Howard News Service, and Scripps employs two editorial writers in its Washington, D.C., office who write about national and international affairs. Then, as now, I turn to the Scripps edits as the basis for my secondary editorial most days (and sometimes for the lead editorial, depending on the topic)." Thus, White argued, he often cannot write two or more local editorials daily. "When it's opinion," he concluded, "or even, the news side, when staff is cut back you're all but forced to shovel more wire copy into the paper." Clearly, ownership decisions that include staffing (and thus budget) can have an effect on newspaper, and editorial page, content.

SHOPPING FOR IDEAS

The marketplace of ideas concept applies to these survey findings in two ways. One is the evidence that the responses provide of communities of vigorous ideological differences and of variances in editorial approaches to various subjects. The subject matter of these differences ranges from presidential endorsements to abortion, capital punishment, and the routing of local traffic. As discussed elsewhere in this book, these differences are found not only in ideological and philosophical discussions and in how opinions are framed, but also in variety of subject matter and more subtle variances that include framing, tone, strength of argument, depth of research, and length of editorial. These kinds of differences, from the overt battles of editorial ideologies to the more subtle nuances of writing style, produce a marketplace of ideas that, as these editorial writers recognize, contributes to a viable democratic government process.

The other marketplace concept suggested by these responses is the variety of beliefs, explanations, and agendas put forth by these editors in their explanations and perceptions of their newspapers' roles. This variety takes in such differences as whether the Internet and cable television pose threats to the newspaper editorial marketplace, the tradition, and history of the newspaper editorial and whether it will survive as it is today, the effects of media conglomeration and ownership trends on newspaper editorials, the contribution of editorials to American society, and how newspaper editorials can differ beyond ideological disagreement.

Also, while the editors agreed that newspaper editorials have been and remain important, they offered a plethora of opinions on why this is so. These range from the contribution of the editorial to the democratic process to establishing a dialogue with the community. So, the editors, in their thoughts on their craft and its role and importance, mirror in their responses the variety of ideas that their editorial pages offer to their communities.

The responses of the editors suggest numerous communication theories carried out in practical application. These include framing, agenda-setting, and perception. Also, the editors' responses offer various explanations for some of the findings of the quantitative research presented in this book. For example, political ideological differences in Fort Wayne, Indiana, in Boston, Massachusetts, and in Pittsburgh, Pennsylvania, might be found in family and ownership backgrounds. Ideological agreements on the editorial pages of the Seattle and Dallas metroplex newspapers can be partially explained by regional cultural tradition; Seattle is historically a liberal community, Dallas/Fort Worth is not. And clearly, ownership patterns and policies play a role—sometimes beneficial, sometimes not—in editorial processes ranging from the amount of time devoted to research for an editorial to the availability of corporate-produced editorials that would therefore lend to homogeneity in editorial stances.

Finally, these responses suggest the existence of editorial writing approaches, of journalistic attitudes and beliefs, that lend themselves to editorial diversity, to a genuine and valuable marketplace of ideas that is vital to a democracy. That twelve editors of pages offering wide-ranging political differences can agree on the need for political discourse, the value of political argument and the testing of ideas in a public forum speaks to communities that for the most part offer laboratories of political discourse that the writers of the U.S. Constitution intended.

CHAPTER 7

The Depleted Shelves of the Ideas Marketplace

Elihu Root, speaking in New York Friday night, denounced as "foul and infamous" the charge that the great corporations have been in this campaign the special prey of the Republican money-gatherers, owing to the inquisitorial powers of the Federal bureau of corporations and to the connection with that bureau which Chairman Cortelyou has sustained while a member of the Cabinet....

Whichever way our sympathies may incline as between parties and candidates, let us not forget that the secret collections and secret use of enormous campaign funds, for whose control no one is responsible under the law, and about which, when once scattered, no one pretends to have the slightest knowledge—let us not forget that all this has become a national scandal, and confronts you and all of us as a deadly peril to the form of government and the institutions which we hold dear.

—Springfield *Republican*, November 11, 1904, on the 1904
presidential campaign[1]

Elliot Carver stood on stage, before a big-screen television beaming the latest world news, preparing to announce to the world the completion of a satellite linkup that would enable him to expand his electronic and print media empire

on a global scale. With the assistance of one of his satellites, he had just brought
the world to the brink of World War III by manipulating a British ship into Chinese territorial waters in the South China Sea, had instigated the downing of a
Chinese warplane by the British, had sunk the British warship and made it
appear that the survivors had been murdered by the Chinese, and he trumpeted
the news on the front page of his tabloid "Tomorrow" even before the British
knew of the sinking of their ship.

As the international crisis simmered, Carver, CEO of the fictional
Carver Media Group Network in the 1997 film *Tomorrow Never Dies*, bade his
subordinates: "I want full newspaper coverage, I want magazine stories, I want
books, I want films, I want TV, I want radio, I want us on the air 24 hours a
day. This is our moment, and a billion people around the planet will watch it,
hear it and read about it from the Carver Media Group. There's no news like
bad news."[2]

This list of "I wants" by the fictional Carver conceivably could be delivered in
the real-world media marketplace of today. Cross-ownership, conglomeration,
and monopoly are commonplace in the media market of the early twenty-first
century.

A few examples of such conglomeration: As this book is being written, the
Walt Disney Company owned one national television network (ABC); ten television stations in eight states and sixty-four radio stations and two radio net-
works, including six stations in Minneapolis-St. Paul, five in Dallas, four each
in Los Angeles, Chicago, and New York City, and three in Washington, D.C.;
three book publishing imprints totaling eight separate publishing outlets; fifteen
magazine titles; eight cable television systems; and six film production and distribution companies.[3]

Many of the large conglomerate holdings involve newspapers that were
included in the studies conducted for this book. For example, the *Dallas Morning
News* is owned by the Belo Corporation, which as this book is written included
seven other newspapers, two of them in Texas; twenty television stations,
including one in Dallas, one in Houston, one in Austin, and two in San Antonio; and six cable television stations, including Texas Cable News.[4]

The Gannett company, which owns the *Cincinnati Enquirer*, also has a
national newspaper, *USA Today*. Its other holdings include ninety-six
newspapers in thirty-eight states and in Guam, all served by the Gannett
News Service; seven newspapers published under its Army Times Publishing
Company subsidiary; nineteen newspapers in the United Kingdom; and
twenty-two television stations in fifteen states and the District of Columbia,
including three stations in Arizona, three in Florida, and two each in Georgia
and Maine.[5]

The *Denver Post* is owned by MediaNews Group, which also owned fifty-two
other newspapers in ten states.[6]

The holdings of the New York Times Company, owner of the *Boston Globe*,
also include eighteen other newspapers in eight states and the France, eight

television stations in eight states, and two radio stations, both in New York City. It also owns half of cable's Discovery Times channel.[7]

The *Chicago Tribune*'s owner, the Tribune Company, has fourteen newspapers in eight states; twenty-eight television outlets in sixteen states and Washington, D.C.; three cable outlets in two states and one radio station. In Chicago, it owns the *Tribune*, television station WGN, radio station WGN-AM, and cable outlets WGN and Chicago Land Television.[8]

Chain ownership is the norm in the newspaper market of twenty-first century America. The purchase of newspapers by groups, in fact, is evidence of the continued interest in newspapers despite declining readership. In 1997, for example, of the sixty-six transactions involving the sales of daily newspapers, fifty-five were by buyers that owned at least two other daily newspapers, continuing a longtime trend toward chain ownership and away from independently owned newspapers.[9] Benjamin M. Compaine and Douglas Gomery reported in 2000 that in 1923, 31 newspaper groups owned 153 newspapers, which accounted for 7 percent of all dailies. The number of chains had tripled to 95 by 1954 and reached 167 in 1978. By 1996, 126 groups owned 1,151 newspapers, which accounted for 76 percent of all U.S. dailies and 82 percent of daily newspaper circulation.[10]

But this trend toward consolidation and concentration of the media is no recent occurrence. The Hutchins Commission on Freedom of the Press warned in 1947 of the dangers of this ownership trend and its negative effect on a democratic society. At that time, the commission members wrote,

> the conditions affecting the consumer's freedom have radically altered. Through concentration of ownership the flow of news and opinion is shaped at the sources; its variety is limited; and at the same time the insistence of the consumer's need has increased. He is dependent on the quality, proportion, and extent of his news supply not alone for his personal access to the world of thought and feeling but also for the materials of his business as a citizen in judging public affairs.[11]

The danger of media concentration, said the commission, is in its monopolistic nature and thus of the power of editorial voice, a danger that poses just as much of a threat to the free exchange of ideas as does government censorship. "Concentration of power substitutes one controlling policy for many independent policies, lessens the number of competitors, and renders less operative the claims of potential issuers who have no press."[12] Indeed, concentrated ownership lessens the ability of the citizen in a democracy to be heard.

> While it is not, like the right of speech, a universal right that every citizen should own a press or be an editor or have access to the clientele of any existing press, it is the whole point of a free press that ideas deserving a public hearing shall get a public hearing and that the decision of what ideas deserve that hearing shall rest in part with the public, not solely with the particular biases of editors and owners.[13]

The worry over the perils of media conglomeration has not abated in the modern era. This is because media competition is an economic rivalry unlike that of other kinds of business in which competition is viewed as beneficial in classical Adam Smithian terms of economic efficiencies; it is one involving news, ideas, and opinions, the stuff of democratic pluralism and diversity. Rifka Rosenwein wrote of this concern in a 2000 *Brill's Content* piece. Media mergers, Rosenwein wrote,

> ...matter in ways that other takeovers don't. Having five or six major widget companies may be enough to safeguard the price and product competition with which traditional economic theory and antitrust law have been concerned. But concentrating much of the power to create and distribute news and ideas in five or six media conglomerates with a vast array of interests raises all kinds of other issues. There is, after all, a virtue in diversity, lots of it, when it comes to expression that transcends widget economic theory.[14]

Another phenomenon accompanying the consolidation and conglomeration of the nation's media is the public-ownership facet of many chain newspapers overseen by corporate boards, many of which feature interlocking board members. A 2004 study of such media boards found advertising and financial concerns among board representation of many newspaper and media companies, including some that were part of analyses in this book. For example, financial and advertising company representatives on the board of the Belo Corporation from 1988 to 2000 included Goldman Sachs & Co. of North America, Scudder Kemper Investments, Kimberly-Clark, and PepsiCo. During that same time period, Gannett listed board members that included American Security Bank, Prudential Mutual Funds, Kellogg, American Express, and Coca Cola. Tribune Company board members included representatives from General Electric Investment Co., Morgan Stanley & Co., K-Mart, Sara Lee, and McDonald's. The New York Times Company board membership included New York Life Insurance, Chase Manhattan Bank, IBM, Bristol-Meyers, and Johnson & Johnson. Knight Ridder's membership included Vanguard Group of Investment Co., Citibank, Bank America Co., Seagram Co., and AT&T.[15]

In-depth analyses of these media ownership traits—conglomeration, monopolies, group ownership, board governance, and interlocks—have been presented elsewhere.[16] The wide-reaching power of such media conglomerates, though, is similar to that found in the James Bond thriller cited above; as with television stations, radio outlets, and newspapers in the American media landscape, truth and fiction merge. In the film, the fictional Elliot Carver, surrounded by admirers, clients, and groupies, boasted to his international viewing audience of his new satellite technology, and he expounded on his company's intentions and news credo. Possessing the media wherewithal to bring down governments, he explained that he built his empire for power: "the power to illuminate the far corners of the globe, not for higher profit, but for higher understanding between the people of this great planet," he told the world as his henchmen were in a back room working over British special agent Bond. "I promise to report the news without fear or favor, I promise to be a force for good in this world, fighting injustice, crushing intolerance, battling inhumanity, striking a blow for freedom at every turn."[17]

If those lofty principles put forth by a madman in control of the world's largest media conglomeration sound familiar, it is because we have heard them before in real-world pronouncements of the benefits of media conglomeration, consolidation, and convergence that promise better, more thorough and swifter delivery of news. For example, in Dallas, where the *Morning News* and WFAA are owned by the Belo Corporation, a *Morning News* top editor argued, using a word uttered by the fictional Carver—"power"—that the newspaper and television station complement each other. "We trade tips and we trade stories and we co-promote," he said. "It increases the amount of reach and our journalism power."[18]

Everette E. Dennis, then of the Gannett Center for Media Studies at Columbia University, arguing in 1991 that media pluralism is on the rise, discounted worries of the growing power of media owners in an era of conglomeration, consolidation, and convergence that he suggested brings about greater diversity. Dividing the meaning of media pluralism into two components, diversity of ownership and diversity of content, he argued that the number of available media voices is only part of the issue. "It is what's in them that counts and there is no easy universally accepted way to measure diversity of content." Seeking to assuage concerns about homogenization of interests due to conglomerate control of newspapers and broadcast stations, he wrote that the electronic revolution, "especially as represented by cable, ought to relieve many fears. Naturally, some large firms have moved into this business (Time Warner, for example, owns Home Box Office and Cinemax), but there are still many alternative voices."

> The diverse sources of information and opinion are almost mind-boggling. These are with us already in greater numbers than any of us can hope to comprehend, let alone use. In an information society with these massive offerings, the real secret of intellectual survival for the consumer lies in understanding the range of possibilities and knowing how to use them to personal advantage. There are, of course, reasons to be concerned about information-rich people versus information-poor people. Information is power and some information will no doubt be priced so high that it will be out of reach of many people. Even then, though, through the prudent use of libraries and other public sources, most of us will have such enormous choices, so rich and varied, that it will be abundantly clear that media pluralism is on the increase.[19]

But as journalism students learn in the classroom, this story, or argument, has more than one side. In this case, another side is one that considers not the abundance of media voices but instead focuses on the dangers of ownership models that limit these voices because of centralized, and thus homogenized, often public, ownership or because of monopoly ownership that by its nature excludes competing voices and viewpoints. Indeed, though the power of the media may not be carried to the extremes of the James Bond film, the premises and concepts of *Tomorrow Never Dies* are based on truth. Recent manifestations of real-world media power demonstrate this. While these examples certainly are not of the magnitude of the fictionalized sinking of British ships and the shooting down of Chinese warplanes brought about by the media megalomania depicted in *Tomorrow Never Dies*, they nonetheless offer evidence of the kind of power over ideas, of a diminished marketplace of opinions and thought, that media monopolization and conglomeration can foster.

In October 2004, a few weeks before the presidential election pitting Senator John Kerry against incumbent George W. Bush, Sinclair Broadcast Group Inc. ordered its sixty-two television stations, representing 24 percent of television households in the United States including the swing states of Ohio and Florida, to air an anti-Kerry documentary two weeks prior to the election. The documentary, "Stolen Honor: Wounds That Never Heal," used sources such as the Swift Boat Vets and POWs for Truth group of Vietnam veterans, who claimed that Kerry had distorted his war record for political gain. As a documentary, it posed as news, not as a paid advertisement.

According to a report in the *Los Angeles Times*, Democratic National Committee Chairman Terry McAuliffe said Sinclair executives had given generous donations to the Republican Party, and the corporation had refused to broadcast a Democratic National Committee ad criticizing Bush. He asserted that the company's news was "notoriously anti-Kerry in its content." The film was produced by Carlton Sherwood, a former reporter for the conservative *Washington Times* who also had worked for eight years for former Pennsylvania Governor Tom Ridge, who at the time was head of Homeland Security for the Bush administration. Also, the public relations firm of Shirley & Bannister, which represented the Republican National Committee, was representing the film, according to McAuliffe.

Federal Communications Commission member Michael J. Copps criticized the broadcast, calling it "an abuse of the public trust. And it is proof positive of media consolidation run amok when one owner can use the public airwaves to blanket the country with its political ideology—whether liberal or conservative."[20]

In that same year, media giant Clear Channel, the nation's largest owner of radio stations with more than 1,200, moved to revoke a contract for a billboard leased by Project Billboard for a 69-by-44-foot display of a stylized bomb and fuse decorated in stars and stripes above the message, "Democracy is best taught by example, not by war." It had been scheduled to be displayed over Times Square during the Republican National Convention in August and until Election Day. Project Billboard, described as a nonprofit group devoted to "diversity, tolerance and free expression," and Clear Channel, a large donor to Republican political candidates, reached an agreement allowing the activist group to lease two billboards during the convention for a compromise message: one displayed a giant peace dove and one showed a ticker that displayed the cost of the Iraq war.[21]

In the previous year, the United States Senate, during deliberations on the effects of consolidation in the radio industry, heard evidence regarding the censorship of music by the Dixie Chicks. Corporate-owned radio companies had banned playing of the group's music because the group's lead singer, Natalie Maines, had disparaged President Bush during a March 2003 concert in London. Senate Commerce Committee Chairman John McCain, an Arizona Republican, said that the ability of large radio groups to ban music because of a political statement was "incredible" and was evidence of how radio consolidation was bringing about "erosion of the First Amendment."[22]

In his 1999 book *Rich Media, Poor Democracy: Communication Politics in Dubious Times*, Robert W. McChesney detailed several examples of newspaper and broadcast executives censoring news stories for reasons that ranged from perceived legal threats cited by company executives to potential damage to the media organizations' financial interests. He cited the following examples:

- An exposé of NBC News by one of its former correspondents, Arthur Kent, who chronicled opposition by NBC owner General Electric "to NBC news examining any of GE's business operations."
- A 1998 instance in which Disney's ABC News "rejected a report by its leading investigative correspondents exposing labor and safety practices at Disney World in Florida." (The coverage of the Disney empire arose again in a 2000 issue of *Columbia Journalism Review*, in which then-Disney Chairman Michael Eisner was quoted as telling National Public Radio that he would "prefer ABC not to cover Disney. I think it's inappropriate. . . . ABC News knows that I would prefer them not to cover [Disney]."[23])
- The retraction in 1998, in the face of a lawsuit (based on allegedly illegally obtained voice mail messages as sources), by the Gannett-owned *Cincinnati Enquirer* of an investigative report of Chiquita Brands International that detailed alleged unethical and illegal business practices even though "the truth of the story itself has never been disproven." Nonetheless, the reporter was fired.
- The 1996 retraction by the *San Jose Mercury News* and the demotion of reporter Gary Webb in connection with his exposé on the connection of the CIA to drug dealing in American inner cities. The retraction came following pressure from the African-American community. "The main gatekeepers—*The New York Times*, *Washington Post*, and *Los Angeles Times*—all published attacks on the *Mercury News* story. After all, if a story like this was true, it called into question the entire 'free press' that had been asleep at the switch for decades while all of this was going on." McChesney reported, however, that "extensive subsequent research effectively supported the thrust of Webb's allegations," and an internal investigation of his charges by the CIA "did not disprove and, indeed, effectively supported Webb's claims, acknowledging that the CIA had relations with drug dealers throughout the 1980s."[24]

Instances such as these, noted McChesney, have led to serious questioning from respected practitioners of American print and broadcast journalism, including Richard Reeves, the *Washington Post*'s David Broder, and former CBS News anchor Walter Cronkite. The latter observed in 1997: "Our big corporate owners, infected with the greed that marks the end of the 20th Century, stretch constantly for ever-increasing profit, condemning quality to take the hindmost." The media companies, he said, are "compromising journalistic integrity in the mad scramble for ratings and circulation."[25]

CBS in the mid-1990s provided a highly publicized example of media putting financial interests—fear of costly litigation, at least—above those of citizen needs, and of a competitive media marketplace righting the situation. The focus of this example was the decision by executives at CBS to withhold an interview with a former big tobacco scientist. In an exclusive interview with CBS 60 *Minutes* correspondent Mike Wallace, chemist Jeffrey Wigand accused representatives of tobacco interests of misleading Congress in their testimony regarding the addictive nature of nicotine. He also revealed that his former company had used a pipe tobacco additive that had been linked to liver tumors in laboratory mice.

Under fear of lawsuit from Wigand's former company, Brown and Williamson Tobacco Corporation (a lawsuit that included the possibility of accusing CBS of tortious interference for the network's role in Wigand allegedly violating his confidentiality agreement), CBS executives without putting Wigand directly on camera aired only portions of the interview, withholding some of the key information. Some suspected that the real reason for this decision by CBS was not the threat of lawsuit so much as it was the fear of disrupting the pending merger of CBS with Westinghouse.[26]

Thanks to tipsters who led other media to the information and sources, Wigand's story and CBS' handling of it eventually did find its way to the public —and to Hollywood in a film that won critical acclaim and that displayed this episode to a national audience.

"In this instance," wrote Lawrence K. Grossman, a former president of NBC News and of the Public Broadcasting System, in the *Columbia Journalism Review* early in 1996,

> clearly...the pending Westinghouse merger played a not insignificant role, whether overt or subconscious, in how CBS management viewed the issue here, if only in influencing outsiders' perceptions of the reasons behind the decision. But the reality is that nothing can be done about such outside factors as ownership and mergers. News decisions must be made on their own merits, recognizing that those factors inevitably play a role.[27]

ETHICAL CONCERNS

This episode is but one example of how journalistic integrity is being eroded in a scramble for profits, a scenario that led the researchers of the above-cited 2004 interlocking study to raise troubling ethical concerns. In their analysis of these interlocking relationships, the study's authors said they had confirmed arguments by media critics that the news media "maintain frequent ties to big business, especially major advertisers." The researchers concluded that the relationship between advertisers and news media led to concern about the influence of the advertisers on content, and they raised ethical questions about such relationships. Citing the Society of Professional Journalists' code of ethics admonishment that journalists should avoid conflicts of interest, the researchers wrote that

> there seems to be a double standard in that what is forbidden for reporters is permissible for publishers and, in fact, encouraged for boards of directors. Newspapers are a business, but they are a different kind of business, one that serves the public interest. Evidence of newspaper interlocks with financial institutions and leading advertisers prompts us to revisit the long-time concern over a tug-of-war between the public ownership and journalism concerns of newspapers.[28]

The problem with interlocks, according to a 1978 analysis of this corporate phenomenon, goes beyond conflict of interest. Such business relationships can lead to "a general tendency to manage the environment by appointing significant external representatives to positions in the organization. Known as co-optation, this is a strategy for accessing resources, exchanging information, developing interfirm commitments, and establishing legitimacy."[29]

A 1988 study of the interlocks of two Canadian newspaper groups, Southam and Thomson, concluded that the presence of financial and insurance institution representatives on these firms' boards "is pervasive, serving to make them indistinguishable from the corporate sector generally, and from each other." The researcher also argued that such interlocking raises concerns about "the potential for conflict of interest for individuals on several different boards of directors."[30]

A 2000 study of what the researchers termed the emerging "institutional conflicts of interest" brought about by media synergy argued that the combination of commercial interests with those of journalism "confounds traditional notions of conflict of interest grounded in the ethics of personal behavior. Instead, media cross-ownership by diversified conglomerates introduces greater potential for perceived conflicts of interest fueled by the desire to maximize commercial gain in an effort to justify the investment in newly acquired businesses."[31]

The trouble, argued the researchers, is not so much considerations of whether journalism improves the bottom line. "Rather, the trouble is that journalism is not really conceived of as 'journalism' at all, but as just another product alongside all the other products from which a diversified conglomerate expects to profit. The former [whether journalism sells] seeks to reconcile the goal of serving the public with the goal of making money; the latter ignores the first goal entirely."[32] Thus, bottom-line concerns that treat information and ideas purely as a commodity bring about decisions to keep the information out of the public domain—or, put in the terms of the context of this book, to decide not to stock the marketplace shelves with particular ideas. Indeed, it is hard to obtain information in the library, a solution suggested by Dennis above, when the information is withheld from publication due to concerns other than the public right to know.

As for arguments on behalf of increased pluralism, University of Maryland media economics and history professor Douglas Gomery, while agreeing that pluralism may be on the rise, concluded in a 2002 study of cross-ownership in newspaper and broadcast media for the Economic Policy Institute that while the number of media outlets has increased since 1975, "ownership has become more concentrated, and today there is less diversity of opinion—and less diversity of news sources—than in 1975." The strengthened market power of a "sharply declining number of corporate voices," he wrote, "has led to negative externalities as well, with media conglomerates stressing profit maximization over concerns of localism and diversity." Finally, Gomery disagreed with the notion that newspaper and television stations complement each other in delivering the news. "There are synergies between broadcast television and newspaper ownership that are not in the public interest," he wrote. "A local television station owned by a newspaper can simply televise a summary of the paper's content, offering no benefits to the consumer, yet it will still be able to dominate the local political and cultural discourse."[33]

In a study of the FCC and cross ownership commissioned by the FCC, University of Wisconsin at Milwaukee journalism professor David Pritchard analyzed news coverage of ten cross-owned newspaper–television combinations during the 2000 presidential election campaign. Focusing on the bias of the coverage, he found that in half of the combinations, "the overall slant of the coverage broadcast by a company's television station was noticeably different from the overall slant of the coverage provided by the same company's newspaper." But in the other five combinations, he found, "the overall slant of newspaper coverage of the 2000 campaign was not significantly different from the overall slant of the local television coverage." Pritchard offered no explanation about the similarities in the second set of combinations, and he concluded that the limited scope of the study "prevents us from drawing firm or sweeping conclusions about the implications of our findings. However, for the markets studied, the data suggest that common ownership of a newspaper and a television station in a community does not result in a predictable pattern of news coverage and commentary about important political events in the commonly owned outlets."[34]

A tally by *Editor & Publisher* magazine of 2004 presidential endorsement editorials by newspaper chains also produced mixed findings. One week before the election, the magazine's web site reported that Knight Ridder newspapers had endorsed Massachusetts' Kerry by an 18-2 margin. The MediaNews Group backed incumbent Bush by a similar margin, 16-2. Lee Enterprise newspapers went for Bush by a 13-6 count, the New York Times group favored Kerry 6-2, Cox newspapers supported Kerry 7-1, Tribune group newspapers were for Kerry 5-2, and the Blethen group also went for Kerry 5-0. Backing Bush were the Copley newspapers 5-0, Morris 3-0, and Belo 2-0. Gannett newspapers split more evenly, backing Kerry 26-19.[35]

So, while the Pritchard study and the *Editor & Publisher* analysis perhaps provide no convincing evidence of homogeneity brought about by group and cross-ownership, these findings do lend support to the argument that some homogenizing effects can be found, depending on the ownership involved. Pritchard's finding that 50 percent of the ownership combinations he studied revealed similar slants, and the *Editor & Publisher* findings regarding certain chains (Knight Ridder, MediaNews Group, Lee Enterprises, New York Times Company, Blethen, Cox, Tribune Company, Copley, Morris, and Belo) could be interpreted as evidence of, if not corporate-mandated homogeneity, certainly a corporate climate that encourages similar opinions, or a "homogenizing effect" as found by researchers in a 1991 study of editorial independence in the Gannett group. Those researchers suggested this effect raised the question of the process that brings about the homogeneity. Among the possibilities put forth by the research were hiring practices, in which "like-minded" editors would be brought in to manage the newsrooms; management procedures; peer pressure; and similarity in news sources, such as use of group-owned wire services.[36]

A troubling aspect of media convergence and conglomeration has been the decline in daily newspapers that has accompanied the increase in media pluralism cited by Dennis and others. As journalism professor John C. Merrill argued in response to Dennis' defense of pluralism, when journalists discuss the dangers of increasing group ownership,

> they are not talking about total media (nonjournalistic) pluralism. Rather they are concerned about the shrinkage of news media. Journalists are talking about newspapers being bought out by groups (like Gannett), about dailies (like the *Washington Star*) that are disappearing from the scene, and about one-newspaper cities, which restrict the news-commentary options of the citizenry. In effect, they are referring to a restriction of journalistic pluralism or diversity, not to a shrinkage of pluralism in the total communications system of the whole country.[37]

This shrinkage is a market trend not confined to independent dailies such as the *Washington Star*. It also has affected members of JOAs, which were intended to preserve newspaper competition when they were approved by Congress in the 1970 Newspaper Preservation Act. Since then, eleven JOAs have ended early, according to a 2000 study. Among these was the renegotiation in 1998 by Cox and Knight Ridder of their JOA agreement in Miami, "which resulted in Cox closing the *News* in exchange for a share of the *Herald*'s profits, which Cox will continue to receive until 2021. That same year, the McClatchy Co. paid $1.2 billion for the *Minneapolis Star-Tribune*, a record for an independent newspaper. The *Indianapolis News* shut down in 1999 after 130 years of publication."[38] As this book is being written, Gannett has informed its JOA partner in Cincinnati of its intentions to dissolve that JOA, and the JOA newspaper partnership in Seattle may be near dissolution. Add in other JOA newspapers that ceased operation, such as those in Cleveland, Pittsburgh, and Tulsa discussed elsewhere in this book, and it becomes clear that while the Newspaper Preservation Act may have succeeded in fostering editorial competition as demonstrated by the research in this book, it has not had the intended effect of preserving two-newspaper communities and continuation of the editorial diversity found in this book.

NEWSPAPERS AS A MEDIA MODEL

This discussion of newspapers within the larger context of media convergence and conglomeration that takes in electronic and broadcasting is appropriate in light of the changing economic nature of newspaper ownership. A 1974 U.S. Supreme Court decision in a case involving application of the broadcasting fairness doctrine to the newspaper industry referred to this altered media ownership landscape. Chief Justice Warren Burger, writing for the court majority, noted that when the First Amendment was ratified in 1791, "Entry into publishing was inexpensive; pamphlets and books provided meaningful alternatives to the organized press for the expression of unpopular ideas and often treated events and expressed views not covered by conventional newspapers. A true marketplace of ideas existed in which there was relatively easy access to the channels of communication." This had changed, though, Burger wrote.

> Newspapers have become big business and there are fewer of them to serve a larger literate population. Chains of newspapers, national newspapers, national wire and news services, and one newspaper towns are the dominant features of a press that has become noncompetitive and enormously powerful and influential in its capacity to manipulate popular opinion and change the course of events....Much of the editorial opinion and commentary that is printed is that of syndicated columnists distributed nationwide and, as a result, we are told, on national and world issues there tends to be a homogeneity of editorial opinion, commentary, and interpretive analysis. The abuses of bias and manipulative reportage are, likewise, said to be the result of the vast accumulations of unreviewable power in the modern media empires. In effect, it is claimed, the public has lost any ability to respond or to contribute in a meaningful way to the debate on issues. The monopoly on the means of communication allows for little or no critical analysis of the media except in professional journals of very limited readership.[39]

This recognition by the court of the problems wrought by conglomeration and consolidation is important; it was the U.S. Supreme Court, after all, that introduced the concept of a marketplace of ideas into the legal realm; it was the federal court system that upheld the constitutionality of the Newspaper Preservation Act in preserving competitive newspaper voices; and it is the federal court system that stands behind the rulings of the Federal Communications Commission in its regulation, in the name of competition, of the nation's publicly owned airwaves.

Burger's comments take on even more importance in his observation that the economic factors leading to the decline in the number of American daily newspapers are the same ones that have "made entry into the marketplace of ideas served by the print media almost impossible....The First Amendment interest of the public in being informed is said to be in peril because the 'market-place of ideas' is today a monopoly controlled by the owners of the market'."[40] So, even though the court ruled in this case against a claimant's assertion that a newspaper owed him the opportunity to reply to allegations that had been brought against him, the decision nonetheless opened the legal door to the notion that entry into the newspaper industry has become limited. And it is this logic—limitations of airwave space—that stands behind the courts and federal government in their regulation of broadcast outlets. At the same time, this ruling in its language underscored the growing threat to the American democratic system by a curtailed marketplace of ideas. It is a threat that newspaper publisher Virginius Dabney of the *Richmond Times-Dispatch* warned against near the end of the first half of the twentieth century, when he rued the tilt of newspaper ownership concerns toward business interests and away from editorial—including the editorial page.

> Today newspapers are Big Business, and they are run in that tradition. The publisher, who often knows little about the editorial side of the operation, usually is one of the leading business men in his community, and his editorial page, under normal circumstances, strongly reflects that point of view. Sometimes he gives his editor a free hand but far oftener he does not. He looks upon the paper primarily as a "property" rather than as an instrument for public service....[The typical publisher] considers the important part of the paper to be the business management, and is convinced that so long as high salaries and lavish expenditures are made available to that management, the editorial department can drag along under a schedule of too much work and too little pay. Of course, such a publisher sees that the editorials in his paper are "sound," which is to say they conform to his own weird views of society, and are largely unreadable.[41]

Dabney may well have been describing a philosophy and editorial page of a newspaper sold on a latter-twentieth-century or early-twenty-first-century news rack.

FINDINGS WARRANT CONCERN

The findings of the studies for this book support the claims of those who worry that something crucial is being lost in the continuing trend toward newspaper consolidation and monopoly. Certainly, defenders of pluralism are correct in pointing out that the nation enjoys a plethora of media voices, including print journalism and its numerous newspapers, book and magazine outlets, free radio and television broadcast outlets with even more electronic information options available through such fee services as satellite radio and cable television, and the rapidly expanding Internet.

But these findings dispute previous research evidence that daily newspaper competition does not assure a marketplace of ideas.[42] They reveal that such a marketplace, which political observers, historians, and media analysts agree is essential to a democratic government, is becoming depleted in ways that previous research has not considered in depth: in localism, for example, and in the variety and quantity of ideas and information. This research has found genuine editorial debates over important issues, ranging from entry into war and who ought to lead this nation to how to battle economic adversity. These sorts of robust public differences, waged in the nation's newspapers in an effort to discern truth, lessen as the differing voices abate.

It has been the purpose of this book's research to discover just what is being lost because of the diminished competitive daily newspaper market brought about by the ownership and market changes discussed above. Thus, it was necessary to limit the research to those few newspaper markets that still support competing newspapers, to the kinds of diversity of ideas found in editorials of newspapers through history, and to include an analysis of a different and, in some cases, relatively new type of competing market, the metroplex market in which newspapers of neighboring communities compete for readers and advertisers in a larger metropolitan market. These analyses enabled the drawing of conclusions based on the process of subtraction: what a community stands to lose if one of its competing newspapers no longer exists and the community becomes a monopoly newspaper market.

The research employed a method of analysis that used a replicable coding scheme to differentiate newspaper editorials according to geographic concentration (localism, regionalism, nationalism, and internationalism), to subject categories (politics and government, economic matters, education and the arts, etc.), and to variance of opinion and conclusion. The method also employed coding, based on general agreement or disagreement with policies of the Republican administration of President Bush, that enabled the categorization of newspaper editorials based on differences in political ideology or partisanship (i.e., Republican versus Democratic and conservative versus liberal).

The research verified previous findings that JOA newspapers tend to resemble separate, direct-competition newspapers in their editorial content. It also found that while metroplex newspapers do not offer a substitute for direct competition or JOA newspapers for editorial comment on local issues, measurable ideological, topical, and geographical focus differences exist among newspapers in all three types of markets analyzed.

The greatest negative impact of the demise of the competing daily newspaper market is at the local level. Despite the claims by defenders of concentration that the nation enjoys an increased wealth of information and voices, the diversity of opinion and information found on the Internet and in broadcast and cable outlets deals primarily with national and international events. The Internet and cable TV for the most part do not provide alternative coverage for local news and opinions found in newspapers. Local broadcast outlets compete minimally, in early morning, midday, and late-night newscasts that provide little more than headline coverage on television broadcast affiliates and in five- to ten-minute radio newscasts on those few local radio stations that still employ news readers or reporters. They rarely editorialize. So, the local news and opinion market is left largely to the community newspapers. Thus, the loss of one of these competing newspapers is considerable, as shown by the diversity and rich local and regional news agendas of the daily newspapers analyzed in the three types of newspaper markets in this research. This diversity of agendas was revealed in the finding that competing newspapers offered a relatively small percentage of editorials on the same topic, which therefore left a wide field of subject matter for opinion. This author has labeled this phenomenon a market basket of ideas. This basket, in which truth may indeed grapple with falsity (several instances were found of newspaper editorials disagreeing for ideological or philosophical reasons), takes in a wealth of ideas and opinions that are important to the community and its politics but that have drawn little or no editorial opposition or verification within that community.

The question of whether newspapers that become monopoly publications will find ways to substitute or replace what has been lost has not been researched extensively. A 2004 study of the Louisville *Courier Journal* in Kentucky before and after Gannett in 1986 purchased that newspaper and its afternoon sister, the *Times*, found no increase in the frequency of local editorials after the purchase and subsequent closure of the *Times*. Thus, there was no apparent effort to make up for the loss of local editorials that had been provided by the *Times*, which had offered a greater focus on local issues.[43]

A 1995 study of the *Courier-Journal* takeover by Gannett found a mixed commitment to editorial quality. Gannett "substantially increased" news and photographic content while decreasing advertising space, but the researchers also found a marked decrease in story length and a decline in news coverage as a percentage of the *Courier-Journal*'s expanded news hole. Also, the frequency of wire stories "greatly out paced staff written pieces which decreased as a proportion of the enlarged news hole."[44]

A 1988 study of the *Winnipeg Free Press* in Canada after it became a monopoly newspaper in 1980 found, as had a 1983 study of the development of monopoly markets in Ottawa and Winnipeg, no benefit for "either the consumer or the advertiser." The 1988 study found that stories had become shorter, and the number of sources for local stories had increased, as did local coverage focusing on city police "possibly of a sensational nature." The researchers also found what they termed a "dramatic" decline in the use of such prestige wire services as the *New York Times*, the *Los Angeles Times*, and the *Washington Post*, no change in the proportion and number of local stories, and a decrease in the number and proportion of national news stories and the number of international news stories.[45] The 1983 study also found a decline in the quantity and quality of municipal government news in both surviving newspapers and a shift in emphasis "to more obvious or higher profile sources of news at the expense of the lower tier decision-making institutions." The researchers concluded that the end of intracity newspaper competition decreased the availability of in-depth information on local government.[46]

So, localism clearly is affected when communities become monopoly newspaper markets. Merrill, cited earlier in his response to Dennis on the issue of pluralism, discussed this issue when he cited distinct "levels" of pluralism, which include what he called a "community level of pluralism."

> This level gets the concept of pluralism closer to home. The important question here is: How much diversity is present at the local level? To many persons, system pluralism is really unimportant compared with community pluralism....I must maintain that pluralism or diversity is shrinking. How does it really affect me here in my locality that throughout the whole country pluralism may be expanding? The diversity that I want is here (in my news media), not what might be available in Oregon, Maine, Florida, or Washington, D.C.[47]

Ed Bishop, a journalism educator and editor of the *St. Louis Journalism Review*, cited in a column A.J. Liebling's adage about freedom of the press belonging to those who own a press and observed, "if that's the case, we have less freedom of the press than ever before because fewer and fewer companies own the presses." Bishop offered his take on localism viewed through the lens of absentee ownership. Of those who determine the structure of newsrooms in St. Louis, he argued, "their scope, their focus, their style—their budgets—are sitting in offices hundreds of miles from here. They have less understanding of the community. They have more responsibility to their stockholders."[48]

So the issue of localism takes in more than decreased local diversity or attention to local issues; it also involves closeness to and understanding of the community; it also involves ownership and economic factors. "The real story of local journalism," wrote Bishop, "is the national consolidation of media ownership and the newsroom's place in corporate America."[49]

No Hollywood movies are being made about vital local issues and the lack of media competition in these one-newspaper towns to fill in the coverage gaps about local issues—issues that for millions of Americans have to do with their public services, including police and fire protection and schools, their local business structures, consumer ripoffs, and environmental threats.

This book's research also found types of diversity other than ideological. These include framing differences, or variances in focus of editorials; differences in editorial tone (use of sarcasm, for example); omission of editorial comment on some subjects altogether; and such subtle differences as placement and length of editorial. These sorts of differences, or combinations of them, affect perception and attitude and can be just as important as ideological disagreements in setting agendas.

Finally, this book employed qualitative research to discern the attitudes and methods of editorial writers. To help understand the editorial process, it is important to discover why and how editors think about their jobs, their roles, and their responsibilities. The findings of the survey of editorial page editors of newspapers involved in this research, along with the editors' responses to open-ended questions, verified the quantitative analyses' historical and contemporary findings of the existence of genuine newspaper editorial debate over subjects and philosophies that ranged from abortion, gay marriage, and the war in Iraq to the routing of state highways and tax policy. The editors' responses also supported the quantitative research's findings regarding variances in tone, framing, and editorial length as providing substantive avenues of editorial difference. That these editors understood and appreciated the value of idea and topic competition, and of a marketplace of ideas, attests to the importance that they placed on their daily work and on the product of their research and deliberations and the meaning of their work in the context of the American democracy and its culture. They are part of a tradition of political and cultural dialogue that has contributed to the dynamics of the nation's society and body politic.

That they shared in an understanding of the value of the newspaper editorial while disagreeing over political, social, and cultural topics attests to the continuing worth of the written editorial. The editorial is a commentary based on research and deliberation and then put forth to the public in an organized fashion, with some tactile permanence for future reference and research. The newspaper editorial is laid out on paper for analysis and discussion as opposed to shouted out on the airwaves or blogged on the Internet; it is grounded in reporting, in give-and-take of editorial board discussion, and thus represents a more institutional, authoritative, and reasoned voice then much of the opinions bantered about in Internet blogs or in broadcast yell-fests.

Bill Kovach and Tom Rosenstiel discussed this nature of political debate in their 2001 *The Elements of Journalism,* in which they analyzed what they termed "the Crossfire Syndrome."

> The media's penchant for talk has increasingly grown into a penchant for polarization. The "discussions" too often have little or nothing to do with journalism's mission of enlightening. On the theory that everyone likes a good fight, instead, all problems begin to seem unsolvable. Compromise is not presented as a legitimate option....The irony is that though it does build a small but passionate following, the shouting matches over time tend to alienate the larger public that increasingly fails to see itself in the debate.[50]

An opinion arrived at through painstaking research and through discussion among newspaper publishers and editors, the newspaper editorial is a more rational, reasoned debate—or half a debate, in the majority of cases involving one-newspaper towns—that speaks to information typically contained within the newspaper based on well-researched and documented information. But it also represents more. Newspaper editorials deal not with blared, shouted opinions, but with ideas, agendas, and perceptions about American society; as such, they offer a unique and useful tool of analysis for a marketplace and market basket of ideas that, though dwindling, remains essential to the dynamic American political experiment. The editorial, as studied in the context of this book, is a representation of the diversity of content present in a marketplace of ideas that exists in a competitive media environment.

WHAT TO DO?

The nation's media market is not poised to return to the past and to resurrect dead newspapers; yet those who mourn the demise of vigorous newspaper competition are correct to worry about the depleted marketplace and market basket of ideas this demise is bringing about, especially at the local level. There ought to be great concern over the loss of diversity on competing editorial pages such as that found in this book's research, not so much because of the sometimes questionable effects of editorials on public policy or because the public clamors to read editorials. If the demand were high for newspaper editorials, the American marketplace would produce more of them. The editorial, besides offering opinion, is an agent of a newspaper's voice and content. Besides producing opinions, it represents the overall content of the newspaper; it puts into the public domain issues, events, and ideas for consumption and discussion in a democratic forum. The editorial, in affirming or questioning aspects of American culture and society, acts similarly to the Greek philosophers and politicians of the agoras, who gathered with townsfolk in the Greek city states to pass judgment on public policy, to question it, and to discuss matters of political, economic, and social philosophy.

Editorial boards deliberate these issues daily and spend most of their deliberations discussing news and information that has appeared in their newspapers, or that they believe needs to be published in their newspapers: information of the public forum. So, comments here regarding the need for diverse and varying editorial voices should be understood to apply to a similar need regarding newspapers and their overall content and newspaper competition and diversity in general.

One way that contemporary American society can restore at least some of the diminished editorial voice is happening already in some communities. This is the existence of university newspapers, published, managed, reported, and written by student editorial boards that frequently enjoy independence from the universities' journalism departments and university administrations. Several university campuses are headquarters for student-run newspapers that operate independently of the universities and that actively compete with the private newspapers in their communities. Some of them offer the only locally written and locally focused editorials in their communities. University administrators and journalism and communications schools, and those at junior and community colleges, should encourage this sort of journalism enterprise through a morally and financially supportive climate and through a culture that encourages investigation, challenge, and watchdog journalistic undertakings. Many do, more should.

Another way in which the local editorial void could be partially filled would be for the federal government to more vigorously enact and enforce antitrust laws to stymie some daily newspapers' efforts to control their markets. Former journalism professor David C. Coulson urged such governmental activism when he called in a 1988 study of antitrust law and its relationship to newspapers for a "carefully crafted legislative approach...which limits large media-enterprise transactions that pose the greatest potential threat to the unfettered exchange of information. Coupled with a broader judicial interpretation of First Amendment policy, such action would help antitrust enforcers to combat conglomerate economic domination of the press."[51] He added:

> As long as the scope of antitrust law is confined to narrow economic concerns, however, antitrust seldom will pose an effective deterrent to newspaper concentration. Successful antitrust enforcement will depend on the Supreme Court's willingness to view newspaper's restrictive business practices as substantially lessening competition in the marketplace of ideas. If the government were to weigh societal interests when considering the desirability of newspaper concentration, antitrust law and First Amendment principles would coalesce to protect freedom expression from the newspaper industry's powerful economic influence.[52]

Finally, policymakers of this nation need to come to an understanding and agreement about the changing market nature and climate of the media. As the U.S. Supreme Court and media analysts have recognized, entry into the newspaper business is much more difficult than it once was. It takes more than owning a printing press, which is a cost by itself that severely discourages entry into the newspaper market. Printed-word journalistic enterprise is limited in a way similar to the limitations of broadcast and cable. Given this restrained newspaper environment, the government should move away from restrictions on public support of newspapers to encourage journalistic enterprise not limited by a dependence solely on advertising and circulation revenue and large start-up costs.

Just as public radio and television stations are granted licenses through municipalities or universities, government could establish local editorial boards, perhaps overseen by public library boards, or school boards, with editorships free from publication oversight, other than financial ones. As Coulson argued on behalf of government enforcement of antitrust legislation to stem newspapers' restrictive business practices, a press that is preoccupied with profit margins ill-serves the public. "The gathering of newspaper ownership into larger and more centralized units justifies government economic intervention to promote diversity of expression" in a way that avoids government regulation, he observed.[53]

The sort of public newspaper boards suggested here would not be licensed, as are public radio and television stations. Because of the obvious negative conflict-of-interest and First Amendment ramifications, government licensure of the press never should be sanctioned. Rather, these local newspaper boards, perhaps with staggered and rotating memberships, would act as publishers in providing (government) funding to take care of printing and distribution. Beyond that, their bylaws would forbid editorial oversight other than establishing a staff and letting it go about its journalistic business.

Government involvement with the press is not unique, nor is government support of endeavors involving research, artistic and journalistic enterprise. The federal government's Department of Defense publishes the *Stars and Stripes;* universities and high schools are tax-supported governmental organizations that publish newspapers and operate student radio and television enterprises. In a less overt system of government support for media outlets, National Public Radio and the Public Broadcasting System are journalistic enterprises partially supported by government subsidy, along with direct audience funding, that provide alternative news voices beyond the private and cable models. Careful crafting of newspaper media advisory boards could bring about the same sort of journalistic competition and choice.

The Swedish model provides a successful example of such government intervention in newspaper operations. Newspaper markets in that nation followed similar trends to those in the United States, in which ownership during the 1970s began to become concentrated in fewer hands. A 1995 study of Swedish media ownership discussed this phenomenon, in which communities that traditionally had enjoyed newspaper competition saw the failure of some newspapers with others experiencing "increasingly dire economic straits. A system of direct state press subsidies was introduced in the early 1970s (indirect political support via political parties had been introduced in 1965), thanks to which it was possible to continue publication of two competing newspapers in some twenty, principally larger, towns and cities."[54]

Fears of competition from practitioners in private enterprise (the newspaper lobby likely would fight this idea just as vigorously as it battled on behalf of the Newspaper Preservation Act) would have to be overcome. But government support of an enterprise that competes with the private sector is nothing new; libraries compete with private book stores; buses, subways, and trains compete with privately owned taxi and airline companies; public hospitals compete with private facilities.

Nor is the notion of government sponsorship of competing newspapers a new or radical idea. The Hutchins Commission in the mid-twentieth century raised the possibility in several places in its report. Arguing that the "cure for distorted information would seem to be more information, not less,"[55] the commission members reasoned that there is nothing in the First Amendment "or in our political tradition to prevent the government from participating in mass communications: to state its own case, to supplement private sources of information, and to propose standards for private emulation. Such participation by government is not dangerous to the freedom of the press."[56]

To that end, the commission recommended:

- Facilitation by the government of "new ventures in the communications industry, that it [government] foster the introduction of new techniques, that it maintain competition among large units through the antitrust laws, but that those laws be sparingly used to break up such units, and that, where concentration is necessary in communications, the government endeavor to see to it that the public gets the benefit of such concentration."[57]

- That "nonprofit institutions help supply the variety, quantity, and quality of press service required by the American people."[58]

Argued the commission report: "Since the consumer is no longer free not to consume, and can get what he requires only through existing press organs, protection of the freedom of the press is no longer sufficient to protect automatically either the consumer or the community. The general policy of laissez faire in this field must be reconsidered."[59] Those words, written in 1947, accurately portrayed the public information dilemma of the era; they spoke to a problem of media concentration that has worsened more than a half century later. Thus, this proposed solution becomes less radical and more practical.

The benefits of such a public enterprise would be numerous. A second editorial voice in a community could look into stories and ideas that the commercial press avoids for reasons ranging from fear of offending advertisers to such conflicts of interest as newspaper ownership involvement in local business concerns, or business or advertiser membership on local newspaper boards. A second editorial voice in a community would provide competition for the existing press, thus bringing about an improved product (research findings on this subject vary, but it is not difficult to find research and, for that matter, newspaper editorials lauding the benefits to consumers that competition brings about). A second editorial voice would provide a richer agenda and a wider range of topics. It would serve as a check on a monopoly newspaper that abuses its power. A second editorial voice in a community would help to restore the diversity in localism, in agenda, and in topics that this book's research has discovered in competing newspapers.

Such a voice may not be necessary in communities served by direct, JOA, metroplex, or umbrella newspaper competition, but it is needed in the thousands of smaller communities in the nation in which monopoly presses enjoy unlimited and unchallenged economic and agenda-setting power. Such a second voice need not be established in numerous communities at once; let it be a pilot project, an experiment, similar to establishment of the TVA during the first term of President Franklin D. Roosevelt to compete with large, private utility companies by producing low-power hydroelectricity cheaply—and successfully.

More recently, the FCC undertook a similar experiment, the establishment of low-power FM public radio stations, licensed to local municipalities and boards, to fill a localism and programming void with broadcast outlets that typically do not reach beyond ten miles.[60] This experiment, undertaken over the opposition of privately owned and some public radio stations, also has been successful and demonstrates how voice diversity can be expanded through public/private media partnerships.

The larger benefit of such an experimental undertaking in expanding idea availability could be a society more likely to find diversity on the streets rather than having to seek it out in libraries or in select journals. It also would be a society with access to the sort of diverse and competing public discussion that Jefferson, Milton, the Supreme Court, and others have found essential.

Surely it can be agreed that a fully-stocked market basket of ideas is in the best long-term interests of this nation.

Notes

PREFACE

1. The three newspaper executives were interviewed by telephone, Burkett on February 23, 2004, and Aregood and Craig on February 24, 2004.

INTRODUCTION

1. Allan Nevins, ed., *American Press Opinion: Washington to Coolidge, A Documentary Record of Editorial Leadership and Criticism, 1785–1927,* (New York: D.C. Heath and Company, 1928), 47–48.

2. Roya Akhavan-Majid, Anita Rife, and Sheila Gopinath, "Chain Ownership and Editorial Independence: A Case Study of Gannett Newspapers," *Journalism Quarterly* 68, 1/2 (Spring/Summer 1991): 61–62.

3. Barbara Funkhouser, telephone interview by author, Las Cruces, N.M., March 21, 2003.

4. Ibid.

5. See Ben H. Bagdikian, *The Media Monopoly,* 6th ed. (Boston: Beacon Press, 2000), 45; Martha M. Matthews, "How Public Ownership Affects Publisher Autonomy," *Journalism & Mass Communication Quarterly* 73, no. 2 (Summer 1996): 342; William A. Hatchen, *The Troubles of Journalism: A Critical Look at What's Right and Wrong with the Press,* 2nd ed. (Mahwah, NJ: Lawrence Erlbaum Associates, 2001): 75, 91.

6. Benjamin M. Compaine and Douglas Gomery, *Who Owns the Media? Competition and Concentration in the Mass Media Industry,* 3rd ed. (Mahwah, NJ: Lawrence Erlbaum Associates, Inc., 2000), 8.

7. See Melvin Mencher, *News Reporting and Writing,* 9th ed. (New York: Columbia University, 2003), 80. The year 2003 is used here because it is the second year of the two years (2001 and 2003) of newspapers studied for the archival content analyses for this book. *Editor & Publisher* magazine's 2005 edition lists forty-five cities with more than one daily newspaper, but many of these are cities where the competing newspapers are owned by the same company, or the competing newspapers are non-English language niche newspapers. For the purposes of analyzing newspapers in the context of a marketplace of ideas, this book will rely on the figures attained by Mencher's research.

8. *Editor & Publisher International Yearbook 1930*, (New York: Editor & Publisher, 1930), 134.

9. *Editor & Publisher International Yearbook 2003*, (New York: Editor & Publisher, 2003), vii.

10. *Editor & Publisher International Yearbook 1971*, (New York: Editor & Publisher, 1971), 13.

11. Bagdikian, *Media Monopoly*, 222.

12. Katharine Q. Seelye, "Players Big and Small are Sifting Through Pieces of Knight Ridder, *New York Times*, March 27, 2006, C1.

13. Debra Gersh Hernandez, "Profiles of the News Consumer," *Editor & Publisher* 130 (January 1997): 6.

14. Benjamin J. Bates, "Breaking the Structural Logjam: The Impact of Cable on Local TV Market Concentration," *Journal of Media Economics* 4, no. 3 (Fall 1991): 47–57.

15. Guido H. Stempel, Thomas Hargrove, and Joseph P. Bernt, "Relation of Growth of Use of the Internet to Changes in Media Use from 1995 to 1999," *Journalism & Mass Communication Quarterly* 77, no. 1 (Spring 2000): 71–79.

16. John Dimmick, Yan Chen, and Zhan Li, "Competition Between the Internet and Traditional News Media: The Gratification-Opportunities Niche Dimension," *Journal of Media Economics* 17, no. 1 (2004): 19–33.

17. "Study Tracks Trends in Profession," *Quill* 92 (May 2004): 7.

18. Janet Kolodzy, "Everything that Rises/Media Convergence is an Opportunity, Not a Curse," *Columbia Journalism Review* 42, no. 2 (July/August 2003): 61.

19. Hernandez, "Profiles of News Consumer."

20. Ibid.

21. Ibid.

22. Guido H. Stempel III, "Where People *Really* Get Most of Their News," *Newspaper Research Journal* 1, no. 4 (Fall 1991): 2.

23. Joey Reagan and Richard V. Ducey, "Effects of News Measure on Selection of State Government News Sources," *Journalism Quarterly* 60, no. 2 (Summer 1983): 211.

24. John Milton, "Areopagitica," in *English Reprints* 1 (New York: AMS Press, Inc., 1969), 74.

25. Philip M. Napoli, *Foundations of Communications Policy; Principles and Process in the Regulation of Electronic Media* (Cresskill, NJ: Hampton Press, Inc., 2001), 100.

26. J.A. Smith, "Freedom of Expression and the Marketplace of Ideas Concept from Milton to Jefferson," *Journal of Communication Inquiry* 7, no. 1 (Summer 1981): 47–64.

27. Robert A. Rutland, "The First Great Newspaper Debate: The Constitutional Crisis of 1787–1788," *Proceedings of the American Antiquarian Society* 97 (Part I, 1987): 58.

28. Steven H. Chaffee and Donna G. Wilson, "Media Rich, Media Poor: Two Studies of Diversity in Agenda-Holding," *Journalism Quarterly* 54, no. 3 (Autumn 1977): 466–76.

29. David Pearce Demers, *The Menace of the Corporate Newspaper: Fact or Fiction?* (Ames: Iowa State University Press, 1996), 321–23.

30. The Commission on Freedom of the Press, *A Free and Responsible Press: A General Report on Mass Communication: Newspapers, Radio, Motion Pictures, Magazines, and Books* (Chicago, IL: The University of Chicago Press, 1947), 9.

31. Ibid., 67–68.

32. Ibid., 60–68.

33. Michael W. Drager, "Measuring the Marketplace: Diversity and Editorial Content" (paper presented at the annual meeting of the Association for Education in Journalism and Mass Communication, New Orleans, LA, August 1999).

34. Theodore L. Glasser, "Competition and Diversity Among Radio Formats: Legal and Structural Issues," *Journal of Broadcasting* 28, no. 2 (Spring 1984): 137.

35. Don R. Pember, *Mass Media Law*, 5th ed. (Dubuque, IA: Wm. C. Brown Publishers, 1990), 591–92.

36. Bagdikian, *Media Monopoly*, 125.

37. Gayle A. Waldrop, *Editor and Editorial Writer*, 3rd ed. (Dubuque, IA: Wm. C. Brown Company Publishers, 1967), 4–5.

38. F. Dennis Hale, "Editorial Diversity and Concentration," in *Press Concentration and Monopoly: New Perspectives on Newspaper Ownership and Concentration*, ed. Robert G. Picard, James P. Winter, Maxwell E. McCombs, and Stephen Lacy (Norwood, NJ: Ablex Publishing Corporation, 1988), 170.

39. Bill Kovach and Tom Rosenstiel, *The Elements of Journalism: What Newspeople Should Know and the Public Should Expect* (New York: Crown Publishers, 2001), 40.

40. Richard B. Morris, ed., *Encyclopedia of American History Bicentennial Edition* (New York: Harper & Row, Publishers, 1976).

41. Stephen Richard Lacy, "The Effects of Ownership and Competition on Daily Newspaper Content" (Ph.D. diss., University of Texas at Austin, 1986), 271.

42. Paul Deutschmann, *News-Page Content of Twelve Metropolitan Dailies* (Cincinnati: Scripps-Howard Research, 1959), 92–95.

43. Ron Rodgers, Steve Hallock, Mike Gennaria, and Fei Wei, "Two Papers in Joint Operating Agreement Publish Meaningful Editorial Diversity," *Newspaper Research Journal* 25, no. 4 (Fall 2004): 104–9.

CHAPTER 1

1. Nevins, *American Press Opinion*, 71–72.

2. Scott Ellsworth, *Death in a Promised Land/The Tulsa Race Riot of 1921*, (Baton Rouge: Louisiana State University Press, 1982), 46–47.

3. Ibid., 52.

4. Neil Henry, "When Tulsa Burned," *Mother Jones*, March–April 2002, 81–82.

5. Ellsworth, *Death in a Promised Land*, 48.

6. See Kenneth Rystrom, "Apparent Impact of Endorsements by Group and Independent Newspapers," *Journalism Quarterly* 64, no. 2/3 (Summer/Autumn 1987): 449–53; Byron St. Dizier, "The Effect of Newspaper Endorsements and Party Identification on Voting Choice," *Journalism Quarterly* 62, no. 3 (Autumn 1985): 589–94; Fred Fedler, Ron F. Smith, and Tim Counts, "Voter Uses and Perceptions of Editorial Endorsements," *Newspaper Research Journal* 6, no. 1 (Fall 1984): 19–23; Robert E. Hurd and Michael Singletary, "Newspaper Endorsement Influence on the 1980 Presidential Election Vote," *Journalism Quarterly* 61, no. 2 (Summer 1984): 332–38; Fred Fedler, Tim Counts, and Lowndes F. Stephens, "Newspaper Endorsements and Voter Behavior in the 1980 Presidential Election," *Newspaper Research Journal* 4, no. 1 (Fall 1982): 3–11; Solomon M. Fulero, "Perceived Influence of Endorsements on Voting," *Journalism Quarterly* 54, no. 4 (Winter 1977), 789–91; Paul L. Hain, "How an Endorsement Affected a Non-Partisan

Mayoral Vote," *Journalism Quarterly* 52, no. 3 (Summer 1975): 337–40; John P. Robinson, "The Press as King-Maker: What Surveys From Last Five Campaigns Show," *Journalism Quarterly* 51 (Winter 1974): 587–94; Maxwell McCombs, "Editorial Endorsement: A Study of Influence," *Journalism Quarterly* 44 (Autumn 1967): 545–48; James E. Gregg, "Newspaper Editorial Endorsements and California Elections, 1948–62," *Journalism Quarterly* 42 (Autumn 1965): 532–38; James L. McDowell, "The Role of Newspapers in Illinois' At-Large Election," *Journalism Quarterly* 42 (Spring 1965): 281–84; and Michael Hooper, "Party and Newspaper Endorsement as Predictors of Voter Choice," *Journalism Quarterly* 46 (Summer 1964): 302–5.

7. William David Sloan and Laird B. Anderson, *Pulitzer Prize Editorials/America's Best Writing 1917–2003*, 3rd ed. (Ames, IA: Iowa State University Press, 2003), 35–36.

8. Ibid., 39.

9. Ibid.

10. Ibid., 113.

11. Ibid., 127.

12. Ibid., 136–37.

13. William David Sloan, Cheryl S. Wray, and C. Joanne Sloan, *Great Editorials; Masterpieces of Opinion Writing,* (Northport, AL: Vision Press, 1997), 99.

14. Ibid.

15. Ibid.

16. John Harper, "Who Reads Us, Who Doesn't, and What that Tells Us," *Masthead* 44 (Winter 1992): 16.

17. Susan Albright, "Editorial Page Readership: A Task Force Report National Conference of Editorial Writers," September 1994: 1–2.

18. Sloan, Wray, and Sloan, *Great Editorials*, 23.

19. Ibid., 24–25.

20. Ibid., 41–42.

21. Charles A. Pilant, "Expressions of Nationalistic Sentiments in Early American Newspapers, 1776–1826" (Ph.D. diss., Marquette University, 1989), 197–98.

22. Nevins, *American Press Opinion*, 4.

23. Ibid., 3, 6.

24. Pilant, "Expressions of Nationalistic Sentiments," 12.

25. Ibid., 13.

26. Sloan, Wray, and Sloan, *Great Editorials*, 43.

27. Ibid., 49–50.

28. Pilant, "Expressions of Nationalistic Sentiments," 105.

29. Ibid., 143.

30. Nevins, *American Press Opinion*, 23.

31. Sloan, Wray, and Sloan, *Great Editorials*, 65.

32. Pilant, "Expressions of Nationalistic Sentiments," 147.

33. Ibid., 167.

34. Ibid., 185.

35. Ibid., 43.

36. Ibid., 193.

37. Nevins, *American Press Opinion*, 109.

38. Ibid., 112.

39. Susan Annette Thompson, "The Antebellum Penny Press" (Ph.D. diss., University of Alabama, 2002), 3.

40. Ibid., 361.

41. Ibid., 129.

42. Nevins, *American Press Opinion*, 143.

43. Fourierism, which advocated the reorganization of society into small communities or phalanxes, was based on the socialist philosophy of France's Charles Fourier and came to be known in 1840s America as Associationism. See Gregory Claeys and Lyman Tower Sargent, eds., *The Utopia Reader* (New York and London: New York University Press, 1999), 199–200.

44. Sloan, Wray, and Sloan, *Great Editorials*, 87.

45. Ibid., 71.

46. Ibid., 86.

47. Ibid., 105–7.

48. Nevins, *American Press Opinion*, 211.

49. Thompson, "The Antebellum Penny Press," 320.

50. Sloan, Wray, and Sloan, *Great Editorials*, 85.

51. Thompson, "The Antebellum Penny Press," 368.

52. Sloan, Wray, and Sloan, *Great Editorials*, 142.

53. Ibid., 143.

54. Ibid., 150.

CHAPTER 2

1. Nevins, *American Press Opinion*, 77.

2. Thompson, "The Antebellum Penny Press," 120–121.

3. Ibid., 120.

4. Rutland, "First Great Newspaper Debate," 55–56.

5. Ibid., 57.

6. Ibid., 44.

7. Ibid., 57–58.

8. Nevins, *American Press Opinion*, 149–50.

9. Ibid., 150–151.

10. Ibid., 150.

11. Ibid., 156–57.

12. Ibid., 158–59.

13. Thompson, "The Antebellum Penny Press," 62–63.

14. Sloan, Wray, and Sloan, *Great Editorials*, 68.

15. Thompson, "The Antebellum Penny Press," 64.

16. William E. Huntzicker, *The Popular Press, 1833–1865*, (Westport, CT: Greenwood Press, 1999), 118.

17. Ibid.

18. James Melvin Lee, *History of American Journalism*, 2nd ed. (Garden City, New York: The Garden City Publishing Co., Inc., 1923), 213.

19. Ibid., 213–14.

20. Thompson, "The Antebellum Penny Press," 220–21.

21. Ibid., 219–20.

22. "A Monopoly Ends," *Badger Herald,* September 10, 1969.

23. Rutland, "First Great Newspaper Debate," 58.

24. Glasser, "Competition and Diversity," 127–42.

25. Ben H. Bagdikian, "The U.S. Media: Supermarket or Assembly Line?" *Journal of Communication* 35, no. 3 (Summer 1985): 97–109.

26. Pember, *Mass Media Law,* 591–92.

27. Stanley K. Bigman, "Rivals in Conformity: A Study of Two Competing Dailies," *Journalism Quarterly* 25, no. 2 (Summer 1948): 127–31.

28. Gerard H. Borstel, "Ownership, Competition and Comment in 20 Small Dailies," *Journalism Quarterly* 52, no. 3 (Autumn 1975): 220–22.

29. Raymond B. Nixon and Robert L. Jones, "The Content of Non-Competitive vs. Competitive Newspapers," *Journalism Quarterly* 33, no. 3 (Summer 1956): 299–314.

30. Robert M. Entman, "Newspaper Competition and First Amendment Ideals: Does Monopoly Matter?" *Journal of Communication* 35, no. 3 (Summer 1985): 147–65.

31. Benjamin M. Compaine, "The Expanding Base of Media Competition," *Journal of Communication* 35, no. 3 (Summer 1985): 81–96.

32. Maxwell McCombs, "Effect of Monopoly in Cleveland on Diversity of Newspaper Content," *Journalism Quarterly* 64, no. 4 (Winter 1987): 740–44.

33. John C. Busterna and Kathleen A. Hansen, "Presidential Endorsement Patterns by Chain-Owned Newspapers, 1976–84," *Journalism Quarterly* 67, no. 2 (Summer 1990): 286–94.

34. John C. Busterna and Robert Picard, *Joint Operating Agreements: The Newspaper Preservation Act and Its Application* (Norwood, NJ: Ablex Publishing, 1993), 89.

35. David Demers, "Effect of Corporate Structure on Autonomy of Top Editors at U.S. Dailies," *Journalism Quarterly* 70, no. 3 (Autumn 1993): 499–508.

36. David Demers, "Corporate Newspaper Structure, Editorial Page Vigor, and Social Change," *Journalism & Mass Communication Quarterly* 73, no. 4 (Winter 1996): 857–77.

37. Roya Akhavan-Majid and Timothy Boudreau, "Chain Ownership, Organizational Style, and Editorial Role Perceptions," *Journalism & Mass Communication Quarterly* 72, no. 4 (Winter 1995): 863–73.

38. American Society of Newspaper Editors, "News and Editorial Independence: A Survey of Group and Independent Editors," *ASNE Bulletin* (April 1980): 13–28.

39. Ralph Thrift Jr., "How Chain Ownership Affects Editorial Page Vigor of Newspapers," *Journalism Quarterly* 54, no. 2 (Summer 1977): 327–31.

40. Daniel B. Wackman, Donald M. Gillmore, Cecilie Gaziano, and Everette E. Dennis, "Chain Newspaper Autonomy as Reflected in Presidential Campaign Endorsements," *Journalism Quarterly* 52, no. 3 (Autumn 1975): 411–19.

41. Cecilie Gaziano, "Chain Newspaper Homogeneity and Presidential Endorsements, 1971–1988," *Journalism Quarterly* 66, no. 4 (Winter 1989): 836–45.

42. Dominic L. Lasorsa, "Effects of Newspaper Competition on Public Opinion Diversity," *Journalism Quarterly* 68, no. 1/2 (Spring/Summer 1991): 38–47.

43. Jan P. Vermeer, "Multiple Newspapers and Electoral Competition: A County-Level Analysis," *Journalism & Mass Communication Quarterly* 72, no. 1 (Spring 1995): 98–105.

44. All circulation figures are from the *Editor & Publisher International Yearbook 2003.*

45. "Listen to Truth-Teller at Treasury," *Chicago Tribune,* January 22, 2001.

46. "Taxpayers Finally Get a Friend in W.," *Chicago Sun-Times*, January 23, 2001.

47. "Let Ashcroft Do the Job He Knows," *Chicago Sun-Times*, January 22, 2001.

48. "The Real Question About Ashcroft," *Chicago Tribune*, January 14, 2001.

49. "A Reluctant Yes to John Ashcroft," *Chicago Tribune*, January 23, 2001.

50. "Freed from Death Row," *Chicago Tribune*, January 12, 2003.

51. "Ryan Has Right on His Side, But He's Gone Horribly Wrong," *Chicago Sun-Times*, January 12, 2003.

52. "Obstruction of Justice," *Chicago Tribune*, January 15, 2003.

53. "Makowski's Legacy is One of County Progress," *Citizens' Voice*, January 5, 2003.

54. "Makowski's Legacy; Much to Look Down," *Times Leader*, January 12, 2003.

55. "Using VC Space for Detention Would be Creative," *Citizens' Voice*, January 24, 2001.

56. "Nursing Home Cannot Sub as a Penal Institution," *Times Leader*, January 28, 2001.

57. "Mayor's Lack of Focus and Follow-Up is Costly," *Times Leader*, January 2, 2001.

58. "Izzo's Exit Should Spur Evaluation of Administration," *Citizens' Voice*, January 8, 2001.

59. Sidney Kobre, *Modern American Journalism* (Tallahassee, FL: Florida State University, 1959), 200.

60. Robert A. Rutland, *The Newsmongers: Journalism in the Life of the Nation 1690–1972* (New York: The Dial Press, 1973), 315.

61. Fred Ney, assistant city editor of the *Citizens' Voice*, telephone interview by author, Wilkes-Barre, PA, January 24, 2005.

CHAPTER 3

1. Nevins, *American Press Opinion*, 325–26.

2. Sinclair Lewis, *Babbitt* (New York: P.F. Collier & Son Corporation, 1922), 2.

3. Ibid., 1.

4. Ibid., 76.

5. Ibid.

6. "The Sinking of the Lusitania," *Pittsburgh Press*, May 8, 1915.

7. "Sinking of Lusitania," *Gazette Times*, May 8, 1915.

8. "The Sinking of the Lusitania," *Pittsburgh Press*.

9. "Sinking of Lusitania," *Gazette Times*.

10. "Being Fair to Germany," *Gazette Times*, May 9, 1915.

11. "Wilson in New York," *Gazette Times*, November 2, 1912.

12. "The Duty of All," *Pittsburgh Press*, November 3, 1924.

13. "Why America Is Republican," *Gazette Times*, November 4, 1924.

14. "The Execution of Sacco and Vanzetti," *Pittsburgh Press*, August 23, 1927.

15. "The Law Claims Its Due," *Pittsburgh Post-Gazette*, August 23, 1927.

16. "A Major Blunder," *Tulsa Tribune*, May 9, 1960.

17. "A 'Spy' Incident With Bad Results," *Tulsa Daily World*, May 10, 1960.

18. "The Wall Is Still There," *Tulsa Tribune*, June 27, 1963.

19. "Ich Bin Ein Berliner," *Tulsa Daily World*, June 27, 1963.

20. "END OF SEGREGATION—EVENTUALLY," *Tulsa Tribune*, May 18, 1954.

52. Tax Cuts/Bush's $674 Billion Plan/A Balanced Approach," *Cincinnati Enquirer*, January 12, 2003.

53. "More Harm Than Good," *Cincinnati Post*, January 9, 2003.

54. "Speed I-69 Project Along Its Way," *Fort Wayne Journal Gazette*, January 12, 2003.

55. "A Little More Fight, Please," *Fort Wayne News-Sentinel*, January 17, 2003.

56. "Give Ashcroft Tough Scrutiny," *Fort Wayne Journal Gazette*, January 4, 2001.

57. "Ask Mr. Ashcroft the Right Questions," *Fort Wayne News-Sentinel*, January 5, 2001.

58. "Bush Plan Should Lose Vouchers," *Fort Wayne Journal Gazette*, January 24, 2001.

59. "A Matter of Choice," *Fort Wayne News-Sentinel*, January 30, 2001.

60. "Case for War Hasn't Been Made," *Fort Wayne News-Sentinel*, January 21, 2003.

61. "The Right War Question," *Fort Wayne News-Sentinel*, January 31, 2003.

62. "Backdoor Ploy on Arctic Oil," *Fort Wayne Journal Gazette*, January 21, 2003.

CHAPTER 4

1. Nevins, *American Press Opinion*, 344–46.

2. "A Cornerstone," *Cleveland Press*, August 5, 1935.

3. "Bills Now Laws," *Plain Dealer*, August 16, 1935.

4. "In War," *Cleveland Press*, December 8, 1941.

5. "History Repeats," *Plain Dealer*, December 8, 1941.

6. "The Atomic Bomb—And After," *Cleveland Press*, August 7, 1945.

7. "Manhattan Project," *Plain Dealer*, August 7, 1945.

8. Jordan A. Schwarz, *The New Dealers: Power Politics in the Age of Roosevelt* (New York: Alfred A. Knopf, 1993), 136.

9. "The Tennessee Valley," *Evening Star*, May 19, 1933.

10. "The Muscle Shoals Boom," *Washington Post*, May 19, 1933.

11. "The New Farm Act," *Evening Star*, May 13, 1933.

12. "An Experiment Begins," *Washington Post*, May 13, 1933.

13. "The Constitution Re-established," *Washington Star*, May 28, 1935.

14. "The NRA Decision," *Washington Post*, May 28, 1935.

15. "Japan's Grave Blunder," *Evening Star*, December 13, 1937.

16. "The Bombing of the Panay," *Washington Post*, December 14, 1937.

17. "American Neutrality," *Evening Star*, September 4, 1939.

18. "The President's Lead," *Washington Post*, September 4, 1939.

19. "Franklin Delano Roosevelt," *Evening Star*, April 13, 1945.

20. "Mr. Roosevelt," *Washington Post*, April 13, 1945.

21. Stephen Lacy, David C. Coulson, and Hiromi Cho, "Competition for Readers Among U.S. Metropolitan Daily, Nonmetropolitan Daily, and Weekly Newspapers," Journal of Media Economics 15, no. 1 (2002): 21–40.

22. Diana Stover Tillinghast, "Limits of Competition," in *Press Concentration and Monopoly: New Perspectives on Newspaper Ownership and Concentration*, ed. Robert G. Picard, James P. Winter, Maxwell E. McCombs, and Stephen Lacy (Norwood, NJ: Ablex Publishing Corporation, 1988), 86; see also Janet A. Bridges, Barry R. Litman, and Lamar W. Bridges, "Rosse's Model Revisited: Moving to Concentric Circles to Explain Newspaper Competition," *Journal of Media Economics* 15, no. 1 (2002): 3–19; K.E. Gustafsson,

"The Umbrella Model-Upside-Down," *Nordicom Review* 1 (Summer 1996): 181–93; Stephen Lacy and A.B. Sohn, "Correlations of Newspaper Content with Circulation in the Suburbs: A Case Study," *Journalism Quarterly* 67, no. 4 (Winter 1990): 784–93; and S.M. Devey, "Umbrella Competition for Newspaper Circulation in the Boston Metro Area," *Journal of Media Economics* 2, no. 1 (Spring 1989): 31–40.

23. Stephen Lacy, "Competing in the Suburbs: A Research Review of Intercity Newspaper Competition," *Newspaper Research Journal* 9, no. 2 (Winter 1988): 69–76.

24. All circulation figures are from the *Editor & Publisher International Yearbook 2003*.

25. Dennis B. Roddy, "Shakeup at the *Tribune-Review*; Layoffs Expected at All Newspapers," *Pittsburgh Post-Gazette*, January 20, 2005.

26. "Texas Senate Equality: Ratliff's Selections Reaffirm Austin's Bipartisan Tradition," *Dallas Morning News*, January 5, 2001.

27. "Redistricting: Will Bill Ratliff's Panel be a Palatable Mix or a Recipe for Disaster?" *Fort Worth Star-Telegram*, January 6, 2001.

28. "Straight Talk: Saddam Has Played the World Long Enough," *Dallas Morning News*, January 29, 2003.

29. "Sending Signals," *Fort Worth Star-Telegram*, January 29, 2003.

30. "M.L. King Day: Lessons are Still to be Learned About Stereotypes," *Dallas Morning News*, January 15, 2001.

31. "Shared Dreams," *Fort Worth Star-Telegram*, January 15, 2001.

32. "A Deal for WQED? Keeping the Public in Public Television," *Pittsburgh Post-Gazette*, January 17, 2001.

33. "Oxymora on the March," *Tribune-Review*, January 14, 2001.

34. "Affirming a Negative: Bush Unwisely Chooses Sides in Admissions Case," *Pittsburgh Post-Gazette*, January 21, 2003.

35. "The Michigan Quotas: Arbitrary and Insidious," *Tribune-Review*, January 16, 2003.

36. "Arbitrary and Capricious," *Tribune-Review*, January 16, 2003.

37. "Death Interrupted/Gov. Ryan Makes a Dramatic Gesture as He Leaves Office," *Pittsburgh Post-Gazette*, January 20, 2003.

38. "Massachusetts Massacre: A Too-Familiar Story of Frustration and Firepower," *Pittsburgh Post-Gazette*, January 1, 2001.

39. "Founders as 'extremists,'" *Tribune-Review*, January 20, 2001.

CHAPTER 5

1. Nevins, *American Press Opinion*, 371–72.

2. CNN.com, Inside Politics/America Votes 2004, "Voter Turnout Highest Since 1968," http://www.cnn.com/2004/ALLPOLITICS/11/03/voter.turnout.ap/ (accessed November 3, 2004; site now discontinued).

3. Greg Mitchell, "Daily Endorsement Tally: Kerry Wins, Without Recount," *Editor & Publisher*, http://www.editorandpublisher.com/eandp/index.jsp (accessed November 5, 2004).

4. *Abrams et al, v. United States*, 250 U.S. 616 (1919).

5. *Thornhill v. Alabama*, 301 U.S. 88 (1940).

6. Pember, *Mass Media Law*, 591–92.

7. Patricia Aufderheide, *Communications Policy and the Public Interest: The Telecommunications Act of 1996* (New York: Guilford Press, 1999), 61.

8. Napoli, *Foundations of Communications Policy*, 24–25.

9. Bagdikian, "U.S. Media."

10. Hurd and Singletary, "Newspaper Endorsement Influence."

11. Fedler, Counts, and Stephens, "Newspaper Endorsements."

12. Ibid.

13. See Rystrom, "Apparent Impact of Endorsements;" St. Dizier, "Effect of Newspaper Endorsements;" Fedler, Smith, and Counts, "Voter Uses and Perceptions;" Hurd and Singletary, "Newspaper Endorsement Influence;" Fedler, Counts, and Stephens, "Newspaper Endorsements;" Fulero, "Perceived Influence of Endorsements;" Hain, "How an Endorsement Affected;" Robinson, "Press as King-Maker;" McCombs, "Editorial Endorsement;" Gregg, "Newspaper Editorial Endorsements;" McDowell, "Role of Newspapers;" and Hooper, "Party and Newspaper Endorsement."

14. "Life, Liberty and Cheap Gasoline," *Chicago Tribune*, May 29, 2004.

15. "Want Lower Gas Prices? Simple—Use Less Gas," *Chicago Sun-Times*, April 5, 2004.

16. "John Kerry's Promises," *Boston Globe*, July 30, 2004.

17. "Kerry's Tough Talk at Odds with Record," *Boston Herald*, July 30, 2004.

18. "John Kerry's Two Vietnams," *Chicago Tribune*, August 24, 2004.

19. "Open the Records and Shut the Speculation," *Chicago Sun-Times*, August 24, 2004.

20. "Edwards Spices Up Democratic Ticket," *Denver Post*, July 7, 2004.

21. "Kerry Chooses a Southern Populist," *Rocky Mountain News*, July 7, 2004.

22. "The Kerry Moment," *Seattle Times*, July 30, 2004.

23. "Kerry Shows Himself, His Case," *Seattle Post-Intelligencer*, July 30, 2004.

24. "George W. Bush for President/Key Difference: Foreign Policy," *Rocky Mountain News*, October 16, 2004.

25. "George W. Bush for President," *Denver Post*, October 24, 2004.

26. "Can Rumsfeld/Iraqi Prisoner Abuses Call for a New Defense Chief," *Pittsburgh Post-Gazette*, May 7, 2004.

27. "The Abuse Scandal," *Tribune-Review*, May 12, 2004.

28. "Star Quality/Kerry and the Democrats Made a Powerful Pitch," *Pittsburgh Post-Gazette*, August 1, 2004.

29. "Our Best Days?" *Pittsburgh Tribune-Review*, August 1, 2004.

30. "A Stalled Discussion," *Fort Worth Star-Telegram*, August 26, 2004.

31. "Clear the Decks: Swift Boats Throw a Fog Over Real Priorities," *Dallas Morning News*, August 24, 2004.

32. "Backing the Old George W. Bush," *Fort Worth Star-Telegram*, October, 17, 2004.

33. "Bush? Kerry? Neither?" *Tribune-Review*, October 31, 2004.

CHAPTER 6

1. Nevins, *American Press Opinion*, 431–32.

CHAPTER 7

1. Nevins, *American Press Opinion*, 488–89.

2. *Tomorrow Never Dies*, VHS, directed by Roger Spottiswoode (MGM/UA Video, 1997).

3. "Who Owns What," The Walt Disney Company, *Columbia Journalism Review* website, http://www.cjr.org/tools/owners/ (last accessed August 15, 2006, dates given here and in the following represent the most recent update of ownership data by the site).

4. "Who Owns What," Belo Corporation, Ibid. (last accessed August 15, 2006).

5. "Who Owns What," Gannett, Ibid. (last accessed August 15, 2006).

6. "Who Owns What," MediaNews Group, Ibid. (last accessed September 11, 2006). These figures do not include newspapers purchased by the group following the 2006 sale of Knight Ridder newspapers.

7. "Who Owns What," The New York Times Company, Ibid. (last accessed August 15, 2006). These figures do not include possible sales of broadcast outlets by the Times company. National Public Radio reported on September 13 that the company may be putting some broadcast outlets on the market.

8. "Who Owns What," Tribune Company, Ibid. (last accessed August 15, 2006).

9. Compaine and Gomery, *Who Owns the Media?* 8.

10. Ibid.

11. The Commission on Freedom of the Press, *Free and Responsible Press*, 124.

12. Ibid., 130.

13. Ibid., 119.

14. Rifka Rosenwein, "Why Media Mergers Matter," *Brill's Content*, December 1999–January 2000: 93.

15. Soontae An and Hyun Seung Jin, "Interlocking of Newspaper Companies with Financial Institutions and Leading Advertisers," *Journalism & Mass Communication Quarterly* 81, no. 3 (Autumn 2004): 586–87.

16. See Bagdikian, *Media Monopoly*; Robert W. McChesney, *Rich Media, Poor Democracy: Communication Politics in Dubious Times* (New York: The New Press, 1999); Robert G. Picard, James P. Winter, Maxwell E. McCombs, and Stephen Lacy, *Press Concentration and Monopoly: New Perspectives on Newspaper Ownership and Concentration* (Norwood, NJ: Ablex Publishing Corporation, 1988); and Compaine and Gomery, *Who Owns the Media?*

17. *Tomorrow Never Dies*, VHS.

18. Alison Miller, "Debate Over Cross-Ownership Continues," American Society of Newspaper Editors website, http://www.asne.org/index.cfm?ID=5204 (accessed March 13, 2005).

19. Everette E. Dennis and John C. Merrill, *Media Debates: Issues in Mass Communication* (White Plains, NY: Longman, 2001), 71–75.

20. "Democrats Attack Plan for Anti-Kerry Broadcast," *Los Angeles Times*, October 12, 2004.

21. Chaka Ferguson, Associated Press, "Deal Reached on Anti-War Billboard," *Mercury News*, July 16, 2004.

22. Bill Holland, Reuters, "Radio Under Fire Over Free-Speech Crackdown," The Freedom of Information Center, July 11, 2003, http://foi.missouri.edu/firstamendment/radio.html (accessed April 4, 2005).

23. Trudy Lieberman, "You Can't Report What You Don't Pursue," *Columbia Journalism Review*, (May/June 2000): 45.

24. McChesney, *Rich Media, Poor Democracy*, 51–60.

25. Ibid., 52.

26. Lawrence K. Grossman, "Lessons of the Sixty Minutes Cave-In," *Columbia Journalism Review* January/February 1996, http://archives.cjr.org/year/96/1/60minutes.asp (accessed January 20, 2006).

27. Ibid.

28. An and Jin, "Interlocking of Newspaper Companies," 592–93.

29. J. Pfeffer and G. Salanick, *The External Control of Organizations* (New York: Harper & Row, 1978), 161.

30. James P. Winter, "Interlocking Directorships and Economic Power," in *Press Concentration and Monopoly: New Perspectives on Newspaper Ownership and Concentration*, ed. Robert G. Picard, James P. Winter, Maxwell E. McCombs, and Stephen Lacy (Norwood, NJ: Ablex Publishing Corporation, 1988), 115.

31. Charles Davis and Stephanie Craft, "New Media Synergy: Emergence of Institutional Conflicts of Interest," *Journal of Mass Media Ethics* 15, no. 4 (2000): 219–231.

32. Ibid.

33. Douglas Gomery, "The FCC's Newspaper-Broadcast Cross-Ownership Rule: An Analysis," Economic Policy Institute website, 2002, http://www.epinet.org/books/cross-ownership.pdf (accessed March 10, 2005).

34. David Pritchard, "Viewpoint Diversity in Cross-Owned Newspapers and Television Stations: A Study of News Coverage of the 2000 Presidential Campaign," Federal Communications Commission, Media Ownership Working Group website, September 2002, http://hraunfoss.fcc.gov/edocs_public/attachmatch/DOC-226838A7.txt (accessed March 10, 2005).

35. Greg Mitchell, "Endorsement Analysis: Breaking Down the Chains," *Editor & Publisher*, http://www.editorandpublisher.com/eandp/news/article_display.jsp?vnu_content_id=100 (accessed October 27, 2004, site now discontinued).

36. Akhavan-Majid, Rife, and Gopinath, "Chain Ownership and Editorial Independence," 59–66.

37. Dennis and Merrill, *Media Debates*, 76.

38. Marvin Kalb and Nicholas Kralev, "The Afternoon Newspaper War," *Harvard International Journal of Press/Politics* 5, no. 4 (Fall 2000), http://www.nicholaskralev.com/PP-afternoon.html (accessed March 10, 2005).

39. *Miami Herald Publishing Co., Division of Knight Newspapers, Inc. v. Tornillo*, 418 U. S. 241 (1974).

40. Ibid.

41. The Commission on Freedom of the Press, *Free and Responsible Press*, 60.

42. Compaine and Gomery, *Who Owns the Media?* 43–44.

43. Steve Hallock, "Acquisition by Gannett Changes Paper's Editorials," *Newspaper Research Journal* 25, no. 2 (Spring 2004): 36.

44. David C. Coulson and Anne Hansen, "The Louisville Courier-Journal's News Content After Purchase by Gannett," *Journalism & Mass Communication Quarterly* 72, no. 1 (Spring 1995): 212.

45. Dores A. Candussi and James P. Winter, "Monopoly and Content in Winnipeg," in *Press Concentration and Monopoly: New Perspectives on Newspaper Ownership and*

Concentration, ed. Robert G. Picard, James P. Winter, Maxwell E. McCombs, and Stephen Lacy (Norwood, NJ: Ablex Publishing Corporation, 1988), 144–45.

46. Katherine Trim, Gary Pizante, and James Yaraskavitch, "The Effect of Monopoly on the News: A Before and After Study of Two Canadian One Newspaper Towns," *Canadian Journal of Communication* 9, no. 3 (1983): 33–56.

47. Dennis and Merrill, *Media Debates*, 77.

48. Ed Bishop, "SJR Expands," *St. Louis Journalism Review* 35 (October 2005): 3.

49. Ibid.

50. Kovach and Rosenstiel, *Elements of Journalism*, 141.

51. David C. Coulson, "Antitrust Law and Newspapers," 195.

52. Ibid.

53. Ibid.

54. Staffan Sundin, "Media Ownership in Sweden," *Nordicom Review* 2 (1995): 63.

55. The Commission on Freedom of the Press, *Free and Responsible Press*, 285.

56. Ibid., 81.

57. Ibid., 83.

58. Ibid., 97.

59. Ibid., 125.

60. Steve Hallock, "A Low-Power Listening Experience," *Dayton Daily News*, February 2, 2004.

Bibliography

BOOKS

Aufderheide, Patricia. *Communications Policy and the Public Interest: The Telecommunications Act of 1996*. New York: Guilford Press, 1999.

Bagdikian, Ben H. *The Media Monopoly*. 6th ed. Boston: Beacon Press, 2000.

Busterna, John C., and Robert Picard. *Joint Operating Agreements: The Newspaper Preservation Act and its Application*. Norwood, NJ: Ablex Publishing, 1993.

Compaine, Benjamin M., and Douglas Gomery. *Who Owns the Media? Competition and Concentration in the Mass Media Industry*. 3rd ed. Mahwah, NJ: Lawrence Erlbaum Associates, Inc., Publishers, 2000.

Demers, David Pearce. *The Menace of the Corporate Newspaper: Fact or Fiction?* Ames: Iowa State University Press, 1996.

Dennis, Everette E., and John C. Merrill. *Media Debates: Issues in Mass Communication*. White Plains, New York: Longman, 2001.

Ellsworth, Scott. *Death in a Promised Land/The Tulsa Race Riot of 1921*. Baton Rouge: Louisiana State University Press, 1982.

Halberstam, David. *The Powers That Be*. New York: Dell Publishing Co., Inc., 1980.

Hatchen, William A. *The Troubles of Journalism: A Critical Look at What's Right and Wrong with the Press*. 2nd ed. Mahwah, NJ: Lawrence Erlbaum Associates, 2001.

Hollinger, David A., and Charles Capper, eds. *The American Intellectual Tradition*, Vol. 1. 4th ed. New York: Oxford University Press, Inc., 2001.

Huntzicker, William E. *The Popular Press, 1833–1865*. Westport, CT: Greenwood Press, 1999.

Kovach, Bill, and Tom Rosenstiel. *The Elements of Journalism: What Newspeople Should Know and the Public Should Expect*. New York: Crown Publishing, 2001.

Lee, James Melvin. *History of American Journalism*. 2nd ed. Garden City, NY: The Garden City Publishing Co., Inc., 1923.

Lewis, Sinclair. *Babbitt*. New York: P.F. Collier & Son Corporation, 1922.

Lippmann, Walter. *Public Opinion*. New York: The MacMillan Company, 1934.

McChesney, Robert W. *Rich Media, Poor Democracy: Communication Politics in Dubious Times*. New York: The New Press, 1999.

Mencher, Melvin. *News Reporting and Writing*. 9th ed. New York: Columbia University, 2003.

Morris, Richard B. *Encyclopedia of American History Bicentennial Edition*. New York: Harper & Row, Publishers, 1976.

Napoli, Philip M. *Foundations of Communications Policy; Principles and Process in the Regulation of Electronic Media*. Cresskill, NJ: Hampton Press, Inc., 2001.

Nevins, Allan. *American Press Opinion Washington to Coolidge/A Documentary Record of Editorial Leadership and Criticism*. New York: D.C. Heath and Company, 1928.

Pember, Don R. *Mass Media Law*. 5th ed. Dubuque, IA: Wm. C. Brown Publishers, 1990.

Pfeffer, J., and G. Salanick. *The External Control of Organizations*. New York: Harper & Row, 1978.

Picard, Robert G., James P. Winter, Maxwell E. McCombs, and Stephen Lacy. *Press Concentration and Monopoly: New Perspectives on Newspaper Ownership and Concentration*. Norwood, NJ: Ablex Publishing Corporation, 1988.

Rutland, Robert A. *The Newsmongers: Journalism in the Life of the Nation 1690–1972*. New York: The Dial Press, 1973.

Rystrom, Kenneth. *The Why Who and How of the Editorial Page*. 3rd ed. State College, PA: Strata Publishing, Inc., 1999.

Schwarz, Jordan A. *The New Dealers: Power Politics in the Age of Roosevelt*. New York: Alfred A. Knopf, 1993.

Severin, Werner J., and James W. Tankard, Jr. *Communication Theories: Origins, Methods, and Uses in the Mass Media*. 5th ed. New York: Longman, 2001.

Shoemaker, Pamela J., and Stephen D. Reese. *Mediating the Message: Theories of Influences on Mass Media Content*. 3rd ed. White Plains, NY: Longman Publishers USA, 1996.

Sloan, William David, Cheryl S. Wray, and C. Joanne Sloan. *Great Editorials; Masterpieces of Opinion Writing*. Northport, AL: Vision Press, 1997.

Sloan, William David, and Laird B. Anderson. *Pulitzer Prize Editorials/America's Best Writing 1917–2003*. 3rd ed. Ames, IA: Iowa State University Press, 2003.

The Commission on Freedom of the Press. *A Free and Responsible Press: A General Report on Mass Communication: Newspapers, Radio, Motion Pictures, Magazines, and Books*. Chicago: The University of Chicago Press, 1947.

Underwood, Doug. *When MBAs Rule the Newsroom*. New York: Columbia University Press, 1993.

Waldrop, Gayle A. *Editor and Editorial Writer*. 3rd ed. Dubuque, IA: Wm. C. Brown Company Publishers, 1967.

ARTICLES AND PAMPHLETS

Adams, Edward E. "Secret Combinations and Collusive Agreement: The Scripps Newspaper and the Early Roots of Joint Operating Agreements." *Journalism & Mass Communication Quarterly* 73 (1996): 195–205.

Akhavan-Majid, Roya, and Sheila Gopinath. "Chain Ownership and Editorial Independence: A Case Study of Gannett Newspapers." *Journalism Quarterly* 68 (1991): 59–66.

Akhavan-Majid, Roya, and Timothy Boudreau. "Chain Ownership, Organizational Style, and Editorial Role Perceptions." *Journalism & Mass Communication Quarterly* 72 (1995): 863–73.

American Newspaper Publishers Association. *'87 Facts About Newspapers*. Reston, VA: American Newspaper Publishers Association, 1987.

American Society of Newspaper Editors. "News and Editorial Independence: A Survey of Group and Independent Editors." *ASNE Bulletin* (April 1980): 13–28.

An, Soontae, and Hyun Seung Jin, "Interlocking of Newspaper Companies with Financial Institutions and Leading Advertisers." *Journalism & Mass Communication Quarterly* 81 (2004): 586–87.

Bagdikian, Ben H. "The U.S. Media: Supermarket or Assembly Line?" *Journal of Communication* 35 (1985): 97–109.

Bates, Benjamin J. "Breaking the Structural Logjam: The Impact of Cable on Local TV Market Concentration." *Journal of Media Economics* 4 (1991): 47–57.

Barnett, Stephen R. "The JOA Scam." *Columbia Journalism Review* (November/December 1991): 47–48.

Bigman, Stanley K. "Rivals in Conformity: A Study of Two Competing Dailies." *Journalism Quarterly* 25 (1975): 127–31.

Borstel, Gerard H. "Ownership, Competition and Comment in 20 Small Dailies." *Journalism Quarterly* 52 (1975): 220–22.

Bridges, Janet A., Barry R. Litman, and Lamar W. Bridges. "Rosse's Model Revisited: Moving to Concentric Circles to Explain Newspaper Competition." *Journal of Media Economics* 15 (2002): 3–19.

Busterna, John C., and Kathleen A. Hansen. "Presidential Endorsement Patterns by Chain-Owned Newspapers, 1976–84." *Journalism Quarterly* 67 (1990): 286–94.

Candussi, Dores A., and James P. Winter. "Monopoly and Content in Winnipeg." In Robert G. Picard, James P. Winter, Maxwell E. McCombs, and Stephen Lacy, *Press Concentration and Monopoly: New Perspectives on Newspaper Ownership and Concentration.* Norwood, NJ: Ablex Publishing Corporation, 1988.

Compaine, Benjamin M. "The Expanding Base of Media Competition." *Journal of Communication* 35 (1985): 81–96.

Chaffee, Steven H., and Donna G. Wilson. "Media Rich, Media Poor: Two Studies of Diversity in Agenda-Holding." *Journalism Quarterly* 54 (1977): 466–76.

Coulson, David C. "Antitrust Law and Newspapers." In Robert G. Picard, James P. Winter, Maxwell E. McCombs, and Stephen Lacy, *Press Concentration and Monopoly: New Perspectives on Newspaper Ownership and Concentration.* Norwood, NJ: Ablex Publishing Corporation, 1988.

Coulson, David C., and Anne Hansen. "The Louisville Courier-Journal's News Content After Purchase by Gannett." *Journalism & Mass Communication Quarterly* 72 (1995): 205–15.

Davis, Charles, and Stephanie Craft. "New Media Synergy: Emergence of Institutional Conflicts of Interest." *Journal of Mass Media Ethics* 15 (2000): 219–31.

Demers, David. "Effect of Corporate Structure on Autonomy of Top Editors at U.S. Dailies." *Journalism Quarterly* 70 (1993): 499–508.

Demers, David. "Corporate Newspaper Structure, Editorial Page Vigor, and Social Change." *Journalism and Mass Communication Quarterly* 73 (1996): 857–77.

Deutschmann, Paul. *News-Page Content of Twelve Metropolitan Dailies.* Cincinnati: Scripps-Howard Research, 1959, 92–95.

Devey, S.M. "Umbrella Competition for Newspaper Circulation in the Boston Metro Area." *Journal of Media Economics* 2 (1989): 31–40.

Dimmick, John W., Scott J. Patterson, and Alan B. Albarran. "Competition Between the Cable and Broadcast Industries: A Niche Analysis." *Journal of Media Economics* 5 (1992): 13–30.

Glasser, Theodore L. "Competition and Diversity Among Radio Formats: Legal and Structural Issues." *Journal of Broadcasting* 28 (1984): 127–42.

Gustafsson, K.E. "The Umbrella Model-Upside-Down." *Nordicom Review* 1 (1996): 181–93.

Entman, Robert M. "Newspaper Competition and First Amendment Ideals: Does Monopoly Matter?" *Journal of Communication* 35 (1985): 147–65.

Fedler, Fred, Ron F. Smith, and Tim Counts. "Voter Uses and Perceptions of Editorial Endorsements." *Newspaper Research Journal* 6 (1984): 19–23.

Fedler, Fred, Tim Counts, and Lowndes F. Stephens. "Newspaper Endorsements and Voter Behavior in the 1980 Presidential Election." *Newspaper Research Journal* 4 (1982): 3–11.

Fulero, Solomon M. "Perceived Influence of Endorsements on Voting." *Journalism Quarterly* 54 (1977): 789–91.

Gaziano, Cecilie. "Chain Newspaper Homogeneity and Presidential Endorsements, 1971–1988." *Journalism Quarterly* 66 (1989): 836–45.

Gregg, James E. "Newspaper Editorial Endorsements and California Elections, 1948–62." *Journalism Quarterly* 42 (1965): 532–38.

Hain, Paul L. "How an Endorsement Affected a Non-Partisan Mayoral Vote." *Journalism Quarterly* 52 (1975): 337–40.

Hale, F. Dennis. "Editorial Diversity and Concentration." In Robert G. Picard, James P. Winter, Maxwell E. McCombs and Stephen Lacy, *Press Concentration and Monopoly: New Perspectives on Newspaper Ownership and Concentration*. Norwood, NJ: Ablex Publishing Corporation, 1988.

Hallock, Steve. "Acquisition by Gannett Changes Paper's Editorials." *Newspaper Research Journal* 25 (2004): 36–43.

Henry, Neil. "When Tulsa Burned." *Mother Jones*, March–April 2002, 81–82.

Hernandez, Debra Gersh. "Profiles of the News Consumer." *Editor & Publisher*, January 1997, 6.

Hooper, Michael. "Party and Newspaper Endorsement as Predictors of Voter Choice." *Journalism Quarterly* 46 (1964): 302–05.

Hurd, Robert E., and Michael W. Singletary. "Newspaper Endorsement Influence on the 1980 Presidential Election Vote." *Journalism Quarterly* 61, 2 (1984): 332–38.

Kolodzy, Janet. "Everything That Rises/Media Convergence is an Opportunity, Not a Curse." *Columbia Journalism Review*, July/August 2003, 61.

Lacy, Stephen. "Competing in the Suburbs: A Research Review of Intercity Newspaper Competition." *Newspaper Research Journal* 9 (1988): 69–76.

Lacy, Stephen. "Content of Joint Operation Newspapers." In Robert G. Picard, James P. Winter, Maxwell E. McCombs, and Stephen Lacy, *Press Concentration and Monopoly: New Perspectives on Newspaper Ownership and Concentration*. Norwood, NJ: Ablex Publishing Corporation, 1988.

Lacy, Stephen. "Effects of Group Ownership on Daily Newspaper Content." *Journal of Media Economics* 4 (1991): 35–47.

Lacy, Stephen, David C. Coulson, and Hiromi Cho. "Competition for Readers Among U.S. Metropolitan Daily, Nonmetropolitan Daily, and Weekly Newspapers." *Journal of Media Economics* 15 (2002): 21–40.

Lacy, Stephen, and A.B. Sohn. "Correlations of Newspaper Content with Circulation in the Suburbs: A Case Study." *Journalism Quarterly* 67 (1990): 784–93.

Lasorsa, Dominic L. "Effects of Newspaper Competition on Public Opinion Diversity." *Journalism Quarterly* 68 (1991): 38–47.

Matthews, Martha M. "How Public Ownership Affects Publisher Autonomy." *Journalism & Mass Communication Quarterly* 73 (1996): 342–53.

McCombs, Maxwell. "Editorial Endorsement: A Study of Influence." *Journalism Quarterly* 44 (1967): 545–48.

McCombs, Maxwell. "Effect of Monopoly in Cleveland on Diversity of Newspaper Content." *Journalism Quarterly* 64 (1987): 740–44.

McDowell, James L. "The Role of Newspapers in Illinois' At-Large Election." *Journalism Quarterly* 42 (1965): 281–84.

Nixon, Raymond B., and Robert L. Jones. "The Content of Non-Competitive vs. Competitive Newspapers." *Journalism Quarterly* 33 (1956): 299–314.

Picard, Robert G. "Pricing Behavior in Monopoly Newspapers: Ad and Circulation Differences in Joint Operating and Single Newspaper Monopolies, 1972–1982." *LSU School of Journalism Research Bulletin,* 1985.

Picard, Robert G., and Gary D. Fackler. "Price Changes in Competing and Joint Operating Newspapers; Advertising and Circulation Differences, 1972 and 1982." *LSU School of Journalism Research Bulletin,* May 1985.

Robinson, J.D. "The Changing Reading Habits of the American Public." *Journal of Communication* 30 (1980): 141–52.

Robinson, John P. "The Press as King-Maker: What Surveys From Last Five Campaigns Show." *Journalism Quarterly* 51 (1974): 587–94.

Rodgers, Ron, Steve Hallock, Mike Gennaria, and Fei Wei. "Two Papers in Joint Operating Agreement Publish Meaningful Editorial Diversity." *Newspaper Research Journal* 25 (2004): 104–09.

Rosenwein, Rifka. "Why Media Mergers Matter." *Brill's Content* (December 1999–January 2000): 93.

Rutland, Robert A. "The First Great Newspaper Debate: The Constitutional Crisis of 1787–1788." *Proceedings of the American Antiquarian Society* 97 (Part I, 1987): 43–58.

Skylar, David. "Why Newspapers Die." *Quill,* July/August 1984, 14.

Smith, J.A. "Freedom of Expression and the Marketplace of Ideas Concept From Milton to Jefferson." *Journal of Communication Inquiry* 7 (1981): 47–64.

Sobel, Judith, and Edwin Emery. "U.S. Dailies' Competition in Relation to Circulation Size: A Newspaper Data Update." *Journalism Quarterly* 55 (1978): 145–49.

Stempel, Guido H., Thomas Hargrove, and Joseph P. Bernt, "Relation of Growth of Use of the Internet to Changes in Media Use from 1995 to 1999." *Journalism and Mass Communication Quarterly* 77 (2000): 71–79.

Stempel, Guido H. III, "Where People *Really* Get Most of Their News." *Newspaper Research Journal* 1, 4 (Fall 1991): 2–9.

"Study Tracks Trends in Profession." *Quill,* May 2004, 7.

Sundin, Staffan. "Media Ownership in Sweden." *Nordicom Review* 2 (1995): 63–74.

Thrift, Ralph Jr. "How Chain Ownership Affects Editorial Page Vigor of Newspapers." *Journalism Quarterly* 54 (1977): 327–31.

Tillinghast, Diana Stover. "Limits of Competition." In Robert G. Picard, James P. Winter, Maxwell E. McCombs, and Stephen Lacy, *Press Concentration and Monopoly: New Perspectives on Newspaper Ownership and Concentration.* Norwood, NJ: Ablex Publishing Corporation, 1988.

Trim, Katherine, Gary Pizante, and James Yaraskavitch. "The Effect of Monopoly on the News: A Before and After Study of Two Canadian One Newspaper Towns." *Canadian Journal of Communication* 9 (1983): 33–56.

Vermeer, Jan P. "Multiple Newspapers and Electoral Competition: A County-Level Analysis." *Journalism & Mass Communication Quarterly* 72 (1995): 98–105.

Wackman, Daniel B., Donald M. Gillmore, Cecilie Gaziano, and Everette E. Dennis, "Chain Newspaper Autonomy as Reflected in Presidential Campaign Endorsements." *Journalism Quarterly* 52 (1975): 411–19.

Willoughby, Wesley F. "Are Two Competing Dailies Necessarily Better Than One?" *Journalism Quarterly* 32 (1955): 197–204.

Winter, James P. "Interlocking Directorships and Economic Power." In Robert G. Picard, James P. Winter, Maxwell E. McCombs, and Stephen Lacy, *Press Concentration and Monopoly: New Perspectives on Newspaper Ownership and Concentration.* Norwood, NJ: Ablex Publishing Corporation, 1988.

LEGAL CASES

Abrams et al. v. United States 250 U.S. 616 (1919).

Miami Herald Publishing Co., Division of Knight Newspapers, Inc., v. Tornillo 418 U.S. 241 (1974).

Thornhill v. Alabama 301 U.S. 88 (1940).

UNPUBLISHED MATERIALS

Drager, Michael W. "Measuring the Marketplace: Diversity and Editorial Content," paper presented at the annual meeting of the Association for Education in Journalism and Mass Communication, New Orleans, Louisiana, 1999.

Lacy, Stephen. "The Effects of Ownership and Competition on Daily Newspaper Content." Ph.D. dissertation, University of Texas at Austin, 1986.

Pilant, Charles A. "Expressions of Nationalistic Sentiments in Early American Newspapers, 1776–1826." Ph.D. dissertation, Marquette University, 1989.

Thompson, Susan Annette. "The Antebellum Penny Press." Ph.D. dissertation, University of Alabama, 2002.

Index